Pride and Prejudice

Pride and Prejudice

School Desegregation and Urban Renewal in Norfolk, 1950–1959

Forrest R. White

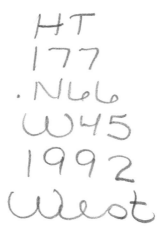

PRAEGER

Westport, Connecticut
London

Library of Congress Cataloging-in-Publication Data

White, Forrest R.
    Pride and prejudice : school desegregation and urban renewal in
Norfolk, 1950-1959 / Forrest R. White.
        p. cm.
    Includes bibliographical references and index.
    ISBN 0-275-94274-0 (alk. paper)
    1. Urban renewal—Virginia—Norfolk—History. 2. School
integration—Virginia—Norfolk—History. 3. Norfolk (Va.)—Race
relations. I. Title.
HT177.N66W45 1992
371.19'344'09755521—dc20   92-7491

British Library Cataloguing in Publication Data is available.

Library of Congress Catalog Card Number: 92-7491
ISBN: 0-275-94274-0

First published in 1992

Praeger Publishers, 88 Post Road West, Westport, CT 06881
An imprint of Greenwood Publishing Group, Inc.

Printed in the United States of America

The paper used in this book complies with the
Permanent Paper Standard issued by the National
Information Standards Organization (Z39.48-1984).

10 9 8 7 6 5 4 3 2 1

Contents

Figures

Acknowledgments

Because every major project of this sort re-
lies at times on the effort of a group of
supporters, advisers, consolers, and consultants, the author would like to take this opportunity to express his thanks to all those
who helped make this group effort successful.
Chief among my supporters and consolers is my
wife, Holly, who endured much in the eighteen
years since the research was first initiated,
abandoned, and finally resumed again. My parents also inspired my early interest in the
period, and my sister, Ann White Pulley gave
tirelessly of her time and talents to prepare
the first draft more than a decade ago. In
addition to those cited in the references,
there were numerous others who encouraged the
project and helped to provide insight into the
people, events, and mood of the era under
study. Special thanks are due to Drs. Maurice
R. Berube, Peter Stewart, James Sweney, and
Ulysses V. Spiva, all of Old Dominion University, for their guidance and assistance during various phases of the project.

Introduction

The twin waves of boom and bust had broken
many times upon Norfolk's shores. Bombarded,
blockaded, captured, and even plundered, the
city had endured its share of misfortune at
the hands of invaders; but Norfolk, too, had
suffered even more mercilessly from enemies
within, having been razed by the patriots,
isolated by trade restrictions, strangled by
intrastate rivalries, decimated by yellow
fever, terrorized by the armed mobs during
Reconstruction, and then very nearly ruined
financially by the disarmament that followed
World War I. Through it all, however, the
promise of prosperity lingered just around the
corner. For more than 300 years the ships of
many nations had sought refuge in her fine
natural harbor. For two centuries the hammer
blows of the ship-building trade had reverberated across her waterfront, punctuating the
bustle of ships' chandlers, sail makers, jack-
tars, tavern keepers, and sailors on leave.
Merchants, upon surveying this hubbub of
activity, dreamed of the day when the harbor
would one day compete with the great ports of
New York, Baltimore, Boston, and Charleston.
It was the pursuit of this dream that brought
them the resiliency to overcome the harrowing
scars of defeat. Over and over Norfolk again
had bounced back from the crushing blows of

misfortune, only to be leveled once more (Wertenbaker 1962).

In short, Norfolk had been washed by the twin tides of hope and despair as often, if not more precipitously, as the other great cities of America. Approaching the middle of the twentieth century, Norfolk appeared to have as great a prospect of prosperity and as little to fear as any city in the nation: World War II was over, and yet there would be no disarmament; her enemies lay far beyond the reaches of her coastline defenses; the ravages of the Depression had been left far behind; and her merchants and captains of industry were eager to get on about their tasks, hopeful that the time was at last at hand to build the great city of their dreams.

At first glance, Norfolk's history during these postwar years does not seem remarkably different from other American cities. The boom and bustle of the war years gave way to a momentary respite, and then raged on in the frantic growth of suburbia. The highways zoomed, the buildings loomed, and the babies boomed in postwar prosperity. The civic elite who ruled Floyd Hunter's Atlanta (Hunter 1953) had their counterparts who reigned over Norfolk's growth, a well-being that extended to every segment of the community: merchants found a seller's market; consumers spied an unbelievable selection of goods and services; employers sensed unrivaled opportunities for growth and expansion; workers faced an unprecedented array of career positions; and even the sick, old, and unemployed discovered a growing national consensus that all should share in the spoils of victory.

Two events alone make Norfolk's history at this time remarkable from that of other cities: one, the voracity of its assault upon urban blight, and two, the ferocity of its resistance to school desegregation. The rate at which the federal bulldozers gobbled up its

slums earned Norfolk all-American honors and
a lasting place in the annals of municipal
achievement; the collision between the advocates of integration and the forces of Massive
Resistance won the city only a footnote in the
history books, and fleeting dishonor on the
national scene. Norfolk's reaction to these
two issues, and, indeed, their very emergence
as historical turning points, may be directly
traced to the rise and fall of two distinct
foci of power--one, economic, and the other,
political--irrevocably tied together in a tale
of pride and prejudice. It is the story of how
boom perverted very nearly came to bust; how
the same forces that launched the tide of
urban renewal acquiesced, waned, and then
finally regrouped to form the last bulwark of
resistance against an even greater surge of
racial antipathy; and how new blood, untutored
and untested in the political conventions of
the era, emerged to eclipse both these elements at the seat of municipal power.

Much that is both right and wrong with
Norfolk today may be traced back to developments during the formative years between 1950
and 1960. Before then, its citizens were far
more attuned to the small town provincialism
of rural Virginia than to the urban dynamism
of the great port cities that were its com-
petitors. The leadership, the vision, and the
progressive policies that could have brought
about such a change never had a chance to rock
the *status quo*; they were too finely filtered,
processed, and forced out through the sieve of
machine politics. It was not until the close
of World War II, when Norfolk stood on the
brink of economic ruin, that its citizens
found the courage to overthrow the political
machine that had dominated its deliberations
and stifled its advance. Norfolkians now
became obsessed with the dream of a revitalized city; they saw at last an opportunity to
discard the unpleasant memories of wartime

shortages and depression deficits, and they
jumped at the chance to advance the kind of
leaders who could make this vision come true.

Many factors were responsible for the fall
of the old political order, but it was unquestionably civic pride, really unbridled
boosterism, that swept new leadership into
office with a mandate for reform and rejuvenation. Pride was the magnet that attracted a
different breed of leader--financially secure,
successful, confidant, and socially superior--
to the helm of municipal government; pride was
the driving force that cleaned house at city
hall, and recruited instead an exciting and
vibrant coterie of professionals, planners,
engineers, and reformers capable of putting
the dreams into practice; and it was pride,
along with a heavy dose of optimism and sense
of adventure, that helped to transform a once-
indolent populace into a dynamic and progressive citizen force. The business and civic
leaders who took over city hall were realistic
enough to realize that they could not achieve
their goals alone without assistance from outside sources, including the federal government. A host of national experts descended
upon the city to help draft the blueprints of
this dream--a vision that would thrust the
city into the forefront of the nascent fields
of municipal planning, redevelopment, and
urban renewal.

By the early 1950s, however, the impetus
for change had waned, and the reformers who
had been swept into office by civic pride and
optimism lost out to others who owed their
allegiance to the old political order, now
more flexible and resilient than ever. The
dream of a New Norfolk had reached the building stage, and it now took on a different form
than had once been envisioned. The planners,
reformers, and out-of-towners who had once
peopled city hall now gave way to a new wave
of bricks-and-mortar men, far more provincial

and politically dependent than their predecessors. There was an attempt at first to
retain the guidance of the business and civic
leaders, but this effort, too, faded with
their falling political fortunes.

Time and events had changed considerably
since the old political machine last ruled
city hall, but its leaders failed to discern
the differences, and in doing so, very nearly
brought the city to its knees. For them,
racial antipathy had always been the *cause
celebré* that rallied supporters and overrode
all other more meaningful divisions in the
white community. Under the reformers, black
leaders had been given an advisory role in
planning and redevelopment, and that now made
them convenient targets for attacks that would
also sting the flanks of the progressives. The
social advances of the postwar era were the
first casualties as the machinery of municipal
government was retooled to conform to racial
antipathy. Discrimination at first took the
more subtle form of the sort of political
tit-for-tat that frequently accompanies the
fortunes of the electoral process, but the
Brown v. Board of Education decision acceler-
ated both the rhetoric and the scope of the
contest. Virginia's Massive Resistance (movement) to school desegregation soon locked both
races into a cut-throat competition with
stakes so high that neither side could afford
to fold its hand. In this contest, prejudice
--the unreasonable adherence to the conventions, traditions, and mores of the past--
reigned supreme and soon became the underlying
force behind every phase of municipal policy.
Even the planners' tools of redevelopment and
urban renewal--the hallmarks of the reformers'
rule--were prostituted to serve this end.

Prejudice brought Norfolk once again to the
brink of ruin: with schools closed, the population divided, neighborhoods threatened, and
development stagnated, its future was indeed

uncertain. The city that had once been so open
to new ideas, innovative approaches, and outside leadership had closed its doors to the
rest of the world, and turned inward upon itself, afraid now to face even the slightest
alteration in the status quo. This time the
voices of pride and boosterism that had once
led the city to municipal glory stood silent.
Only a handful of public-minded citizens--bit
players up to now--dared to oppose the politics of prejudice; they lacked the resources
to mount a challenge to the established order;
so, instead, they sought to diffuse the confrontation. In the end their strategy was
successful, and their opposition inspired the
major business and civic leaders to finally
speak out. Aroused at last, the forces of
pride and boosterism stepped in to avert the
ultimate conflict, but their move came too
late to seize for themselves the mantle of
municipal office; it passed instead to those
few brave citizens who had initiated the
challenge.

Norfolk at mid-century had faced an uncharted sea of opportunity that had induced
its business leaders to dream of splendors
far beyond the city's grasp; in striving to
achieve those ends, they had miraculously
transformed this once sleepy little port into
a dynamic and modern metropolis. Along the way
their leadership peaked, ebbed, and was then
replaced by a surge of prejudice that very
nearly ruined the city. This rush of events
destroyed both the old political order and the
newer forces of boosterism; leadership in the
future fell instead to a new group of citizens
without identifiable cause or calling, certain
only that the city would have to live in a
world in which neither pride nor prejudice
reigned supreme.

By 1960 Norfolk had come to face a less
certain future: its grand visions had been
scaled down to encompass a lesser reality, but

one in which all citizens could share on equal terms; and the city had learned that it could not afford either the economic costs of re-birth or the social toll of racial antipathy. The monuments to this era are many: they are cast in concrete, steel, and glass, but they may also be seen in the trail of bulldozed rubble, vacant buildings, and bombed-out open spaces; the evidence may also be found in the toll of suffering and despair; its record may still be read in this tale of pride and preju-dice.

Prologue:
Norfolk Before 1950

Four sailors with a barmaid in tow steamed out
into Granby Street and launched into a chorus
of "Roll Out The Barrel." A single car cut
out of traffic and pulled to the curb, jubi-
lantly sounding its horn over their slurred
rendition of the chorus. This mild commotion
on an otherwise still August afternoon stirred
onlookers from their shaded refuge in the
shops and storefronts that lined the street; a
few quick words were exchanged, and the news
flashed through the gathering crowd. Other
cars began sounding their horns in salute, and
soon a blaring procession of automobiles was
inching its way past the swelling throng. The
taverns along Beer Barrel Row began closing
their doors as patrons rushed to join the
melee in the street. The "Roll-Out-the-Barrel"
boys had by now picked up a chorus line of
converts that was snake-dancing arm in arm
through the stalled traffic. Streamers of
toilet paper drifted down from the offices
above, the opening salvos in a furious fusillade of impromptu confetti that belied the
constraints of wartime rationing. The merry-
makers dancing in the streets below were the
precursors of one of the most raucous, brawl-
ing, celebrations in Norfolk's history. The
day was Tuesday, August 14, 1945--V-J Day--and
the radio had just signaled the end of World

War II. Not since Patrick Henry's army of
patriots burned this Tory stronghold to the
ground had the nation's domestic military
forces had such a grand night on the town. One
solemn sailor surveyed the jubilant commotion
surrounding him and summed up the frequent
lament of his colleagues, "Of all the damned
places to be when this thing happened, we had
to be in Norfolk (*Norfolk Virginian-Pilot*
8/15/45)."

   The following day dawned quietly for the
city; half of its population was nursing their
worst hangover of modern times. The other half
--Norfolk's more permanent residents--faced an
even grimmer morning after. The city's streets
were empty, its shops, banks, and government
offices having been closed for a day of prayer
and thanksgiving. Gone were the sailors, the
shipyard workers, the snake dancers, the
blaring automobiles, and the drunken carousers
of the night before; even the taverns and the
bawdy houses of East Main Street were closed
for the day. Here and there the white "dixie
cup" of a sailor's cap bobbed among the flot-
sam of confetti and other jetsam of the cele-
bration. A handful of bleary-eyed strangers
still ruled this empty roost from perches
tucked away well off the beaten path (*Norfolk
Virginian-Pilot* 8/16/45). To Norfolk's more
permanent residents this panorama of desertion
served as a grim reminder of what the city
would be like without its navy. While the war
was raging overseas, they had thought only of
tolerating this domestic military invasion
until they could reclaim the city as their
own--they had given little thought to really
making a "home" for the transient population.
Now that the war was officially over, however,
the thought of empty streets and the fleet's
departure struck the community to the core,
rousing it from its civic stupor, and infusing
it with a thirst for fresh leadership and new
direction.

Control of city hall had long been in the hands of the city's professional politicians, a group that had always shown tremendous willingness to run the show without external interference. The "Prieur Machine," as the local affiliate of the statewide (Harry F.) Byrd Organization was called, was run by Clerk of Courts William "Billy" Prieur. Time and circumstances over the course of the Depression and the war years had combined to make the Prieur Machine far more powerful than either the perks of office or the patronage of political organization would have indicated. Since they were powerless to influence the deliberations at city hall, and unwilling to risk the ire of the Organization that controlled so many jobs in a hard-strapped economy, Norfolk's business and financial leaders turned their attention instead during the Depression to a more receptive arena, the sphere of civic involvement. Not only did they find great success in these endeavors, well separated from the political operations of the city, they also forged key alliances and learned to build a community coalition of their own that would one day rival the more entrenched political operatives. Through the Community Chest and a number of related charities, the businessmen worked tirelessly to relieve the suffering of their fellow citizens; by means of the National Recovery Administration and its volunteer successor, the Emergency Relief Commission, they also learned to rely on federal support in this effort. Through their own Citizens Crime Commission they studied the harsh economic impact that slums had, not only upon city services, but also upon the lives of their inhabitants.

The war years had brought incredible hardships to the citizens and great turmoil to city government. Norfolk experienced a tremendous period of growth at the start of the war, and its population would double, even

triple on the weekends, as thousands of
sailors, soldiers, and shipyard workers on
leave descended upon the downtown area for
entertainment. This put an enormous strain
upon both the city's municipal services and
its aging housing stock; the politicians were
so reluctant to provide even essential municipal services for these new, more "temporary,"
residents that the Navy Department had to step
in to build schools, parks, playgrounds, highways, recreation areas, utilities, and a host
of other projects. The businessmen forged
their own alliance with the navy, and, acting
as the Norfolk Housing Authority, built
several thousand new housing units for the
servicemen.

The first postwar problems, however, began
to appear almost immediately as the specter of
closed stores and empty streets served as a
grim reminder of the fact that, in peacetime,
Norfolk would again have to stand on its own
financial feet: the navy would no longer be
willing to foot the bill for some much-needed
and long overdue municipal improvement. That
prospect was so frightening, that the City
Council called for a cutback in planned improvement projects and current levels of
service (Schlegel 1951, 361). This proved to
be the final straw for Norfolk's business
establishment: it had endured the national
vilification of the city in the media and
halls of Congress for its sordid nightlife,
but they would not now stand for a self-
imposed recession. Area businessmen knew that
the city could not maintain its position in
the world of trade by depending solely upon
merchant shipping and local industries;
Norfolk needed the navy, now more than ever,
and local merchants turned their efforts
furiously into remaking the city into a place
where the navy would want to stay, rather than
remain known infamously as the world's worst
liberty port. The subsequent uproar of mer-

chants and businessmen over proposed municipal cutbacks prompted a dramatic turn of events. The powder keg of civic unrest was finally ignited.

Almost as suddenly as the tides of war began to recede, a new wave of community pride and civic boosterism rose to take its place. The war years that had witnessed a dramatic upsurge in citizen activity to accommodate and alleviate the bombardment of navy personnel (Curtin 1969, 130-49) now gave way to a new direction in civic involvement. The civic leaders who had gone all-out to beef up the wartime charities to serve the new, transient population were not now content to rest. The club ladies who had knocked themselves out to provide wholesome entertainment for "the boys" were no longer content to sit at home. The volunteers who had staffed the bandage brigades and peopled the U.S.O.'s were looking for a new cause. The transient residents who had poured into the city during the war years were now almost as established as the old-timers; they would not tolerate a cutback in the very services and facilities designed to meet their needs. Thus, all of these diverse elements--the civic, the business, the volunteer, and the transient communities--had a hand in forcing the issue of Norfolk's postwar renewal out into the open; all of them urged a dramatic reversal of municipal policy.

Another issue seethed beneath the surface of this desire for change. During the war, crime had become big business in the city. Gamblers, prostitutes, racketeers, and bootleggers had invaded the area--as they invariably do to all boom towns--to cater to the more salacious desires of sailors out on leave and shipyard workers out on the town. Norfolk's finest citizens began to feel that too many of these mobsters and racketeers controlled city hall, replacing their own more legitimate voice with bribes and payoffs. The

blatancy with which the city's "other element"
conducted its venal activities shocked and enraged the citizenry. It was no wonder that
such conduct was the talk of the town, and an
open link between the gangsters and the politicians was widely suspected (Darden). Norfolkians had long endured the shenanigans of
all sorts of wartime carpetbaggers and entrepreneurs, but the prospect that these gangsters and racketeers would continue to control
the city's fate in peacetime now became too
great a burden to bear, and thus the closing
months of 1945 became the winter of discontent
for many residents.

    Political conformity had bred a closed
society in Norfolk--a society afraid to accept
outsiders, new ideas, or even dissension among
its provincial little community. The city's
close proximity to the navy and government
workers during World War II had been a positive force that had done much to erase that
stagnation. The war years had been a bitter
experience in many ways--with the crowding,
inconvenience, crime, and hedonism--for both
the hometowners and the sailors alike, but in
the end, the war had opened the minds of many
of the citizens to a world beyond their own
parochial realm, while others had found their
mission in ministering to strangers from all
parts of America. Norfolk had opened its doors
to the navy slowly, cautiously, and even
grudgingly, but now a fear was growing that
those doors, once closed, would remain forever
shuttered.

    The next few months would witness some re-
markable changes for a city overly conditioned
to accept the narrow scope and dreary conformity of its venerable political leaders. The
citizens that had so recently focused their
attention upon fighting despots overseas would
suddenly turn their efforts towards resisting
a more home grown version of totalitarianism.
The hometown folks who had so recently des-

pised the visiting sailors as an army of occu-
pation would turn instead to welcome them as
economic liberators. That bleak specter of
closed stores and empty streets in Norfolk's
downtown commercial district would prompt a
fondness for the profligacy and crowded jubi-
lation of sailor's revelry, and that longing
would in turn provide the public mandate for a
remarkable chain of events that would sweep
this once-seedy little backwater port into the
forefront of a national municipal reform movement, bringing as well an era of unheralded
progress and prosperity.

Pride and Prejudice

1

Planning the New Norfolk

When bulldozers ripped into the wall of a house in the 700 block of Smith Street on December 11, 1951, they marked both a new beginning and a crumbling end. At long last the city was moving from the quiet haunts of its earlier infamy into the spotlight of national attention. The house that first shuddered, shook, and then crumbled that wintry morning marked the beginning of the first federally financed slum clearance project in the country (*Norfolk Virginian-Pilot* 7/23/61); it also signaled the passing of a very special style of government in Norfolk, and served as both the legacy and the tombstone of the final retreat of progressive reform in the city.

Those first bulldozers were propelled by a force of civic pride and boosterism that would project Norfolk into the forefront of the Age of Redevelopment before it peaked, and then dissipated altogether. The muffled applause of the gloved dignitaries who had gathered to witness this event faded as the bulldozers tore into the sagging structure. In their eyes the memories of yesteryear were giving way to a dynamic effort to build the metropolis of the future. Those first bulldozers were the most dramatic and tangible evidence that the

dreams of an indolent age were at last on
their way to becoming a reality.

That first house stood as well as a sad
omen of what would come. As the small crowd
gathered, crewmen bound the house in chains
and clamped them to the bulldozer designated
for the job. At the appointed moment, the
machine started and lurched forward, dragging
its chains through the underpinnings of the
structure. The house shook, but did not fall
(*Norfolk Virginian-Pilot* 12/12/51)--a remarkable augury of blight's resistance to eradication. As if to prophesy the unseen forces of
the future that would chart the city's course
--as if to warn of invisible props that underlay Norfolk's renewal--the house still stood,
its underpinnings completely destroyed. Embarrassed crewmen reattached their chains to a
more elevated point, reporters and dignitaries
chatted idly by, news photographers reloaded
for a second shot, and history paused momen-
tarily in the making. The second time the
bulldozers lurched, the chain took hold, and
the frame collapsed in a shower of crumbling
plaster, rotting boards, billowing dust, and
scattering functionaries.

Norfolk was irreversibly embarking upon a
whole new approach to municipal activity, but
it was more than just a fervent desire to
erase the memories of an unpleasant past that
had put the city in the vanguard of urban renewal. It was more than just the aimless longing for the golden dream of "A New Norfolk;"
more than just the fulfillment of campaign
promises. Norfolk had reached this pinnacle of
regeneration because a specific group of men
had possessed the courage to not just dream,
but to act. Theirs was a bold vision, and it
was shared by men and women all across the
country, but the difference in Norfolk was
that they were just the sort of individuals
who could make that aspiration a reality. All
were committed to the cause, and all were

conditioned to success. They had made their
reputations, both business and civic, by over-
coming long odds; they knew how to gamble for
high stakes, but, more importantly, they knew
how to win. The individuals who sparked Norfolk's redevelopment were business leaders who
wielded the power and prestige to overcome
almost any opposition and drag the city into
nearly any venture. Certainly the fine points
of that redevelopment--the stakes, expense,
delay, social costs, and suffering--were as
misunderstood by the general public in Norfolk
as in any city in the country, but it was here
that the city's leading citizens put their
reputations on the line behind renewal. And
that made all the difference.

The council-manager type of reform government was designed to be a "businessman's
rule." The system was intended to take the
power out of the hands of the political hacks,
and give it to the true leaders of the community, and then back them up with the technical and professional expertise necessary to
make the very best decisions for the community. City government, the theory went, had become too complex, its myriad services so vast,
its management too technical, and its planning
too vital to be left to amateurs. That was the
ideal, but in far too many council-manager
cities, the power had merely passed from one
group of parochials to another. In most cities
the real leaders, the real opinion-makers, had
lost interest in municipal affairs; the result
of their abdication was that a group of small
businessmen and petty interests took over in-
stead--a group that was still businessmen, but
only second-rate ones; they were capable only
of dreaming small dreams, and often failed to
comprehend the bigger picture. In most cities
directorship of the taxpayers' multi-million
dollar municipal corporation had settled into
the grasp of people scarcely off the assembly
line--foremen, at best, who could only hold

the machinery of government on course until
the real leaders returned to take control.

In Norfolk, however, a peculiar set of circumstances had befallen the city and was forcing a different sort of leader to the top. The
little people had so bungled the prerogatives
of power that the first team had been forced
out of their board rooms and counting houses
to take over. At the close of World War II
Norfolk faced the prospect of folding altogether in the hands of the "little people" who
ran most other cities; the lure of wartime
profiteering, the power to control the expansion of municipal services, and the opportunity to promote political or parochial interests
had been too much for them. The transfusion of
new leadership that was taking place in Norfolk's reform movement came from the bluest
blood in the city. At last the real corporate
minds hoped to take over the directorship of
city government. They understood management on
a large scale, and knew that even if they
could promote themselves to the city's board
of directors, they could not fulfill their
aspirations for the city alone; just as in
their own private enterprises, they would need
an army of specialists, planners, and consultants to plot and carry out their vision.
Although they dreamed big dreams, they possessed the dynamism, energy, and wherewithal
to carry them out.

Even so, any move to snatch control of the
city from the political organization that had
ruled it for decades would be no mean accomplishment, especially in a Virginia election
system that used every conceivable means, including the poll tax and early registration
deadlines, to keep the voting population small
and manageable. In fact, when the frustrations
of the business and civic leaders first began
to surface and take on a political bent in the
winter of 1945, the poll books for the June
election had already been closed, precluding

any effort to register new voters who shared this hope of reform (*Norfolk Virginian-Pilot* 6/11/46). It was the stormy resignation of Colonel Charles K. Borland, Norfolk's long-suffering and usually staid city manager, in "a violent temper" over the City Council's proposed cutback of essential services (*Norfolk Virginian-Pilot* 6/5/46) that proved to be the culminating event. Both his resignation and his parting blast at machine politics took the community by surprise, especially since Borland was just a few months away from becoming eligible for a substantial retirement pension (*Norfolk Ledger-Dispatch* 2/21/46). Talk at a testimonial dinner hastily arranged by the business community soon turned to a political agenda. At first the businessmen sought an audience with local Organization chieftain Billy Prieur, hoping to convince him that a change in city leadership was needed, (Darden; Gornto) but when these efforts at appeasement proved futile, the People's Ticket of Richard D. Cooke, Pretlow Darden, and John Twohy was born.

The men who now proposed to take control of Norfolk had two undeniable loci of power: the one financial and the other civic. These were not the ordinary group of downtown merchants hoping to harness municipal spending to keep the central business district alive. There was not a single retailer in the lot; instead they were the heavyweights of the area's business community: bankers, brokers, builders, corporate attorneys, and building supply dealers--they had more than just a personal interest in Norfolk's rebirth and redevelopment, they had a financial stake in it. They were also the foremost representatives of the city's civic pride and community spirit; throughout the Depression and war years the city's charities had turned to these individuals for leadership, and they had built up their own independent civic following as a consequence.

Although it was left to corporate attorney
Richard D. Cooke, automobile dealer Pretlow
Darden (younger brother of Virginia's popular
wartime governor), and concrete magnate John
Twohy to carry their standard, this was a
group effort that found almost every substantial business and civic leader in the city
aligned against one of the most powerful,
well-financed, and experienced political organizations in the state; failure meant great
risk and personal sacrifice for all who par-
ticipated in this coup. All had benefitted
from their alliance with the Byrd Organization
in the past, and now had much to lose if the
selective enforcement, special treatment, and
red tape of municipal government were suddenly
turned against them. All relied too heavily in
their corporate ventures on the rapid pro-
cessing of building permits, legal documents,
inspections, and applications not to fear a
significant threat of intimidation if the
venture were to fail. Once committed, they had
to succeed, and they threw themselves into the
exhausting work of the political campaign with
the same vigor, skill, and determination evident in their civic and corporate achievements. It proved to be a hotly contested race
--"the hottest political campaign in Norfolk's
history (*Norfolk Virginian-Pilot* 6/12/46)."

The "Silkstocking Ticket," as the Cooke-
Darden-Twohy group was immediately labeled in
the hardball oratory of the Prieur Machine
stalwarts, hoisted the "Time For A Change"
standard and ran carefully against the lack-
luster record of the wartime City Council.
They were determined to run as three conservative businessmen who had close ties to the
Byrd Organization, thereby avoiding at least
the appearance of challenging Prieur directly.
It was a clever strategy, but it meant they
had to both outdo the existing administration
in conservative rhetoric and out-organize the
Prieur Machine on its home turf. As part of

that effort, they pledged not to seek reelection, thereby hoping to convince the traditional Organization voter that they only meant to revitalize Norfolk's governmental structure, not found another political dynasty.

Fortunately the People's Ticket had both the personal credibility and the backing to pull off one of the most dramatic upsets in the otherwise closed conformity of Virginia's political arena. Their election by a better than 2-to-1 margin in the largest voter turnout the city had ever witnessed, gave them a mandate to bring progressive government to Norfolk (*Norfolk Virginian-Pilot* 6/12/46). As if to seal their pledge of "business-like government, free from political influence and control," their first order of business was to set about hiring the "best city manager money can buy. . . not to get the best would be money wasted (Darden)." They turned to Charles A. Harrell, past president of the International City Manager's Association. In addition to having a strong national reputation for long-range planning and careful administration, Harrell had grown up in Norfolk, started his career in its service, and maintained close ties to the area. Even so, it was the promise of the new City Council not to interfere in his administration--not the money or the hometown connection--that proved successful in luring him away from his post in Schenectady, New York (Darden).

Harrell set busily about the task of re-building Norfolk's tarnished national image and cleaning its squalid municipal house. The promise not to succeed themselves lent a sense of urgency to the actions of the new City Council: "We knew what we had to do, and we knew we were only there for four short years; so we did it (Darden)." As part of its campaign promise, the People's Council gave Harrell free reign to bring in an army of professionals and consultants to help chart the

city's rebirth. But Harrell went beyond this
charge, and skillfully involved as many of the
city's critical business and civic leaders as
possible into a new hierarchy of appointed
boards and commissions that further removed
the political functionaries at city hall from
the decision-making process.

The task of municipal house cleaning, however, ran into some serious opposition, especially from the well-entrenched forces in
the Public Safety (Police and Fire) Department. A fortuitous event, however, helped to
break the back of the Prieur Organization in
this arena as well. A young captain of detec-
tives, Claude "Bubba" Staylor, who later
served as both chief of police and a city
councilman, took the initiative when the Organization's police chief was out of town to
raid Norfolk's "protected" gambling and numbers rackets. The raid sent off howls of protest, especially when the police chief quickly
returned to drop the charges against several
of what the newspaper labeled as the city's
"most notorious gangsters (*Norfolk Virginian-
Pilot* 12/3/48)" for lack of evidence, while
more than a hundred of their customers lan-
guished in jail (*Norfolk Virginian-Pilot* 12/
4/48). The blatant partiality of this treatment, plus the fact that Staylor had uncovered
evidence of bribes and payoffs to more than
half the force, helped to unravel a comprehensive scheme of municipal corruption. A special
grand jury of the city's business and civic
elite used this opportunity to bring down both
the protected rackets and the police hierarchy
(*Norfolk Virginian-Pilot* 3/13/49). The Silkstocking Takeover was thus complete, and the
Organization's grip on city hall broken.

City Manager C. A. Harrell was not one to
delay once he had achieved the circumstances
conducive to action. The scandal in the police
department and the publicity generated by its
subsequent investigation had given him the

mandate for reform he sought; skillfully he shifted people to promote his professionals to a larger grasp of power. Although many of the experts who had descended upon the city returned quickly to their previous haunts in industry, commerce, and academia, they left behind the blueprints for progress in their voluminous charts, statistics, and analyses. Knowing that the work of these boards would outlast the electoral mandate of the People's Council, Harrell conspired to shift as much of the burden of charting municipal expansion as he could from the offices in city hall to the volunteer boards and commissions that established the policies. The People's Council exercised such a strong personal pull that others of similar talent were drawn from industry, commerce, professional callings, the arts, and the charities into volunteer service to the city, and this level of civic involvement became one of the most enduring legacies of their reign. By staffing these independent boards and commissions with his own professional advisors, and then feeding them the reports of the hired consultants, Harrell knew that he could broaden his mandate beyond the limitations of the work force at city hall.

The roster of the postwar City Council, Redevelopment and Housing Authority, and the Planning Commission read like a listing of local Community Fund chairmen, charitable benefactors, First Citizen Award winners, and civic headliners—just the type of individuals who so rarely get personally involved in running the day to day operations of municipal enterprises. The men who had been forced to take over the rebirth and redevelopment of Norfolk were the true opinion leaders in the community. They had the power, the prestige, and the respect to personally dispense with the types of objections that hamstrung so many similar dreams of rebirth across the country (Stinchcombe 1968, 129-50).

Harrell's plan worked better than anyone could have expected. Not a single community leader ever refused the Council's call to volunteer service (Darden), and the city's boards and commissions began calling for new ventures that would have been unthinkable just a few years earlier. Norfolk's citizens soon began to discern the fruits of their labor: a municipal airport, water treatment plant, modern bus system, a bridge-tunnel link to Portsmouth, new super highways to the downtown, and a host of other new highway and municipal ventures. Only a portion of C. A. Harrell's program was cast in concrete; the rest was set in careful planning and legislation. As part of the city's new house-keeping system, Harrell advocated a vast upgrading of the municipal statutes regarding property. The business and civic leaders who peopled the various volunteer boards and commissions took the lead in recommending revamped zoning ordinances, new building codes, stronger health and safety ordinances, and one of the nation's first enforced minimum housing codes (*Norfolk Virginian-Pilot* 7/23/61). It was such an ambitious program that it would never have passed without their support. The new ordinances would require major renovations to half the houses in the city; had the recommendations come from bureaucrats, instead of established community leaders, the public would have quickly suspected that partisan motives or selective enforcement were involved. Yet here were Norfolk's First Citizens, the leaders of its charities, financial institutions, industries, and businesses calling for an uplifting that began with their own boot-straps.

The Norfolk Housing Authority, born of the navy's need for wartime dwellings, had been among the first to catch the spirit of rebirth. The Authority was determined not to die out with the end of the war; it knew how much the city still had to accomplish to provide

adequate housing for its citizens. "Redevelopment" was added to its title for the first
time at the close of the war, and now the new
Norfolk Redevelopment and Housing Authority
began to revise its calling. Instead of just
serving as the navy's link to additional housing, the N.R.H.A. hoped to provide the means
to eliminate much of the city's crime- and
disease-infested slums (Curtin 1969, 140). It
began to formulate a plan that included two
phases: phase one entailed the renovation of
more than 1,000 wartime housing units to
accommodate civilian public housing tenants;
the second phase included an aggressive proposal to build 1,890 more public housing units
in order to clear the path for slum removal.
The Authority's sales pitch was accompanied by
the release of a graphic pictorial publication, *This Is It*, designed to sell both the
human and the economic elements of the plan.
The N.R.H.A. did not mince its words, the
booklet was clearly designed to sell public
housing as the essential first step to the
rebirth of the rest of the city:

> A 1937 study showed that the city was
> spending $5 for every $1 collected from
> real estate taxes and other income from
> five slum areas. Public housing cuts
> these service costs to a minimum. Public
> housing reduces the subsidy that tax-
> payers contribute every year to perpetu-
> ate nineteenth century hovels which
> injure the value of nearby property,
> impede the city's growth, and threaten
> the whole population with crime and
> disease. . . . The citizens of Norfolk
> will not, we believe, be satisfied with
> anything less than the complete elim-
> ination of every unfit dwelling in the
> city. Year by year, house by house, the
> reconstruction must go on until the com-
> bined efforts of the Norfolk Redevelop-

ment and Housing Authority and private
builders enable every family to enjoy a
decent home (Norfolk Redevelopment and
Housing Authority, 1946: 30, 47-8).

It was an argument skillfully designed to
appeal to the business and civic leaders that
the commissioners felt comprised their natural
constituency; indeed, even under the wartime
administration of the Prieur Machine, the
former Housing Authority had been the sole
prerogative of the business and civic elite
that now constituted the Silkstocking Takeover. Now that the People's Ticket was in
power, the Norfolk Redevelopment and Housing
Authority became the showpiece of the new administration. Not only were the commissioners
the very pillars of the city's new businessmen's elite, these men, by virtue of their
very extensive civic and charity work, had
also gathered a constituency that was far
larger than just the Silkstocking group they
seemed so adequately to represent. Of the
seven commissioners who had helped to formulate the N.R.H.A's postwar program, five had
headed the Community Fund, four had been named
First Citizen, and all seven had actively
studied the dreadful conditions of Norfolk's
aging housing stock. All had hung their heads
in shame when Nathan Straus, a federal housing
official rounding out his tour of 137 cities,
remarked of Norfolk's blight, "I have travel-
led all over the United States, from one end
to the other, but I have never seen anything
as bad as this (Norfolk Virginian-Pilot
7/26/61)." All seven were convinced that the
unsafe health and sanitary conditions that
existed in the slums posed a very great danger
to all the citizens of Norfolk (Norfolk
Virginian-Pilot 11/29/48), and they seized
upon this rare opportunity to convert the
navy's wartime projects to civilian use as
public housing.

It was more than just shame, however, more than just crime, taxes, health, property values, and housing conditions that motivated these men. All had lived through a most peculiar period in the history of Norfolk's growth: crisis proportions of wartime con-scription had strangely welded the entire citizenry into an active and cohesive civic force (Schlegel 1951). As members of the wartime Housing Authority, they had seen how quickly the people of Norfolk could respond to alleviate the most intolerable hardships. The sense of shared emergency had made the city vibrant and alive; it had carried over into a post war boom that was unique for the city; it had provided the impetus for the reform move-ment that was the first tenet of their faith; and finally, it had awakened the citizens to the fact that for a community united, all things were possible. If they could once more promote the sense of shared emergency, once again cultivate enough civic shame to prompt action, then, the commissioners believed, they could translate these forces into a renewed impetus for growth in general and a personal mandate for redevelopment and public housing specifically. Theirs was an ambitious plan, and they knew that citizen support was essen-tial to its adoption.

A series of timely events, however, helped to underscore the need for public housing, careful community planning, and quick munici-pal action. The Brambleton section of the city had for some time been convulsed with racial turmoil when several blacks sought to defy the community's strict standard of segregated housing. During the war years the vast influx of families into the city had put a premium on housing space in the few small areas of the city reserved for blacks. More than half of the black families in the city had been forced to either take in boarders or double up, just as in the white community, but in the black

neighborhoods, this meant two or more families
living in a one- or two-room apartment. There
had been almost no private housing built for
blacks in more than a decade and a half, and
Brambleton appeared to be the ideal site for
black expansion: it was a small (1,100 homes)
white community bounded on two sides by black
developments, and isolated by industrial properties and the Elizabeth River on the other
two. Once the first few black families began
to push across the traditional dividing line
between the black and white communities,
whites responded with attacks, threats, broken
windows, and minor acts of vandalism (*Norfolk
Journal and Guide* 6/8/46). After a series of
stormy City Council sessions, an interracial
committee was appointed to study the situation. The Council had hoped that some way
would be found to guarantee "the separation of
white and Negro homes in the area (*Norfolk
Virginian-Pilot* 6/1/46)," but the city's black
newspaper, the *Journal and Guide*, refused to
let the issue drop. The aggressive attacks of
the editors helped to convince the white
community that further violence would occur
unless something was done:

> It cannot be emphasized too strongly, and
> it is worth repeating again and again,
> that the housing situation affecting
> Norfolk's Negro citizens is not only
> acute, but desperate, while, by a fair
> comparison, no such problem faces the
> white population. The housing predicament
> with which this community is confronted
> cannot be resolved by the simple expedi-
> ent of viewing it as a racial matter. It
> is based upon an elementary human need
> and its amelioration must be on this
> basis alone. It is an age-old story of
> the law of supply and demand. Norfolk's
> Negro population has grown by some 25,000
> in the last few years, but little new

housing has emerged to shelter this
population increase. . . while, on the
other hand, construction of new white
units has been over 5,000. Even assuming
that private capital were available and
homes [for blacks] could be built, under
present restrictive conditions, where
could the necessary land be found (*Norfolk Journal and Guide* 6/1/46)?

The black and white communities remained at
odds, and the interracial committee appointed
by the City Council failed to devise a new
color line in the Brambleton area. The turmoil
did not cease with the first few incursions,
and soon the breakdown of time-honored color
lines began to affect other blocks in the
Brambleton section. The situation failed to
stabilize, and soon whole neighborhoods were
in flight. The *Journal and Guide* continued to
intimate that further incidents would occur
unless the city began to take some quick
measures to provide housing for blacks. The
fact that the *Journal and Guide*'s threats of
racial strife were reprinted for the white
community in the *Virginian-Pilot* helped to
build the momentum for public intervention--
some step that would alleviate the housing
crisis for blacks, yet also work to preserve
the separate status of white neighborhoods.
Thus, the N.R.H.A.'s push for public housing
struck a core of need recognized by both
blacks and whites, and public support for the
proposal began to build rapidly.

By 1948 a solid consensus in the community
had been achieved: the Norfolk Redevelopment
and Housing Authority had been angling for two
years for official endorsement of its slum
removal program; during that time the events
in Brambleton and its surrounding neighborhoods had been simmering; Public Health
Director Dr. John Huff had sounded repeated
warnings regarding the epidemic dangers of

crime and contagion in the city's slums; and
opinion in the black community had coalesced
around the single, dominant theme of their
housing crisis. The City Council was at last
ready to take official action, but the nature
of their commitment was, as yet, still undiscernible. The Council was, however, quick
to agree upon two points: the city faced a
"critical shortage of housing meeting the
minimum health standards in Negro and some
low-income white areas," and that "this condition is a matter of concern to all other
Norfolk residents, regardless of their own
pleasant living surroundings (*Norfolk Virginian-Pilot* 11/28/48)." For more than ten
years a succession of city councils had agreed
that it was "time to do something," the situation was "acute," the housing shortage was
"serious (*Norfolk Virginian-Pilot* 12/4/38),"
so the debate this time focused upon what
official actions, other than following earlier
councils in encouraging private developers to
enter the normally unprofitable low-income
housing market, could be taken to alleviate
the crisis. One councilman recommended that
the city "should be among the first in line"--
those words would prove prophetic--for new
federal redevelopment funds then under consideration by the U.S. Congress (*Norfolk Virginian-Pilot* 11/28/48). The suggestion touched
off such a response that the City Council, already saddled with an enormous array of capital projects, was prepared to embark upon "a
pure gamble (Darden)" and appropriated $25,000
for the N.R.H.A. to study the prospects of
slum removal even before such a program was
either legally or financially feasible!
    The Council's gamble for federal support
was not an idle gesture to ameliorate an increasingly exacerbating situation; it was a
carefully calculated risk. World War II and
the Depression had left the core of most other
cities in a condition comparable to Norfolk's;

it seemed only a matter of time before the
federal government cleared the way for such
action. Norfolk, however, had every intention
of leaping into the national limelight as the
first municipality to embark upon a program of
redevelopment; grabbing the headlines of urban
renewal seemed the city's best opportunity to
shake its sleazy wartime reputation and focus
attention instead upon all phases of its postwar renaissance. Publicity, however, was only
one-half of the quotient: Norfolk, more than
any other city its size, had seen clearly how
federal funds could provide the needed transfusion for massive community expansion. For
almost a decade the City Council under the
Prieur Machine had refused to embark upon any
municipal project or extend any public service
unless the navy dangled the carrot of federal
funding as an incentive. Federal funds had
aided in the construction of more than 3,400
dwellings; had upgraded numerous municipal
facilities, including schools, parks, playgrounds, highways, recreational centers, water
and sewer projects; had poured millions of
dollars into the area's economy (Curtin 1969);
and had helped, with both these new facilities
and the multiplier-effect of federal investment, to immeasurably increase the standard of
living for all the citizens of Tidewater
(N.R.H.A. 1946, 8).

The Norfolk Redevelopment and Housing Authority had already sought to allay fears that
its actions would be competing with the private market by challenging the city's builders
to begin their own redevelopment programs.
This Is It, the N.R.H.A.'s official promo-
tional tract, recalled earlier objections to
its plans and sought graphically to explain
how the city could embark upon a mammoth rebuilding effort, even under existing legislation, and not expend any local funds. The
commissioners knew firsthand that federal
funds had provided the impetus for the city's

economic expansion over the past decade; all
were experiencing, along with the rest of the
city's business leaders, the fruits of a local
boom that had been financed largely with
federal support. There was thus little reason
why Norfolk should not be first in line for
federal dollars as soon as the funds for urban
renewal became available.

The N.R.H.A. hired planning consultant
Charles K. Agle to study Norfolk's downtown
slums and develop a master plan for a major
urban renewal project. His report was a shock
even for natives who had long known that
housing conditions around the downtown area
were deplorable. Methodically he studied each
block and hovel to reach his conclusions:
"large scale redevelopment is the only chance
the city ever has had to accomplish a drastic
modernization of its heart (*Architectural
Forum* 1950, 137)." Map after map, table after
table, showed the same concentration of irre-
versible blight choking the central business
district: blocks where every structure needed
major repairs, where almost all of the houses
dated back to the nineteenth century, where
there were 13 or more fires over a two-year
period, where there were 17 or more arrests in
the previous months, and where there was a
heavy concentration of tuberculosis (*Norfolk
Virginian-Pilot* 7/26/61). As in many other
cities, the streets of Norfolk's downtown area
were the descendants of cow paths and carriage
ways upon which a gridiron street pattern had
been imposed (*Architectural Forum* 1950, 135).
All of the major highways that linked the
suburbs to the downtown area terminated a mile
short of the central business district, dis-
charging their traffic into a complex maze of
back alleys and clogged feeder roads (Beall,
Price and Locke 1950, 7). The feeling was almost universal in the business community that
unless the city took some strong steps to
increase traffic flow and provide parking,

property values and retailing in the downtown
area would collapse (Norfolk City Planning
Commission 1950, 5-15).

The Agle Report was a sobering eye-opener
in other respects. In addition to just reporting the slum conditions that cried out for
renewal, it also attempted to confront all of
the potential obstacles to successful redevelopment. It was in this regard that many
citizens found the report most shocking. Few
individuals realized how very profitable slum
properties--even in an area as blighted as
Norfolk's central ghetto--could be to its
owners, and some of the city's finest families
were shown to have heavy investments in slum
housing. The report showed that even under
rent control, an average slum dwelling with an
assessed value of $400 could achieve contract
rents of $142 a year per room, out of which
very little besides the $10.80 per year real
estate tax bill had to be paid for maintenance and upkeep. One example, pointed to as
typical of the inflated value of slum housing,
sheltered 32 families in a rickety, wood frame
building that had only four sinks and four
toilets; it brought in $4,500 a year in rent
and paid out only $98 in taxes (*Architectural
Forum* 1950, 136-37). Another complex (the
Tidewater Apartments) provided an even more
notorious example of slum profiteering: there
were 152 single-room units that netted the
owners $23,400 a year in rent. There were no
baths or showers; instead, the only facilities
for cooking, cleaning, washing, drinking, and
sanitation were six cold-water privies con-
sisting of a single faucet and toilet. The
total tax bill for the complex was less than
$600 a year (*Norfolk Virginian-Pilot* 7/26/61)
--a highly profitable investment!

Thus Norfolk was compelled by a number of
powerful motivators to become the first city
in the nation to qualify for federal funds the
following June, when President Truman signed

the U.S. Housing Act of 1949 into law. The act
granted municipalities both the legal authority and the necessary funding support to buy up
such properties. Before the act was passed,
the city could rely upon its powers of *eminent
domain* to purchase private property only if
were reused for "public" purposes, such as
land for schools, highways, and parks, but
additional public investment in a deteriorating neighborhood would have been foolish.
Before this new power of redevelopment passed
to cities, nothing in the municipal arsenal
would permit cities to buy up private property, tear it down, and then resell it to other
private residential, commercial, or industrial
de-velopers--the essence of urban renewal. The
act empowered cities to buy up large quanti-
ties of slum housing for a "fair" price--
roughly 60 percent above their assessed value,
or less than two years' rent on most build-
ings--and to acquire the rest through condemnation proceedings (*Architectural Forum* 1950,
137). The Agle Report had predicted that "the
future of Norfolk for the rest of its history
will be fixed by the action of the next ten
years (*Norfolk Virginian-Pilot* 7/26/61)"; it
might just as well have added that the legislation and supporting federal funding would be
the city's only real chance to have much of a
future at all.
     At last assured of both federal funding and
community support, the Norfolk Redevelopment
and Housing Authority forged ahead with its
program--the first urban renewal initiative
in the country. N.R.H.A. Project One bore a
striking resemblance to the blustery, full-
speed-ahead approach of its sires; it proposed
to bulldoze 120 acres of blighted land to make
way for broad highways, light industries, new
commercial districts, civic improvements,
schools, playgrounds, and a giant convention
hotel. It also bore the mark of City Manager
C. A. Harrell's balanced approach of careful

planning and community concern: almost all of
the 1,800 families uprooted by the bulldozers
would be relocated in modern, sanitary public
housing units, and many would eventually move
back into their own neighborhood, once it had
been rebuilt at public expense. No one doubted
the legitimacy of the undertaking: the slum
properties cleared represented some of the
most squalid, festering hovels in the nation
(N.R.H.A. 1957, 5-6); the municipal projects
undertaken were those seen as most essential
to salvaging the central business district;
and the land cleared for renewal was critical
to the city's efforts to restore its flagging
real estate tax base. Before demolition even
began, however, the N.R.H.A. rushed to completion several hundred new public housing
units on vacant land in order to absorb the
first wave of redevelopment refugees (*Norfolk
Virginian-Pilot* 8/15/50). Each time the bulldozers poised to bite off another chunk of
blighted land, the N.R.H.A. rushed to completion new housing projects to absorb the relocated residents. Indeed, this was all part
of the careful, humanistic approach of the
Silkstocking Takeover that promised "to
alleviate as much as possible the hardships
which are the by-products of such a project
(*Norfolk Virginian-Pilot* 8/22/51)."

Partly because this was the first redevelopment project in America, and Norfolk was
aware that the rest of the nation was watch-
ing, and partly because the city had been so
long prepared for this endeavor, N.R.H.A.
Project One was a masterfully planned and
conceived undertaking; certainly it was one of
the most-studied proposals ever advanced by a
municipality. Ever since Colonel Borland's
Citizens Crime Conference of 1937 exposed the
financial and human cost of slum life, the
city's business elite had dreamed of downtown
renewal. The N.R.H.A.'s own study in 1946
(*This Is It*) and the 1949 Agle Report had

added depth and dimension to the vision. It took five years to complete N.R.H.A. Project One, but the enormity of its carefully planned success was apparent to all. In the end, the project offered something for everyone: broad new thoroughfares provided downtown merchants with their first really modern link to the rest of the area; a new light industrial zone on Tidewater Drive was attracting so many private investments that it was prompting its own multi-million dollar construction boom (*Norfolk Virginian-Pilot* 3/22/56); new businesses were already moving into the redeveloped commercial areas; backers of a major new convention hotel (the Hotel Norfolk) were examining a corner site in the project (*Norfolk Virginian-Pilot* 7/26/61); and the former residents of some of the most dilapidated dwellings were able to reclaim their old neighborhoods, now completely rebuilt as planned communities. More importantly, the whole city was caught up in the boom psychology that accompanies such a dynamic undertaking, and the spin-off effects could be seen in hundreds of other unrelated expansions, investments, rehabilitations, and modernizations (Hebert 1950, 10). Urban renewal proved to be the spark that kindled the entire business community into action, and Norfolk raced to blot out the sorry memories of its sordid past.

A more complete description of the size and scope of N.R.H.A. Project One is necessary in order to comprehend its full impact. The project included one 80-acre section that is bounded by Virginia Beach Boulevard on the north, Lincoln Street on the east, Brambleton Avenue on the south, and Monticello Avenue on the west. It then extended east along Brambleton Avenue to include a broad strip surrounding Tidewater Drive--roughly 127 acres. New York's Stuyvesant Town was then the biggest housing project in existence, but it was a little more than one-third the size of Project

One; New York had forty times the population of Norfolk in 1950, but less than twice the slum clearance acreage contained in Norfolk's undertaking (*Architectural Forum* 1950, 132). Land acquisition cost $5.7 million, of which the U.S. government paid two-thirds ($3.8 million). Norfolk's $1.9 million share was not a cash loss; it was worked off instead in land set aside to build new schools, a recreation center, fire and police stations, utility lines, and street improvements, which the city would have built anyhow. The project generated an additional $18 million in public expenditures--more than half of which came from the state or federal government for public housing and highway costs--and $15.6 million in private construction (N.R.H.A. 1974, 46; *Architectural Forum* 1950, 132; Hanna 1967, 92). The total cost to the federal government for building the 3,000 public housing units planned by the N.R.H.A. was close to $30 million (*Architectural Forum* 1950, 132)--a sizeable multiplier in any economy.

The business leaders who sired N.R.H.A. Project One saw redevelopment as more than just a means to eradicate blight, relieve deprivation, and cure downtown traffic congestion; they were focusing as well on a more serious situation that struck deep at their own sense of financial security. Norfolk had too many of its economic eggs tied up in one basket; its huge naval installations made the city essentially a one-industry town (*Architectural Forum* 1950, 134)--an enterprise that was virtually exempt from real estate, personal property, and other local tax assessments. After World War I Norfolk paid a heavy price for this over-reliance when disarmament left the nation with a one-ocean navy that, after the outbreak of war in Manchuria, sailed for duty stations on the West Coast. A brief inspection of the waterfront gave ample evidence of the fact that coastwise shipping--

once the economic staple of the area--had been
almost completely absorbed by rail and truck-
ing facilities. Other than ship-building and
coal export, the city had no other private
industry of any magnitude (Agle 1956, 79) and,
in fact, suffered a severe shortage of available industrial land. A few million dollars
clipped from a naval appropriation by an errant congressional committee could well send
the area into an economic tailspin.

Since the end of the war, the city's economic leaders had given serious attention to
attracting new business as a hedge against
such congressional capriciousness, but they
had achieved little success. City Manager C.A.
Harrell had already recommended an aggressive
plan of annexation, or, he warned, "the city
would die by inches (Harrell 1949, 9)." In
spite of his insistence, annexation under the
present state of Virginia politics proved to
be both a costly and a risky course, although
one to which Norfolk was deeply committed.
Even if they could acquire vacant land through
annexation, however, the city's business
leaders still had to face the harsh reality
that Norfolk could not hope to serve as a
major industrial hub because it lacked a cheap
source of power (*Architectural Forum* 1950,
135). A plan to attract light industry into
newly developed sites close to the heart of
the area's financial and commercial district--
a scarce commodity in any community--was the
city's only hope for a competitive alternative. For this reason, a major redevelopment
project that entailed massive clearing of land
close to the downtown financial district was
seen as the one best hope for the area's
continued financial success. More than a third
of the land cleared in N.R.H.A. Project One
was thus dedicated to developing prime industrial and commercial sites with both rail and
major highway access (*Norfolk Virginian-Pilot*
4/16/52). The catch was that in order to be

able to provide new land for these kinds of
critical business and industrial uses, the
majority of the land cleared under redevelopment powers had to be "residential" in nature.
Federal law at the time also mandated that
after redevelopment the majority of the land
must continue as residential property. Thus
cities, like Norfolk, could clear a slum, but
they had to balance residential, industrial,
commercial, and public uses in the type of
carefully planned undertaking exemplified by
N.R.H.A. Project One (Housing and Home Finance
Agency 1950).

Finally, N.R.H.A. Project One was successful at alleviating a part of the housing
shortage for poor blacks. Not only did it
create 3,000 new public housing units, it
proposed to split these between the project
site and newly acquired vacant land on the
outskirts of the downtown area. This was in
keeping with the housing pattern in the rest
of Norfolk at the time: black neighborhoods
were spread across the city, instead of just
concentrated in a single downtown district, as
in most Northern cities (Taueber and Taueber
1965, 35-96). Since only 1,800 families would
be moved out of the project area during demolition (N.R.H.A. 1957), this represented a
significant net gain in housing for blacks.
The fact that the new black housing area would
be carefully isolated by broad new thoroughfares that would serve as solid color barriers
was also viewed positively by whites fearful
of encroachments into nearby neighborhoods. In
addition, a new recreation center, police pre-
cinct, fire station, and the first elementary
school (Young Park) built for black students
(*Norfolk Journal and Guide* 4/19/58)--the
others were hand-me-downs from the white
community, a standard practice in the South--
were included as part of the project. Because
the new school, park, and recreational facilities were designated for use by blacks, the

city hoped to relieve some of the pressure to
integrate white facilities in adjoining neighborhoods (Ervin 1956, 32-3).

City Manager C. A. Harrell also saw redevelopment as a panacea for many of the city's
other municipal needs. Throughout his tenure
as manager, Harrell placed a strong emphasis
on neighborhood needs: upgrading schools and
residential streets, decentralizing police and
fire facilities, and building new parks, playgrounds, community centers, and recreation
areas. N.R.H.A. Project One also bears the imprint of his careful approach to community
planning. Besides meeting the obvious commuter
transportation needs of the area by building
two additional highway approaches to the downtown area, the project represented the city's
first full attempt to create a planned public
community for its black residents. Although
surrounded by the updated highway system,
Young Park, a 752-unit public housing project
(named for P. Bernard Young, Sr., founder of
the *Journal and Guide*), would be built upon a
neighborhood street concept virtually inacces-
sible to through traffic. Population density
would be reduced from the preredevelopment
levels of 50 families per acre to only 20. In
addition, the phased development of the area
was designed so that every family would have a
place to go as the project gained momentum
(*Architectural Forum* 1950, 134)--a goal that
was far easier to work out on paper than put
into practice, especially since a number of
families and single individuals were ineligi-
ble for public housing.

As part of his concept of professional
community planning, City Manager Harrell was
taking active steps to prevent future slums
from occurring in the ring of older middle-
class housing which separated the downtown
area from the newer postwar subdivisions on
the outskirts of the city. Roughly one-third
of the city's residential structures could be

described as in danger of slipping from relatively good housing for its era into the dilapidated state that precedes a full-fledged slum (*Architectural Forum* 1950: 136)--all of it in this middle-class ring that included all or portions of the city's first streetcar and automobile suburbs. The tremendous influx of people attracted to Norfolk during the war--Norfolk's population increased by 48 percent, or almost 70,000 people, between 1940 and 1950--placed a premium upon existing houses, and many of the homes in these areas either took in boarders or were cut up into multifamily dwelling units. The transient nature of this new population and the slapdash quality of the remodeling jobs left deteriorated dwellings in even the finest neighborhoods.

The major weapon in Harrell's arsenal against blight was the newly-formulated minimum housing code, which was not scheduled to go into effect until January 1, 1954. Housing codes were still a relatively new concept when Walter Hoffman (later, a federal judge) and his committee of lawyers and building officials had to put one together for Norfolk; in fact, less than a dozen other cities across the nation had begun experimentation with code enforcement as a way to prevent blight. Housing codes specified "livability standards" for dwellings, rather than concentrate on the more limited coverage afforded by fire, building, and health codes. Examples of provisions in Norfolk's new code included at least one window per room, running water inside the building, a flush toilet connected to a sewer (but not necessarily inside the dwelling), adequate means of garbage disposal, and a safe form of central heating with a flue to the outside of the building--none of them extravagant standards by any measure, but all represented a distinct improvement over the conditions that existed in many semi-blighted areas. The Norfolk code writers were obviously setting their

standards on the low side of "livability" because they realized that strong enforcement
would be the key to its effectiveness as a
slum deterrent (*Architectural Forum* 1950, 136-
7). As a tribute to the wisdom of the code
writers, almost 2,500 dwellings were rehabilitated during the first two years of the code's
operation; only 173 buildings were vacated as
a result of enforcement, and most of these
were reoccupied later after completion of the
required renovations (*Norfolk Virginian-Pilot*
10/11/56).

The small crowd of dignitaries and city
officials who gathered outside the hovel at
755 Smith Street that wintry morning in 1951
had come to cheer the revitalized spirit of a
New Norfolk as much as to applaud the singular
event they were witnessing. The New Norfolk
was as blustery, bold, and bullish as its
sires in the city's business establishment; it
was as compassionate and humane as the civic
leaders and charity workers who presided at
its birth; it was as levelheaded, pragmatic,
and professional as the planners, designers,
and consultants who fussed over its infant
developments; and finally, it was as careful,
concise, and well directed as the city manager
who tutored it. In electing the Silkstocking
Ticket, the voters had opted for a change from
the cautious, humdrum course plotted by the
wartime City Council; they got more than that
for which they had bargained. In 1946 the
people had been swept up in the vision of a
New Norfolk; by 1951 they were witnessing the
bricks and mortar, the concrete, steel and
glass, of its realization. A revitalized redevelopment and housing authority was plotting
eradication of the city's blight; a new port
authority was bent on reclaiming the glory of
its past; new zoning laws and subdivision
regulations extended the promise of orderly
expansion; annexation initiatives held out the
assurance of continued growth; revamped build-

ing, health, housing, and fire codes served as an omnipresent guard against future deterioration; a massive capital improvements program was rapidly solving the needs for more parks, schools, water, sewage, street lighting, traffic control, and transportation facilities; construction was already underway on a new bridge-tunnel link and a modern airport terminal; new highways promised an end to the city's isolation (Harrell 1950b, 9-14); and everywhere there was evidence that the citizens themselves had caught the spirit of these ventures and were embarking on their own fix up, expansion, rebuilding, and modernization campaigns in thousands of smaller endeavors.

For many, N.R.H.A. Project One represented the high-water mark of the city's effort not just to tear down the old and build the new, but to do it with such style and vision that it would capture the attention of the nation, and thereby erase some of the taint of its earlier infamy. It marked a sharp contrast between the foot-dragging of the wartime City Council and the foot-racing of the Silkstocking administration. Buoyant of spirit, newly confident, and optimistic once again in outlook, Norfolk's citizens were finally prepared to face the future without trepidation. Project One represented as well a remarkable diversity of personalities, a fortuitous display of insight, and a timely turn of events. Foremost among these was the leadership and vision provided by Charles L. Kaufman and the other citizen-elites who served as commissioners of the Norfolk Redevelopment and Housing Authority. Profiteering from blight and overcharging the poor were as widespread among Norfolk's slumlords and a certain segment of its real estate community as anywhere in the nation (*Architectural Forum* 1950, 137); in many instances the profits were collected by families and individuals that had almost parallel standing in the community. But the

commissioners of the N.R.H.A. had the sheer
force of commercial and financial persuasion
to stare down opposition from even the most
well-connected property owners. Their standing in the community was so high that these
individuals were able to launch the city
boldly and irrevocably into what was in most
of the other council-manager cities of the
nation a torturous and easily sidetracked
course (Stinchcombe 1968, 129-50).

The silkstocking People's Ticket of Richard
Cooke, Pretlow Darden, and John Twohy, in
combination with a loose voting alignment with
independent Councilman Rives Worsham (Darden),
possessed much the same kind of community
power and prestige. By ripping political control of city hall from the grasp of the Prieur
Machine, they restored faith in municipal
government--a step that was necessary before
any progressive measure could be taken with
citizen support. The people of Norfolk would
never have stood for the impositions provided
by the revamped building, fire, health and
minimum housing codes if they had feared
indifferent or selective enforcement for
political gain; neither would they have stood
for either the cost or the inconvenience posed
by massive municipal construction initiatives
if they had doubted the motives behind these
efforts; they would never have granted their
city the power to acquire private property and
destroy it in preparation for eventual resale
to other private investors--the very essence
of the redevelopment process--if either end of
urban renewal had been controlled by ring
politicians.

The People's Ticket maintained dignity and
devotion to principal in spite of the controversy that raged about them. Nobody doubted
their motives or questioned either their
integrity or their purpose, but a group that
embarks on so many unparalleled municipal
endeavors must inevitably make enemies and

provoke opposition. The City Council chambers reverberated with the hubbub of both civic support and fierce opposition throughout the brief tenure of the People's administration, but the Council plunged onward despite the controversy, always careful to explain each step of the undertaking to those who would follow. This was the true mark of their partisan independence, for no political group could have long endured the intensity of the public debate, the level of criticism, or the unpredictability of popular support posed by each new initiative. Even so, the People's group had the courage to persevere and risk being judged only by their accomplishments.

City Manager Charles A. Harrell was the right man at the right time to carry out the initiatives of the People's City Council. He represented absolute incorruptibility and professionalism at a time when both were sorely needed at city hall. Twenty years after his reign as manager, Norfolk was still completing the final phases of the ambitious program he had set forth. More than any other single individual, Harrell understood the true potential for municipal planning and government. He was responsible for snatching the operation of city hall from the grasp of short-sighted governmental functionaries, and then tutoring both citizens and municipal workers alike on what could be accomplished. His was a vision of greatness for city government that would be hard to forget, even long after he had passed from the local scene. Harrell brought the best technical and professional minds in the county to study the city's problems and to help chart its growth; many of them decided to stay and lend a hand in achieving the realities promised in their reports. Harrell made Norfolk City Hall one of the most desirable locations in the country for aspiring public servants: not only was the city continually at the forefront of the newly developing fields of muni-

cipal planning, urban renewal, and code enforcement, the People's Ticket promised that
these new powers would be used exclusively for
municipal services, free from the taint of
political interference or partisan purpose
that was apparently so prevalent elsewhere.
Harrell dared to empower the citizens--both
the spark-plugs of its neighborhood leagues
and the dynamos of its civic and business
elite--to help plan and promote municipal
endeavors. He inspired the best from his own
employees, and was able once again to restore
a sense of pride and accomplishment to city
offices. Harrell's vision, backed up by the
proposals of numerous citizen groups and
consultants, provided Norfolk with the basis
for a master plan for city growth and devel-
opment--a step that put it almost two years
ahead of other areas in the competition for
federal urban renewal dollars. Other writers
have bemoaned the lack of unity and leadership
that plagues most council-manager cities and
precludes, for the most part, decisive action;
thanks to City Manager C. A. Harrell and his
close connection and cooperation with the
People's City Council and its corporate elite,
Norfolk suffered no such disability. In fact,
Norfolk, because it had such leadership,
thrived in the area of urban renewal precisely
because it had truly achieved such a professional and non-partisan atmosphere. Because
politics was mixed in with their administration, most other council-manager cities failed
to achieve the level of consensus that was
possible to sustain such activities--a level
of unanimity that was ordinarily only possible
in the highly partisan strong mayor cities
(Stinchcombe 1968, 129-50).

Lawrence M. Cox, the executive director of
the Norfolk Redevelopment and Housing Authority, headed a promising staff of planners and
designers who moved quickly to seize their
opportunity before the momentum for progress

dissipated. "Hustling young Larry Cox," as he was described by one trade magazine (*Architectural Forum* 1950, 136), was ambitious and demanding enough to get results. The relocation program, as well as the total design for Project One, set a standard for the rest of the nation. Cox had been head of the N.R.H.A. almost from its founding, and over the years, especially during the hectic war effort, had developed a capable staff that was both loyal to him and fully committed to redevelopment. Close collaboration between Cox, the City Council, the commissioners, and the business community helped to push N.R.H.A. Project One off of the drawing boards and into reality.

The support of Norfolk's two major daily newspapers, the morning *Virginian-Pilot* and the evening *Ledger-Dispatch* (later the *Ledger-Star* after a merger with the *Portsmouth Star*), was also instrumental in advancing both the cause of the Silkstocking movement and the accomplishments of its administration. The two papers, although fiercely competitive, were owned and published by the same family group; together they served as the spokesmen for the city's business elite, and the accolades of triumph from the newspapers for the latest ground breaking or achievement frequently sounded brassier than any possible press release. The support of the papers, especially the more progressive *Virginian-Pilot*, was critical to the People's efforts to win election, maintain momentum through the police scandal, and promote its program of redevelopment, code enforcement, and bonded indebtedness. Reporters for both papers were insiders to both the events and the intrigue at city hall, and this access to the decision-makers, as well as the fact that a reporter in this era kept a fixed beat for years, gave them a stake in protecting their sources (Mason).

Finally, the spirit of adventure and self-sacrifice that prevailed among Norfolk's citi-

zens helped enormously in clearing the hurdles
inherent in redevelopment. The People's Ticket
had been elected in 1946 with an overwhelming
mandate for progress, and the citizens waited
patiently through the initial stages of planning and development. Seizing control of city
government took more, however, than winning a
single election, yet the citizens did not lose
faith even during the darkest hours of the
police scandal--an event which could have
easily wrecked all hope of progressive activity in most administrations; in Norfolk,
instead, it helped to assure success. The
people were prepared for action, and they
watched patiently as each new step unfolded.
Norfolk's growth during the war years had been
enormous, and municipal services had suffered
greatly under this additional burden, but the
people never lost faith that City Manager
Harrell and the Silkstocking members of the
City Council would eventually catch up to this
level of growth with their own ambitious program of expanded municipal services.

Other cities that were similar to Norfolk
found their own plans for growth and redevelopment stymied because their citizens lacked either the vision or the spirit of sacrifice to participate in progress; not so with
Norfolk. Redevelopment, especially of the
magnitude that had been planned, called for
enormous personal hardships from many individuals, especially from those who could least
afford to suffer more, and yet they bore their
discomfort, and for the most part, bore it in
silence. The People's Ticket and its attendant
push for progress truly represented the efforts of a rejuvenated body politic; the bulldozers that ripped through the sagging walls
of that first Smith Street structure and the
adjacent areas in N.R.H.A. Project One represented the high point in the momentary blaze
of glory that characterized Norfolk's Silkstocking Takeover.

2

Premonitions of Crisis

Norfolk Redevelopment and Housing Authority Project One would take five years to complete, but even before the bulldozers ripped through that first house on Smith Street, the men who had charted the meteoric rise of Norfolk's corporate stock had already retreated to the plushness of their board rooms and counting houses. The individuals who had so carefully planned and nourished its inception were already fading from the scene. Each new groundbreaking or ribbon-cutting ceremony marked the passing of the old order: the planning phase was over, and now it was time for the builders. The Silkstocking Takeover had run into a snag: as part of their promise to clean up city government and make it more responsive, the People's Ticket of Cooke, Darden, and Twohy had promised not to seek a second term; now the very events that served as tributes to their triumph stood as tombstones to their passing. The Silkstocking Ticket was unable to propagate successors, and the spirit of renaissance and reform that had vaulted it to victory had, by 1950, dissipated, and then dissolved completely.

At first, as their term drew to a close, the reform movement sought to find others who would carry their banner (Darden), but none of the city's business or financial leaders was willing to again risk openly opposing Billy Prieur or his political machine. The sense of urgency and shared emergency that had brought the reformers to power had passed; the Outs had become the Ins in the kind of political perversity that always hastens the doom of such reform movements (Sugg 1967, 368); and dramatic change had become altogether too commonplace in Norfolk. Business was booming, and the citizens were no longer forced to turn to the corporate community to avert financial ruin. Local prosperity, aided by the Cold War state of military readiness, had lulled the citizens into a false sense of contentment, fully prepared to count their blessings in the privacy of their homes, untouched by and undemanding of municipal government.

When their search for successors came up dry, the People's group again sought an audience with local Byrd Organization chieftain Billy Prieur, hoping to find some middle ground that would continue their legacy of progress within the more limited confines of machine politics. Finding compromise candidates was no easy matter, especially because Prieur would not agree to anyone who had played even the slightest role in the Silkstocking Takeover. Eventually the political negotiators were able to agree upon one man who emerged at the top of everyone's list of potential contenders (Darden). W. Fred Duckworth was an ideal choice to head the Harmony Ticket that would emerge from these backroom discussions: because he was a relative newcomer to Norfolk, he had no close financial, civic, or personal ties to the Silkstocking crowd. On the other hand, he possessed the type of managerial skills necessary to head up Norfolk's complex municipal organization. Duckworth had been brought to the area from rural North Carolina in 1936 by the Ford Motor Company to manage its South Norfolk plant, one of the few major industrial concerns in the area not directly owned by the People's reformers. Several years later he left that position to manage the area's War Production Board, a post that expanded his circle of community contacts. After the war he started his own car dealership, Cavalier Ford (*Norfolk Virginian-Pilot* 7/23/61), a project that received Silkstocking financial support. Even though he was not a Norfolkian, the People's group was impressed by his managerial acumen, his considerable array of skills, and the extent of his commitment to his adopted city (Darden; Mason).

The People's group was not as pleased with Duckworth's two running mates, both of whom were chosen less for their accomplishments than because nobody could find solid grounds to scratch them from the list. Lawrence C. Page had served on the City Council just before the war, but had shown the good sense to excuse himself from office before being branded for its wartime failures. Although he was a real estate broker, he had no close ties to the powerhouses of the People's group, and since he had also run as a Republican for the U.S. Senate against Organization scion Harry F. Byrd, Sr. (*Norfolk Virginian-Pilot* 6/10/42; 6/14/50), he was obviously no longer associated with Prieur's crowd. N. B. Etheridge, an independent garage owner, was a political unknown without any apparent ties to either the Organization or the Silkstocking crowd. For the People's forces, the Harmony Ticket of Duckworth, Page and Etheridge represented a marriage of necessity, rather than a bond of trust between these two disparate political groups (Darden).

Shortly after the bulldozer ripped through the wall of that first house on Smith Street, City Manager Harrell, the one man who more than any other had been responsible for the rebirth and rejuvenation of Norfolk, departed

abruptly to accept a similar position in San
Antonio, Texas. At the time, the most common
explanation for his departure was that he and
Duckworth, the new mayor, had clashed bitterly
over who would run the operations at city hall
(*Norfolk Virginian-Pilot* 7/25/61). Cleraly the
city could not endure two chief administrators
pulling in opposite directions, and Duckworth,
with his "bulldozer drive and directness," was
bent on running the city from the mayor's office, a marked contrast to the free-wheeling
independence granted C. A. Harrell by the
People's City Council (*Norfolk Virginian-Pilot*
7/4/75). For his part, Harrell had always
indicated that he would resign before sur-
rendering his judgement to partisan considerations (*Norfolk Virginian-Pilot* 6/4/50); the
arrival of Duckworth and the Harmony Ticket,
however, meant that the Organization was again
advancing a foothold in city hall. When C. A.
Harrell left, with him went all hope of continuing the municipal reform brought about by
the People's group; soon his police chief and
a number of other key administrators who had
been instrumental in carrying out his program
also departed with indications that they had
been fired by the new City Council (Staylor).

Mayor W. Fred Duckworth was the perfect man
to step in now and fill the gap in leadership
left by Harrell's departure: he offered a
continuation of the progress and prosperity
without necessitating any further decision or
dissension on the part of the citizens. He was
an unusually able leader, and if the decorum
of democracy was somewhat abridged under his
tutelage, the voters did not seem to mind very
much. The Planning Stage had passed, the
Builder had taken over, and the people seemed
to approve unquestioningly the fruits of his
labor, giving credit equally to the planners
and builder alike. Duckworth was above all
else a bricks-and-mortar man, and he presided
daily over the construction of the New Nor-

folk. As the building blocks of its bright facade were laid in place, nothing, not even the heavy storm clouds of racial disunity building on the horizon, seemed capable of diverting that progress.

The Prieur Machine made no attempt under Mayor Duckworth to return to the corrupt and profligate practices of its wartime administration; its members had been absent long enough from the seats of power that they were content to settle for positions, without demanding authority. Although hardheaded, and occasionally dictatorial, Duckworth had no problem adapting to the programs begun under the People's group. He continued Harrell's administrative innovations, merely rerouting the technical advisors through the mayor's office. Although he was decisive and extremely aggressive, like Harrell, he never moved until satisfied that all the conditions were favorable. C. A. Harrell's departure threatened the continuance of the Harmony coalition, but Duckworth stepped in to take personal control of city government, and so assuaged some of the fears of machine politics.

During the Duckworth era, Norfolk was run almost exclusively from the mayor's office: it was there that city council made its decisions during private presessions before the regular public meeting, and those not in attendance were told later how to vote. He throve on consensus, and minor differences between council members at the public sessions took on major proportions in his mind. Although protective of the Byrd Organization's interests, Duckworth would not brook incompetence. He rose quickly to the top of the local Organization and soon, along with Prieur, dominated its decisions as well. This combination of elected authority, political power, administrative expertise, and driving personal force was devastating to city employees who faltered or got out of line.

Duckworth did not have to bargain for acquiescence from the People's group; he won it through strength. The Silkstocking crowd respected Duckworth's ability and integrity, or at least they feared crossing him without a guarantee of victory. Although more political than they had been, Duckworth's program did not differ perceptibly from their own: they saw that city hall was still well run; there was little evidence of corruption; business leaders were still consulted; the authority of the expert consultants and advisors was still intact; and the framing of Harrell's blueprints was well underway. All in all, the business establishment had few complaints, although plenty of reason to feel uneasy: such power, concentrated in one man, if misdirected, could prove disastrous. The citizens, too, seemed relatively content with Duckworth's administration, and councilmanic contests during this time produced very little in the way of a challenge to the Mayor's preeminence. This was truly the "Era of Good Feeling," as one local historian labeled it (*Norfolk Virginian-Pilot* 7/25/61), for even the corporate and civic leaders who had wrested control of the city's growth from the court-house ring politicians now breathed as well the chloroform of prosperity. Business as usual prevailed at city hall: "the reformers had grown tired, the regulars had taken over, and things would have to get pretty bad before the reformers would stir again (Sugg 1967, 368)."

The U.S. Supreme Court's decision in the *Brown v. Board of Education* case struck like a thunderbolt through the false sense of local optimism that prevailed in May of 1954. By the time the citizens of Norfolk looked up to discern the dangers ahead, they found the state's political leaders scurrying in panic for punitive structures and hastily contrived extralegal shelters as a means to divert the raging force of racial discontent that had been building for centuries in the backwaters that surrounded the city. It was clear from the outset that Norfolk would not be allowed the freedom to pursue its own independent course, separate from the rest of the state, even if its leadership were so inclined. The very fact that Duckworth was now so entrenched at the throttle of municipal control meant that Norfolk would follow the dictates of the statewide Byrd Organization.

Norfolk, one of the most liberal cities in the South, now ironically became the main battlefield upon which the fate of Virginia's Massive Resistance Plan would be decided. Vast segments of its population had little use for those racial codes and institutions, both written and unwritten, that were primarily Southern. The storm-whipped waves of Massive Resistance would break as well over Arlington, Charlottesville, Prince Edward County, and Warren County, but these would be small-scale tests of its voracity when compared to a city Norfolk's size. At the time, Norfolk had a population rapidly approaching 300,000, and was earning new status as the state's largest city. More than one-third of its population represented the liberalizing influences of its naval or N.A.T.O (North Atlantic Treaty Organization) forces; the rest benefitted in their day-to-day contact with these and other representatives of vast national and international interests. Under the able leadership of C. A. Harrell and the People's group, Norfolk had forsaken its obligatory glance to Richmond for guidance, and instead looked to the rest of the world for approval.

The many, varied opportunities of government service in Tidewater had made Norfolk a mecca for Southern blacks hoping to improve their lot in life. The desegregation of the military forces that had taken place under President Truman meant that blacks could rise to positions of leadership in an integrated

society that existed just on the periphery of
Norfolk's own. The lure of steady employment
in the area's shipyards and rework facilities
prompted a continual stream of job-hunters
that started even before the hostilities had
even begun. Whereas most blacks in Norfolk
were of relatively low economic status when
compared to their white neighbors, a black
middle class was growing at a faster pace than
elsewhere in the South. Although most of the
major trade unions had not yet been cracked,
the door of opportunity to nondiscriminatory
positions in government and war-related industries had just been opened, and opportunities
in the private sector would become available
as soon as blacks had achieved success in
these endeavors.

All in all, the history of race relations
in Norfolk had been good, especially under the
even-handed municipal management of C. A.
Harrell and the Silkstocking crowd. Only 27
percent of Norfolk's 300,000 citizens were
black, a segment "large enough to provide
leadership, but not so large as to be believed
to threaten established patterns (Reif 1960,
1)." But to Duckworth, the black leadership
had already proven itself a thorn in the side
of municipal unanimity, and Duckworth was not
one to overlook even the slightest irritant.
Even though black council challenger P. B.
Young had posed no real threat in the 1952
race, Duckworth was apparently miffed that the
black community had opposed his own "harmony"
slate. There were other, more serious signs of
a growing challenge in the black community,
far more significant than the periodic offer-
ing of token opposition candidates. By 1954
blacks were growing increasingly antagonistic
to the Mayor's housing, development, recreation, and municipal finance policies. The
Supreme Court's decision in May of that year
only made that dissension more readily visible
to the general public.

Ever since the first blacks began moving into the white section of Brambleton in the mid-1940s, a succession of city councils had been incapable of halting the demise of traditional barriers to integrated neighborhoods. The tub-thumping of the Organizations' wartime City Council gave mute sanction to a wave of white violence and vandalism that temporarily halted the spread (*Norfolk Journal and Guide* 6/1/46), but the election of the People's Ticket in June of 1946 gave new impetus to that transition. The People's group tried to maintain an air of orderly calm and reasonableness; their approach was to talk out differences with committees comprised of members of both races. In the atmosphere of calm that prevailed under their reign, traditional racial barriers in Brambleton fell quickly. Brambleton had always led a somewhat tenuous existence as the sole white community in the zone of the city dominated by blacks, and its white residents had relied heavily on the combination of natural, geographic, and traditional barriers to keep it that way. Once the color barrier at Corprew Avenue had been breached and violence had subsided, the area fell quickly to growing pressure to provide homes for the emerging black middle class. In 1949 Ruffner Elementary was opened for the diminishing white population of Brambleton and the Stonewall Jackson School was turned over to the black school system (*Norfolk Journal and Guide* 6/1/46). The John Goode Elementary School, ironically named for Norfolk's Confederate congressman and president of the Constitutional Convention that stripped blacks of the power to vote (Rorer 1968, 207) was shifted to the black school system in 1950. Two years later (1952) Ruffner was reassigned to the black system as a junior high school, thereby signaling the final defeat of the last white holdouts (*Norfolk Journal and Guide* 4/19/58).

Once the color line had been successfully
breached and finally broken in the Brambleton
section, it fell more easily in other parts of
the city as well. Norfolk in the 1950s, like
many other older Southern cities, was unlike
its Northern counterparts: it did not have a
single, central, black ghetto surrounded by a
ring of white suburbs (Taueber and Taueber
1965, 35-96). Instead, Norfolk contained a
number of small communities, most of which had
their own sections for black housing (see
Figure 1). Successive annexations had brought
these communities within the city boundaries,
but the result was that Norfolk's black population occupied, in addition to a central slum
area, a number of isolated black communities
that existed next to whites in the Atlantic
City, Lamberts Point, Granby (Bollingbrook),
Sewells Point (Titustown), Tanner's Creek
(Oakwood), Berkley, and Campostella sections
of the city (U.S. Census 1952:II). There was
some pressure to expand the color lines in
these areas, but the traditional proximity of
blacks and whites in the city had forestalled
the white exodus that had taken place in
Brambleton, Chesterfield, and in some areas of
Berkley (*Norfolk Virginian-Pilot* 5/29/46).
Thus, there was little danger of open racial
conflict when the Supreme Court's desegregation decision was handed down in 1954: the
city's traditional residential patterns, its
history of good race relations, opportunities
for advancement in the military and government
service, already-integrated military housing,
and the increasing desegregation of the city's
private charitable, health religious, welfare,
and educational boards (Reif 1960, 1) seemed
adequate to surmount any submerged hostilities.

Increasingly, however, local attention began to focus on the working class neighborhoods of the Tanner's Creek District of old
Norfolk County, scheduled for annexation into

Figure 1
Norfolk's Black, Mixed Race, and Transition Neighborhoods

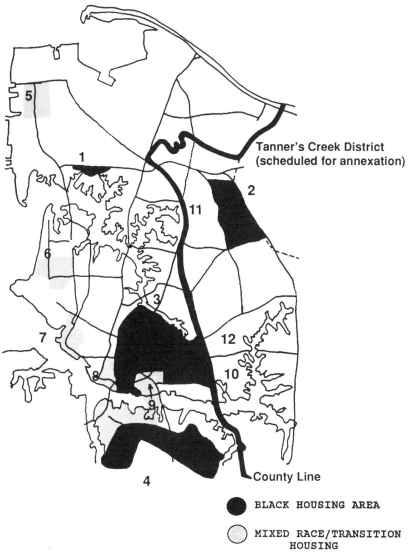

Tanner's Creek District
(scheduled for annexation)

County Line

● BLACK HOUSING AREA

◎ MIXED RACE/TRANSITION
   HOUSING

1	Titustown/Carney Park	7	Atlantic City
2	Oakwood/Rosemont	8	Downtown
3	Uptown/Project One	9	Brambleton
4	Berkley/Campostella	10	Broad Creek Shores
5	Benmorrell Navy Housing	11	Coronado
6	Lambert's Point	12	Broad Creek Navy Housing

Source: Norfolk Chamber of Commerce, 1954, pp. 10-12.

the city on January 1, 1955, as a result of
Harrell's earlier initiatives. Portions of the
area had unpoliced cesspools of crime, prostitution, gambling, and debauchery that operated
under quasi-official auspices just beyond the
reach of city enforcement; other areas held
vast tracts of substandard housing without
adequate plumbing or water. The condition of
the area had already prompted bickering on an
otherwise harmonious City Council over the
unexpectedly high cost of annexation versus
the necessity to find new space for industrial
and suburban expansion (*Norfolk Virginian-
Pilot* 3/15/54). By the summer of 1954, Norfolk
County officials had all but washed their
hands of the area until the city took control.
The Tanner's Creek District thus existed in a
state of limbo: county officials refused to
maintain costly municipal services in an area
they would soon lose, and the City of Norfolk
had not yet acquired title or authority to
deal with its problems. Norfolk's eleventh-
hour hesitations over the exorbitant asking
price only served to increase the area's sense
of isolation from governmental authority. For
this reason, residents began to grow accus-
tomed to the idea of handling matters on their
own without any official intervention.

By mid-summer, the area's sense of helplessness and isolation was further increased
by the breakdown of color barriers in the
formerly all-white Coronado section. Coronado
was a small (300 homes) community of white,
middle-class wage earners across from (white)
Norview High School. Since a large number of
its families were military, the area had a
more rapid turnover of ownership than would be
otherwise expected. Thus, Coronado, with its
plentiful supply of middle-class housing, city
improvements, and high rate of turnover, was a
natural target for black expansion. Only narrow Widgeon Road separated white houses from
the black neighborhoods of Oakwood, Oakwood

Park, and Rosemont (*Norfolk Virginian-Pilot* 8/22/54). Although most of the homes in these traditional black sections were little more than tarpaper shacks (*Norfolk Journal and Guide* 8/6/55), new black developments in Mamie Homes, Incorporated (150 homes), Chesapeake Manor Apartments (332 units), and Chesapeake Manor Gardens (389 homes), all built since 1950, made the northern boundary of Coronado a haven for black middle-class families, many of them displaced by N.R.H.A. Project One. The black community faced a severe shortage of available middle-class housing, and the long waiting lists at all of the properties north of Coronado had put a premium on housing there (*Norfolk Virginian-Pilot* 8/22/54). Moreover, a number of black leaders complained that most black neighbor-hoods "were generally denied city improvements (*Norfolk Virginian-Pilot* 8/31/54)" such as curbs, gutters, parks, play-grounds, paved streets, and sewers that were already available in Coronado.

Trouble began when a black couple was view-ing a house in the black section on the north side of Widgeon Road; a white navy housewife spotted them, walked across the road, and asked them if they wanted to buy her house. Because of the huge demand and short supply of middle-class housing for blacks, this first navy family received a higher price than a white buyer would have offered. Other navy families followed suit, and soon panic gripped Coronado's more established white residents. At about this time the market in Coronado for sale to white buyers all but disappeared; the white banking establishment, realizing the inevitable, refused to finance white buyers in Coronado, and the Veteran's Administration appraisals were dropped as they "generally do go down in areas where Negroes are moving into what was once all-white territory (*Norfolk Virginian-Pilot* 8/22/54)". Once the pattern had begun, white home-owners found it impossi-

ble to reverse: they were trapped by powers
beyond their grasp.

The harassment of black buyers began inno-
cently enough: two elderly white ladies had
allowed a bundle of papers to blow out of the
car window; other passing motorists stopped to
help them retrieve the papers. When residents
learned that the phenomenon of stopped automobiles lining both sides of the street had
frightened off a prospective black buyer, the
idea of neighborhood caravans began "to show
that it was a white neighborhood (*Norfolk Ledger-Dispatch* 8/30/54)." The idea caught on immediately; although a number of homes had been
sold to black buyers, the caravans proved successful in keeping blacks from moving into
their new homes. As word spread, outsiders
began to join in the caravans, and soon random
acts of violence, especially aimed against
unoccupied dwellings already sold to blacks,
became commonplace. Bricks and bottles were
hurled as missiles, a "No Nigers (*sic*) wanted"
sign appeared, the pipes to one house were
ripped out, a bomb was thrown at another, a
dozen white youths attacked the car of a black
couple, another house and automobile were
bombed, bullets were fired into black homes,
and soon armed caravans of whites and blacks
began roaming the area looking for trouble
(*Norfolk Virginian-Pilot* 8/19/54, 8/25/54,
9/11/54, 9/20/54, and 8/22/54). The prospect
that the present rate of property damage, if
not halted, would escalate into human tragedy
became more and more evident.

Blacks in and around the Coronado area were
clearly terrified by the racial turmoil they
confronted. The Norfolk County Police, still
the legal authority in the Tanner's Creek District, were not much help in appeasing their
fears. Although the County Police came promptly when called, they engaged in only minimal
defensive patrolling. Often they stood among
crowds of jeering whites and were indistin-

guishable from the taunters. County officials
were understandably eager to play down the
extent of the threat that existed in Coronado,
but one officer's characterization of the site
of a bomb blast, "the hole appeared to be that
left by a dog trying to bury a bone (*Norfolk
Ledger-Dispatch* 8/30/54)," only aroused blacks
to the fear that little was being done to protect them. Black leaders turned first to the
Norfolk City Council for help (*Norfolk Virginian-Pilot* 8/19/54), and then to the governor
when their pleas for assistance were denied.
Duckworth refused to provide police protection
for black families because the city would not
acquire jurisdiction until January 1, 1955;
Governor Thomas Stanley was powerless under
state law to commit the State Police or
National Guard unless the local governing body
first requested aid. The fact that former City
Council challenger P. B. Young carried the
request to the Governor over the protestations
of the City Council, further enraged Duckworth
(*Norfolk Virginian-Pilot* 9/12/54). After a
month of escalating violence had passed since
the request for assistance, the *Virginian-
Pilot* stepped in with some harsh words of
criticism for the Mayor and his City Council:

> The leadership in the Norfolk City gov-
> ernment has been short-sighted in de-
> ciding not to show any interest in
> Coronado. . . . It does not make good
> sense for a city to use its authority one
> mile beyond the city limit to make a
> numbers racket raid, such as was made
> Thursday by Norfolk police, but to with-
> hold its influence and authority from a
> problem which has potentially much more
> tragic consequences than a numbers game.
> It would be better to provide too much
> law enforcement than what may tragically
> prove later to have been too little and
> too late. The hoodlum elements ought not

to be left in any doubt as to what con-
fronts them if they continue to make an
unpleasant situation worse (*Norfolk Virginian-Pilot* 9/11/54).

In desperation, the black leaders finally
approached their old contacts in the Silkstocking crowd who, although no longer in
control of any governmental authority, still
possessed enormous financial power and corporate authority. The *Journal and Guide* summed
up the resultant beefed-up county patrols this
way: "The powers-that-be Downtown, after
caucusing with the Uptown [black] leaders,
brought pressure to bear upon county officials, and the tragedy that could have been
Coronado was averted (*Norfolk Journal and
Guide* 1/7/56)."
A serious breach between the city's black
community and its white political leaders was
growing, and the fact that P. B. Young and
others had effected, with Silkstocking backing, a successful flanking maneuver around the
Council only made matters worse. Duckworth and
the Organization appeared to oppose any further expansion of the black population within
the city, and they severely chastised anyone
who strayed beyond the acceptable boundaries.
The city government had done all that it could
do legally to block a group of black developers from acquiring a large tract of land off
Broad Creek Road (see Figure 1, page 47); the
white leaders were strongly opposed to any
development that allowed blacks to settle
along the city's major approach route from the
suburbs (now Virginia Beach Boulevard). Once
they saw that the deal could not be prevented,
the City Planning Commission stepped in to
prevent residential use by blacks, and zoned
as much of the tract as possible for industrial and commercial purposes (*Norfolk Virginian-Pilot* 8/31/54). When black leaders persisted in attempting to develop the remaining

acreage into an attractive subdivision (Broad Creek Shores), the city employed its powers of *eminent domain* to buy up the remaining 40-acres as a buffer zone, ostensibly to be used as a park or school site. Black leaders were enraged and could see "no other apparent valid reason for seizing the land, other than to prevent colored home owners from locating on it (*Norfolk Journal and Guide* 8/6/55)," and threatened to call for a referendum to block the ordinance from taking effect.

Newly appointed Councilman Roy B. Martin, Jr., rose with the Organization's response, a proposal to "study" the question, with an eye towards amending the section of the city charter that allowed referendums. The black community had proposed the petition drive in order to affect some sort of compromise with the city (*Norfolk Virginian-Pilot* 7/6/55), but since the last race had been one of the "no-contest" elections for which Duckworth became famous, they were able to collect 2,488 signatures in less than two days, more than enough to force a vote. At last, with the day of the referendum fast approaching, the Organization agreed to a compromise; it was wisely unwilling to test its strength at the ballot box in what was seen by many whites as an illegal and arbitrary use of power. The city agreed to take only 24 of the original 40 acres in the site, and leave the other sixteen acres, already platted and under contract, for development as Broad Creek Shores. The city's chief concern, that (white) Ingleside Elementary School remain widely separated from black housing, was met (*Norfolk Virginian-Pilot* 9/19/55; Roy B. Martin), and the blacks were able to keep a large tract of waterfront property, carefully separated by the city's acquisition and natural geographic barriers from nearby white communities, for expansion. Councilmen Page, Abbott, and Ripley dissented because it included paying a premium price to the black developers for the city's share of the original tract. The final ballot produced one of the few split votes ever recorded on the Duckworth City Council (*Norfolk Virginian-Pilot* 4/29/56), and ensured the Mayor's bitter enmity for cracking the facade of his previously united front. The black community left the Council chambers congratulating themselves for their victory, unaware that Mayor Duckworth, a sore loser at the game of power politics, was already plotting their demise.

At the height of the Broad Creek Shores controversy, the city had appointed a three-man committee to study "the need and desirability of obtaining additional sites for use in constructing private homes for our colored citizens (*Norfolk Journal and Guide* 8/6/55)." At the time of its appointment, the Land Committee, or Kaufman Committee as it was called in the black community, had been a part of Mayor Duckworth's efforts to resolve the impasse short of granting land in the Broad Creek area to black developers. Recognizing the city's "desperate need" for additional suitable sites for black houses, the Mayor turned to the Silkstocking crowd in an attempt to solve the dispute peacefully. The three most powerful representatives of the old People's group still left in the city's government--N.R.H.A. Chairman Charles Kaufman, Planning Commissioners Henry Clay Hofhemier, II, and John S. Jenkins--were appointed to the committee. Privately the committee was charged with finding additional room for black expansion in areas that would not threaten white neighborhoods or segregated schools; no one wanted a repeat of the racial strife that characterized Coronado.

Initially the committee received a hostile reception from the black community because of its association with the Mayor's position on Broad Creek shores, but gradually the reputation for fairness and the high esteem in which its members were generally held won over some support and cooperation. The editors of the *Journal and Guide* apologized for their initial inhospitality, terming it "a natural reaction to an unnatural determination on the part of City Council (*Norfolk Journal and Guide* 8/6/ 55)." Even after careful study and consultation with black leaders, however, the committee failed to find appropriate sites for new development; indeed Norfolk's desperate need for space for all types of expansion was the driving motivation behind its costly annexation initiatives.

Instead, the Land Committee proposed to undertake an extensive redevelopment project in a portion of the new Tanner's Creek District that included Oakwood, Lincoln Park, and Rosemont--a 370-acre site that had more than 1,000 dwellings, all of them already occupied by black families (see Figure 1, page 47). Oakwood began its existence as a shantytown on the outskirts of established (white) settlements before the turn of the century. For as little as $50 a black family could purchase a small tract of land and then scrounge enough scrap lumber, tarpaper, and materials to build a shack. Eighty-five percent of the homes were substandard; few had adequate sanitary facilities; and even fewer could ever be rehabilitated to comply with existing codes (*Norfolk Virginian-Pilot* 4/29/56). Even the *Journal and Guide* recognized that the area contained "some of the worst imaginable slums," and applauded the committee's decision (*Norfolk Journal and Guide* 8/6/55). The committee proposed a massive redevelopment and reclamation project that would rebuild the community to accommodate 2,500 families--an addition of 1,500 units--in individual homes, semi-detached houses, and garden apartments. Like N.R.H.A. Project One, the plan included playgrounds, an elementary school, and a small shopping center (*Norfolk Virginian-Pilot* 4/29/56).

The proposal was well received by members of both the black and white communities; "inasmuch as the site proposed for reclamation has been occupied by colored people for the past sixty-five years, the segregation factor does not enter the package (*Norfolk Journal and Guide* 8/6/55)." In point of fact, no other alternative existed for the area. Most of the homes would have to be condemned and torn down anyway under existing health, fire, safety, and building codes, and the city would be unwilling under current spending formulas to extend sewer and water lines to the area, pave streets, or provide sidewalks, streetlights, and gutters. The N.R.H.A. sought to allay the fears of Oakwood residents by promising to give a "liberal" appraisal for existing homes, relocate those homes sound enough to save, provide financing for new homes, give residents priority in site selection, and even trade comparable land for redeveloped sites (*Norfolk Virginian-Pilot* 4/29/56).

Kaufman and the N.R.H.A. were surprised to hear the strength of Oakwood's opposition to renewal. Most residents knew they were too poor to afford the new development, even if their current substandard dwellings were generously appraised; they lived in Oakwood because there they could survive on little or no regular income. "We old people can't buy new homes," said one resident, "If you take our homes, we'll just be out in the street (*Norfolk Virginian-Pilot* 4/29/56)." Because they had heard horror stories from other blacks who had been resettled during N.R.H.A. Project One, homeowners were understandably unwilling to wait in the line for a unit in Norfolk's already overcrowded public housing; instead they wanted to stay where they were, as they were. This strong anti-redevelopment sentiment forced a critical re-examination of the project by Norfolk's black leadership. Attorneys J. Hugo Madison and Joe Jordan objected that the project tended to perpetuate residential segregation (*Norfolk Journal and Guide* 3/31/56). Others began to question the advisability of crowding an additional 1,500 families in an area that already held more than 1,000. Most stated they would oppose it until the current residents were given sufficient guarantees, written or otherwise, to sway a majority of local support. Thomas Young, president of the *Journal and Guide*, and Rev. W. L. Hamilton, pastor of Shiloh Baptist Church, Dr. Lyman Brooks, president of the Norfolk Division of Virginia State College (now Norfolk State University), and other black leaders who maintained links to the Silkstocking crowd still favored the project, but the growing split in the black community over the city's use of its redevelopment and housing powers was quickly pushing younger, more activist leaders to the fore (*Norfolk Virginian-Pilot* 4/29/56).

The Oakwood Redevelopment controversy was an important episode in the history of the period for a number of reasons. First, it marked the emergence of an important coalition between Mayor Duckworth and the remnants of the People's group still in power. Both groups were committed to continuing the city's informal practice of segregated housing and eager not to repeat the horrors of Coronado. Mayor Duckworth may have been rebuffed at his premature attempt to forestall a Broad Creek Shores settlement, but with the Silkstocking crowd and the Norfolk Redevelopment and Housing Authority firmly in his camp, further efforts would be both more calculated and more successful. Oakwood represented the willingness of the People's representatives to harness the powers of redevelopment to insure segregated housing developments. More importantly, it also indicates the most natural target for the next phase of redevelopment activity; Oakwood was a *bona fide* slum, readymade for a redevelopment project: few of its

homes could ever hope to pass the city's minimum housing codes, and blight and dilapidation
were evident throughout the neighborhood.

Finally, Oakwood points to a growing split
in the black community between the older,
business-oriented leaders like P. B. Young,
Rev. Hamilton, and W. T. Mason, and the younger, more aggressive activists like Joe Jordan,
Victor Ashe, and J. Hugo Madison. The next
round would be fought in the courts, and the
younger leaders had neither the commitment to
compromise nor the bargaining skills possessed
by their elders. Oakwood proved that these
younger leaders were gaining a ready audience
willing to hear the message that new tactics
were necessary to defeat the state and local
forces arrayed against them. The more established black leaders still commanded enormous
respect in both the black and white communities, but all their powers of amelioration
would be needed to avert future strife between
their charges and the forces of the Organization (Suggs 1988, 186).

3

First Reactions to *Brown*

The intensity of the school desegregation controversy may best be seen within the context
of the ongoing power struggle between the
black and white communities; in both instances, Norfolk's pattern of residential
segregation, because it brought black and
white neighborhoods within close proximity to
one another, was the cause of friction between
the races. Even so, the initial reaction in
Norfolk to the Supreme Court decision was
decidedly calm. School Superintendent J. J.
Brewbaker's response was typical: "We must
accept these decisions and give them considered judgment and not let our emotions get
in the way. . . . We will do everything we can
from an intelligent point of view." He then
went on to forecast "very little mixture" of
races due to the residential "lines" within
the city. Councilmen Ezra Summers and Roy
Martin expressed the political sentiment:
"Norfolk will probably be less effected than
any city in the state because of the geograph-
ical set up here [that includes] well-defined
residential districts." The *Virginian-Pilot*
pointed to the bulwark of *de facto* segregation
that stood against integration encroachments:

In Norfolk and other Virginia cities
where Negro and white schools are built
largely in conformity with the white and
Negro patterns of residence, where the
Negro population is distinctly in the
minority, and where the two races respect
each other, adjustment to the new order
will be gradual and not likely to produce
deep change for a considerable time. The
majority of Southerners, and the best of
Southern leadership will strive to work
out their civilization in accord with the
constitutional requirements (*Norfolk Virginian-Pilot* 5/18/54).

Newly elected Governor Thomas Stanley,
fresh from his narrow victory over Republican
challenger Ted Dalton, reacted calmly as well.
He contemplated "no precipitate action" and
stated that the "views of leaders of both
races will be invited" in approaching the
problems created by the court. Stanley's pro-
nouncement was met with a hail of abuse from
Southside Virginia, the string of counties and
small towns which formed the state's tobacco
belt South of Richmond. Because many areas of
the Southside had majority black populations,
racist sentiment and opposition to school
integration there was stronger than elsewhere
in the state. Under pressure from the Southside, the heart of the Byrd Organization's
constituency, Governor Stanley soon adopted a
more militant posture, "I shall use every legal means at my command to continue segregated
schools in Virginia." Former Governor Bill
Tuck expressed the Southside's sentiment,

There is no middle ground, no compromise.
If the other [areas] won't stand with us,
I say make 'em. . . .If you ever let them
integrate anywhere, the whole state will
be integrated in a short time (*Norfolk
Virginian-Pilot* 5/18/54).

A new political group, the Defenders of State Sovereignty and Individual Liberties, was then being formed in the Southside to feed the venom of the state politicians who promised to oppose integration at all cost. The Defenders did not represent the night-rider, confederate-flag-waving brand of resistance found farther South, but as a state-wide organization, they gave backbone to all politicians who similarly pledged unyielding opposition to integration in any form (Dabney 1971, 528-31).

In spite of the hysteria that characterized the Southside in general and the leadership of the Byrd Organization specifically, the reaction on the part of Norfolk citizens remained one of tranquility. A sampling of letters to the editor revealed that by a two-to-one ratio the writers expressed "a calm, rational attitude towards desegregation and/or a strong disapproval of the public stand of Virginia officials." A local group for interracial cooperation concluded that: "There exists in this area of the South a body of moderate, informed, thoughtful, educated, and earnest public opinion which would accept desegregation easily. Extremist opinion is always noisy, and people who are against anything shout louder than those who are simply acquiescent (Women's Council for Interracial Cooperation 1955)."

One predictable response from Norfolk officials was the immediate halt and quiet reassessment of the city's school building program and redevelopment efforts. The Oakwood Plan was set aside for almost a decade, but the postwar baby boom had brought the need for classroom space to crisis proportions all across the state. For this reason, Governor John Battle had set aside $75 million in state funds for school construction during his four year (1951-1955) term. The localities had previously been held responsible for all such construction--a fact that put Virginia's

school system at the bottom of any listing of
quality or funding effort. In 1950 Virginia
had the lowest percentage of high school
attendance in the nation, the next-to-the-
highest percentage of high school dropouts
before graduation, and the next to the smallest percentage of school-age children in
school, but the state had never before done
much to help its localities meet their pressing needs (Dabney 1971, 522-24). Norfolk, in
the waning days of the People's administration
and City Manager C. A. Harrell's tenure in
office, jumped at this chance to receive state
funding, and embarked upon an aggressive $13
million school construction program that included new buildings and improvements to both
the black and white school systems alike (*Norfolk Ledger-Dispatch* 1/28/55). This program
included the first new school buildings for
blacks in the city, the others having been
hand-me-downs from the white community (*Norfolk Journal and Guide* 4/19/58). Four new
schools (Bowling Park, Young Park, Diggs Park,
and Lindenwood), three of them built in part
with federal funds under the redevelopment
effort, had been added to the black system
prior to the *Brown* decision (Sullivan 1956),
and other funds were spent on additions or
improvements to existing black schools (*Norfolk Ledger-Dispatch* 1/28/55).

At the time of the *Brown* decision, the
school system had several projects under
consideration which were jeopardized by the
explosive new issue of desegregation. In
addition to Oceanair Elementary, which was
already in the planning stages, three other
sites were under active consideration for new
schools (see Figure 2): a "Southside Junior
High School" for blacks in the Berkley/Campo-
stella area; a large parcel of land in the
Ballentine area was supported as a replacement
for the aging Lafayette School (white); and a
site just west of Titustown Elementary, an

Figure 2
School Sites Under Consideration in 1954

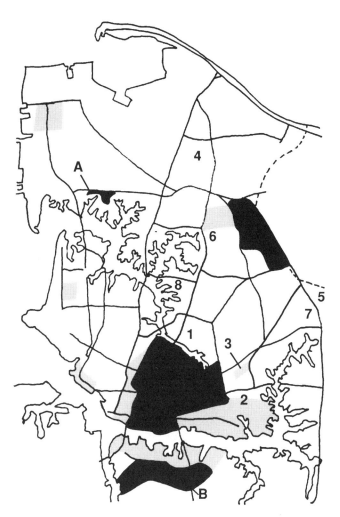

■ BLACK HOUSING AREA

▨ MIXED RACE/TRANSITION
HOUSING

BLACK SCHOOLS
A   Titustown Elementary
B   Southside (Campostella)
      Junior High site

WHITE SCHOOLS
1   Maltby Avenue site

2   Ingleside Junior High site
3   Atterbury Road site
4   Cottage Toll Road site
5   Military Highway site
6   Norview Junior High site
7   Lansdale Junior High site
8   Lakewood Junior High site

aging school for blacks near the naval base,
was proposed as a replacement facility (Brewbaker 11/11/54). All three projects now faced
new scrutiny, apparently as a result of the
Brown decision, and the School Board's intention to continue building new schools for
blacks seemed to dissolve: "Southside" (Campostella) Junior High was not built for almost a
decade; the Ballentine tract was sold to a
private developer; and, even though an addition was built on a portion of the third site,
Titustown Elementary was never rebuilt as
originally intended.

    In addition to these, the City Planning
Commission was helping school officials select
five other sites in the Tanners Creek district
scheduled for annexation, where there was an
"urgent need" for two new junior high schools
and three 700-pupil elementary schools. The
Norfolk School Board proposed building one of
the junior high schools on additional land
around Ingleside Elementary, and a 33-acre
tract in the Sherwood Forest area was being
considered for both an elementary and a junior
high school; the other tracts included a
20-acre site in the Northern portion of the
city, a 12-acre tract in the East near the
airport, and an 8-acre site north of Norview
High School (Brewbaker 11/11/54). New school
construction had, however, been halted as a
result of the *Brown* decision (*Norfolk Ledger-
Dispatch* 10/13/54), and there quickly followed
a period of quiet reassessment. In spite of
the urgent need for new facilities, only the
Norview site was found acceptable. Ingleside
Junior High School was never built, apparently
because the site was too close to Broad Creek
Shores and other black housing developments
(see Figure 2). Although the Board did decide
to build an elementary school on the Sherwood
Forest tract, the site was also apparently too
close to black housing to win approval for a
junior high; the northern tract, site of a

city nursery, was found to be unsuitable for
development (three decades later it became
Northside Park); the eastern site was rejected
because it was in the path proposed for Interstate 64; and the smallest site, the 8-acre
tract north of Norview High, was used to
satisfy the critical need for a junior high
school (Norview).

Because of the urgent need for new school
buildings, there followed a furious period of
planning by the Board. School Board files indicate that a number of plans were considered
by the school administration over the next few
months, but the Board advanced only those that
could clear all of the possible political objections. Gone was any focus on rebuilding aging black facilities; also abandoned were any
sites that might prove to be too close to
nearby black communities. When construction
plans for 1955 were finally announced, School
Superintendent J.J. Brewbaker assured the city
manager that:

> Desegregation will have no effect on this
> building program. With the exception of
> the addition to Oakwood [an elementary
> school for blacks], all other construc-
> tion is for and needed for white children
> (Brewbaker 8/8/55).

In a carefully worded press statement, the
Board indicated that it was preparing to meet
the new threat posed by *Brown* with "reasoned
planning (School Board 7/1/55)."

Even so, finding suitable sites for badly
needed junior high schools in the Tanner's
Creek District proved to be a difficult task.
In addition to the rejected Ingleside and
Sherwood Forest tracts, plans to locate in the
Lansdale and Lakewood areas were also submit-
ted to the City Council for approval (School
Board 9/14/56). The Board even went so far as
to hire architects to design Lakewood (Pente-

cost and Courtney 1957) and Lansdale Junior
High schools. In the end, after much behind-
the-scenes maneuvering, the Council scratched
these sites from an extended list of projects,
and instead converted Willard Elementary into
a junior high (School Board 3/25/58). Even
though a consultant had indicated that the
city's school population would increase by
more than 4,000 students per year for the next
few years (Norfolk Virginian-Pilot 9/17/55)--
the equivalent of five new schools a year--
Norfolk elected to move slowly and deliberately, even if this meant badly overcrowding some
existing facilities and adding a double shift
at others (Norfolk Virginian-Pilot 2/10/56).
Instead of launching an aggressive new building program as originally envisioned, the
Board opted to adopt a safer course, and moved
instead to add new wings to its most overcrowded, but existing, facilities (Rorer 1968,
346). One of the schools marked for immediate
construction was a combination elementary-
junior high for black pupils in the Oakwood
area, where a large number of plaintiffs in
the suit filed by the National Association for
the Advancement of Colored People (N.A.A.C.P.)
lived. In a letter to City Manager Thomas Maxwell, Superintendent J. J. Brewbaker hinted at
the need for the combination school:

> Negro junior high pupils attend Jacox,
> which is approximately seven miles from
> the section in which they live. The near-
> est junior high is Norview (Brewbaker
> 2/13/57).

Reporter Luther Carter went even further when
he surveyed the proposed building program in
light of the desegregation suit: "One obvious
effect of a combination school would be to
accommodate some Negro junior high pupils who
might otherwise want to attend Norview Junior
High, a white school and by far the closest

junior high to the Oakwood-Rosemont area (*Norfolk Virginian-Pilot* 10/24/56)." The Board also pressed its case to build "Southside" (i.e., Campostella) Junior High School to accommodate the growing black population in the Berkley area (*Norfolk Virginian-Pilot* 1/26/57). Again reporter Luther Carter noted the changing racial composition of the city as a motive for the proposed facility: "School officials have noted a pronounced tendency for whites to leave Berkley, and for Negroes to move in (*Norfolk Virginian-Pilot* 10/24/56)."

In fact Norfolk had made tremendous progress under the Battle funds and $13 million building program advanced by C. A. Harrell and the People's administration. By 1953 the Norfolk School Board could say for the first time that the cost of educating a white pupil and a black in the city's schools was equal (*Norfolk Ledger-Dispatch* 8/21/53). Before Harrell, the city's effort was determined by a complicated formula that was weighted heavily upon the percentage of total revenues received from black and white taxpayers. By 1950, however, the city was actually paying more to its black teachers, because they had both more degrees and more seniority, than to its white, having raised the salary of black teachers some 62 percent since the Prieur Machine's wartime city council dominated school spending (*Norfolk Ledger-Dispatch* 12/13/51). In fact Norfolk was cited by Senator Sam Ervin of North Carolina, for its efforts to improve its black educational system. In an article he wrote for *Look* magazine defending continued school segregation in the South, a picture of Norfolk's newly constructed Young Park School (built in part with federal redevelopment funds) bore the caption: "New Negro schools, like this one in Norfolk, Va., attest [to] efforts of [the] South to meet [integration] problems in its own way (Ervin 1956, 32-3)." In spite of this momentum, the impact of the *Brown* decision and

the overreaction of the state's political
leaders forced the city to halt its school
construction plans (*Norfolk Ledger-Dispatch*
10/13/54) at the very time it was most in need
of new classroom space, as a result of both
annexation and the baby boom, (*Norfolk Virginian-Pilot* 1/16/55). The *Ledger-Dispatch* summed
up the attitude of those in charge of school
construction:

> In recent years Southern states have been
> making great financial outlays to put
> Negro schools on a par with those for
> white students. . . however, once the
> court's rejection of separate but equal
> theory became known, there was no longer
> any great pressure on local officials to
> continue the special and costly attention
> to [the] Negro school building programs
> (*Norfolk Ledger-Dispatch* 10/13/54).

In spite of the official "go slow" attitude
of the City Council, the School Board began to
take its first few cautious steps toward compliance with the spirit of the *Brown* decision.
First, it advanced a proposal to create a
biracial study group to recommend possible
courses of action. The move was endorsed by
the Education Association and the Council of
Parent Teacher Associations (P.T.A.) (*Norfolk
Virginian-Pilot* 6/3/55), but opposed by the
N.A.A.C.P. leadership. One black leader broke
the deadlock with his endorsement, "There is
no harm in studying and bringing integration
about in an orderly manner." Next the School
Board voted down Virginia's model 30-day
notice-of-termination clause in its teacher
contracts, a step recommended by the state's
political leaders as a way to prepare for the
possibility of closed schools (*Norfolk Virginian-Pilot* 6/18/55). Gradually the School
Board's commitment to keep schools open and to
comply with the spirit of the Supreme Court

decision began to win it both accolades from the international press and a few denunciations from Southern writers. Typical of the positive reaction was this statement from the *Roanoke World News*:

> [The Norfolk School Board has supplied] the first official word of calm in Virginia's heated integration debate. In so doing it has broken the solid front of opposition to the Supreme Court's decision and decree (*Norfolk Ledger-Dispatch* 7/11/55).

Norfolk School Board Chairman W. Farley Powers appeared somewhat embarrassed by the sudden notoriety and stated:

> I do not want to get into any controversy [with the rest of the state]. We might make some preliminary moves [to keep schools open], but we must abide by state law (*Norfolk Virginian-Pilot* 6/3/55).

School Superintendent Brewbaker was equally aware that Norfolk's progressive attitude marked it in some sections of the state as a "hotbed" of liberalism because:

> We have been conscious that a change [from segregation] is inevitable. We have not been trying to think up ways to circumvent the ruling (*Norfolk Ledger-Dispatch* 7/11/55).

Indeed the rest of the state appeared to be preoccupied with thinking up legal angles to somehow block the eventuality of the Supreme Court's ruling. *Richmond News Leader* editor James J. Kilpatrick happened upon the century-old doctrine of "interposition"--whereby a state supposedly has the right to "interpose" its own authority between an unjust action of

the federal government and its local political
subdivisions--and the interposition craze was
begun. The state's official reaction was the
Gray Plan--named for State Senator Garland
Gray--that provided numerous ways for Virginia
to "interpose" its authority and so block integration. The plan called for a state pupil
placement board that would take over the pupil
assignment duties of the local school boards;
special tuition grants to parents of school
children who attended private schools, parochial establishments, or public schools in
another jurisdiction to escape desegregation;
and an amendment to the compulsory attendance
laws that suspended them in areas where public
schools were desegregated. Few politicians and
only the *Virginian-Pilot* of all the state's
newspapers opposed the Gray Plan. Provisions
within the plan that would have allowed local
subdivisions to desegregate on a local option
basis if the federal courts persisted were
scrapped by the Legislature when Senator Harry
F. Byrd, Sr., leader of the statewide Byrd
Organization, pointed out the need for all local governments to stand together in "massive
resistance" to the dictates of the Supreme
Court. In response, the State Legislature proposed the Stanley Plan, which required the
Governor to close any school under court order
to integrate, and cut off all state funds from
any school district which tried to reopen in
spite of the governor's interposition (Dabney
1971, 532-39).

While the rest of the state was reeling
under the bombast prompted by the Gray Plan,
Kilpatrick's doctrine of interposition, the
Stanley Plan, and Harry Byrd's Massive Resistance, the citizens of Norfolk had another plan
with which to contend: the Summers Plan. Under
Duckworth's rule, Ezra Summers was the closest
thing Norfolk had to an independent voice on
the City Council (*Norfolk Virginian-Pilot* 3/6/
56). In July 1955, Summers introduced a sur-

prise proposal whereby the city could achieve integration if it ever came under a court order: the first step would be to have every parent in the school system, both black and white, fill out an intention card which indicated whether or not they wanted their children to attend an integrated or segregated school. The School Board would then determine how many schools it would have to operate on an all-white, all-black, or integrated basis, and then assign each pupil to the school of his parent's choosing. One of the unwritten elements of the Summers Plan was the hope that few white parents would choose to send their children to integrated schools; those who did would be punished by isolating all the "troublemakers" in the same school; if white parents did not choose integrated schools, then schools would not be integrated. Local politicians extolled it as "in keeping with the Supreme Court's decision" because it allowed every child to attend the school of his or her choice (*Norfolk Virginian-Pilot* 7/27/55).

Obviously the Summers Plan added little positive thought to the discussion of the day, but it does indicate the political mood of obfuscation and deceit that ruled. There were people in Norfolk who understood the *Brown* decision and its ramifications, but by and large they refused to believe that Norfolk schools would have to be integrated or that public schools would have to be closed. They placed too much faith in the hands of local and state politicians who could promise them a plan, any plan, no matter how ill-conceived and contrived, to circumvent the ruling (Reif 1960, 2). The true leaders of public opinion in Norfolk, the business and civic elite who had earlier ruled the city, had been so effectively removed from the political process by the Organization that they were quiet while this irrationality gripped their city. The

School Board, too, was all but ignored as the public rushed to seize each new political panacea.

Undaunted by the political bombast of the period, the Norfolk School Board went quietly about its business, hoping to keep a low profile and thus avoid confrontation with the Organization leaders who dominated city hall. Taking a page from the old People's book, the Board went ahead with its plans to appoint a biracial committee to recommend action; then it commissioned an exhaustive study of the Board, its policy, practices, and the future needs of the Norfolk school population. Local politicians pointed frantically to the need to stand toe-to-toe in Massive Resistance with the rest of the state--as one local legislator did with this rhetorical outburst concerning the Southside counties with their heavy con- centrations of black population,

> Their house is on fire. They want us to send fire trucks to help them. I think it is our Christian duty to help put out the fire for them [by opposing integration] (*Norfolk Virginian-Pilot* 9/19/55).

Even so, the School Board resisted these im- passioned pleas with great aplomb. School Board chairman Paul Schweitzer pointed to how Norfolk's situation differed from the South- side's:

> There are only thirty percent Negroes in the Norfolk school system . . . geograph- ically located so that they are well taken care of in their present schools. If we adopt a gradual plan of integra- tion, there would be so little you wouldn't notice it.

School Superintendent Brewbaker echoed this theme:

> There would be few Negroes in white
> schools because of existing "residential
> segregation. . . . We are all in favor of
> segregation. . . . It is just a question
> of what is the best plan. . . . I'm not
> in favor of integration, I'm in favor of
> carrying out the Supreme Court decree
> with the least harm to pupils . . . and
> to the schools (*Norfolk Virginian-Pilot*
> 9/15/55).

Other school officials pointed to the navy,
N.A.T.O. (North Atlantic Treaty Organization,
headquatererd in Norfolk), and government service as liberalizing influences that had exposed many Norfolk students to a variety of
cultures without undue harm. One principal
stated that more than a third of his students
had already attended integrated schools elsewhere without problems (*Norfolk Virginian-
Pilot* 1/5/56). In fact, when Norfolk Catholic
High School was integrated by the Catholic
diocese following the *Brown* decision, the
event passed without comment from the press or
protest from the public (Reif 1960, 2).

The School Board's air of official calm had
bought a year of grace from legal pressures to
integrate; its members had hoped to use that
year to prepare the public for calm compliance
with the desegregation dictates, but time and
events had conspired against it to block this
intention. Unlike its counterparts in other
parts of the country, the black community in
Norfolk had not rushed into court to force
immediate integration of the schools; instead
local black leaders had followed the more tem-
porizing course of petitioning the School
Board to desegregate (*Norfolk Virginian-Pilot*
7/14/55). Of course the threat of court action
lay behind that petition, but it was an important first step towards finding a peaceful
solution to the desegregation controversy. The
School Board unfortunately could not respond

in kind: too much had transpired in the year
since that initial petition had been filed,
and the state and local political leaders had
moved to block any authority it might have had
to comply. The Broad Creek and Coronado controversies had bred a climate of racial mistrust and resentment--a feeling that cut off
all previous channels of communication between
the races. Unfortunately, and without its
choosing, the Board was now caught up in a
larger political confrontation in which neither side could accept defeat. Similarly, any
opportunity it might have had to defuse the
crisis with token gestures was now gone. The
year of grace had passed, and only the courts
could decide the outcome.

In the mounting atmosphere of racial tension that now prevailed, the local chapter of
the N.A.A.C.P. began to step up the fire power
of its assault upon the city's racial institutions. Accordingly, in May 1956, almost two
years to the day after the Supreme Courts'
landmark ruling, attorneys Victor Ashe and
Hugo Madison formally abandoned the petition
process and filed their school desegregation
suit in the U.S. General District Court, Eastern District of Virginia, (*Norfolk Virginian-
Pilot* 5/11/56). Their suit reflected the
changing mood of the black community: a
majority of the petitioners were from the
still racially tense Oakwood and Coronado
sections of the Norview area; most of the rest
were from the transitional neighborhoods of
Atlantic City and Broad Creek, where racial
boundary lines were not yet clearly drawn
(*Norfolk Virginian-Pilot* 7/14/55). In spite of
this late start, litigation in Norfolk quickly
proceeded, and was soon two or three steps
ahead of that in the rest of the state. Part
of the reason for this fast pace was Federal
Judge Walter Hoffman's no-nonsense approach to
litigation in his court. Even though he was a
Norfolk native and law partner of Organization

stalwart State Senator Edward L. Breeden,
Hoffman was rapidly earning a reputation as a
distinguished and independent jurist who would
not brook the obfuscation and delaying tactics
common elsewhere. For their part, the local
N.A.A.C.P. attorneys pressed vigorously on the
case, obviously encouraged by the fact that
Hoffman had already struck down segregated
barriers in the city's parks (*Norfolk Virginian-Pilot* 8/29/56) and public transportation
systems (*Norfolk Virginian-Pilot* 4/25/56).

The School Board closely followed this judicial trend, and proceeded cautiously under
the assumption that Norfolk's schools would
soon be under court orders to integrate. The
Board appeared in its pronouncements to be
fully prepared to operate a desegregated
school system under such auspices. The city's
political leaders, however, were cognizant of
the fact that integrated classrooms, no matter
how slight their impact might be upon the
functioning of the local school system, were
diametrically opposed to the policies of the
state:

> Norfolk is already looked upon with sus-
> picion by some sections of the state; if
> we are forced by federal courts to be the
> first in Virginia to integrate, it would
> be held against us by the rest of the
> state for the next twenty years (*Norfolk
> Virginian-Pilot* 5/13/56).

Norfolk faced the real possibility that the
state would shut down its schools indefinitely
to avoid integration, just as it had closed
nearby Sea Shore State Park when ordered to
desegregate it (Reif 1960, 1).

Since there had as yet been no shred of
sympathy for Norfolk's predicament, the School
Board sought a closed-door audience with Mayor
Duckworth, the City Council, and the city's

legislative delegation; its members hoped to
develop some plan of action that would protect
the city from political reprisals from the
rest of the state. Norfolk's only real hope in
this regard lay in taking the final decision
to desegregate out of the hands of the local
School Board and passing the onus back to the
state for resolution; thus, if the state government could be forced to take the blame for
ordering desegregation of Norfolk's schools,
then there would be no reason for imposing
economic sanctions or exacting legislative
retribution against the city for complying. To
Norfolk's political leaders the threat of reprisals from the rest of the state was very
real, and one that they feared more than the
authority of the federal courts: the confrontation at Little Rock had not yet taken place,
and no one knew just how forcefully the federal government would move to back up court
orders to integrate. On the other hand, the
city's desperate wartime financial experience
provided ample evidence of just how devastating the consequences of reduced state funding
could be to its economy. Simply put, the
city's plan was to ask the state to "interpose" its own sovereignty between the federal
courts and the School Board. To Norfolk's
leaders the logic was clear:

> We can't put a window in a school without
> the state telling us what size it must
> be, and on a matter as far reaching as
> segregation, the state should be willing
> to stand up to it. This is clearly a
> matter in which the state should tell us
> what to do (*Norfolk Virginian-Pilot*
> 5/13/56).

The meeting broke with the resolve that the
city would request a special session of the
General Assembly in order to assure timely
enactment of the necessary legislation. Public

pronouncements of Norfolk's interposition plan
were highly touted by members of the State
Legislature and City Council in attendance;
almost immediately the School Board began to
back away from the inflammatory language emanating from the closed-door session. Members
of the Board felt that interposition really
meant "imposition"--that the plan only gave
the rest of the state a chance to impose its
more conservative, provincial philosophies
upon the errant liberalism of its urbane sister city--and that shutting down the Norfolk
school system was a step the rest of Virginia
might be willing to take, especially if Norfolk were to bear the consequences alone. This
was a move the Board meant to resist at all
cost: its members had been charged with the
responsibility of running the largest school
system in Virginia, and this meant keeping
schools open under any circumstances, even if
the rest of the state disapproved. Members of
the Board, therefore, attempted to soften the
impact of the city's interposition plan by
stating that Norfolk was merely seeking "the
advice and guidance" of the Legislature. They
recognized that they were unable to act alone
in the face of court-ordered desegregation,
but spokesmen stressed that the Board "wants
to conform to state policies, but the continued operation of public schools here is of
utmost importance (*Norfolk Virginian-Pilot*
5/13/56)."

The School Board's reluctance to back Norfolk's interposition plan publicly was the
first sign of a coming confrontation between
the appointed members of the Board and the
elected officials that made their appointments. Unlike the City Council, the members of
the Board were not responsible to any particular partisan constituency, and not dependent
upon popular reelection for continuance; they
were thus free to choose the course they felt
best for the community without all the postur-

ing and puffery of the politicians. Partly for this reason, researchers all across the South were reporting that appointed school boards dealt far more moderately with the desegregation crisis than their elected counterparts (Crain 1968, 339). In Norfolk, the City Council had a particular reason to mistrust any evidence of independence emanating from the School Board: in the past the Council had used the Board as a convenient dumping ground for business leaders from the People's ranks who still deserved special recognition because of their high standing in the community. The School Board had always been a relatively powerless body, and Council's strict control of the budget served as a powerful check on even the most errant body. Previously there had been little danger in stacking the School Board with key business leaders closer to the People's persuasion--membership on the Board carried high status without any of the spoils potential of the city's housing, planning, zoning, or various inspection appeals boards-- and the City Council felt that a display of strong business support for public education was important for the city. Finally, the Council had sometimes employed the tactical strategy of blaming the School Board for community ills when it came time for reelection, and had thus always sought to avoid placing any of the Organization's faithful in such a role. It was this scapegoat role that most concerned the City Council now: they feared that the public pronouncements of the School Board indicated a willingness, however reluctant, to serve as a whipping boy for the state by accepting desegregation if it was ordered. Thus the move to embrace the philosophy of interposition may be seen as a timely ploy to subvert the authority of local boards, and make sure the power to resist desegregation was in the hands of more partisan operatives.

In spite of the School Board's apparent willingness to accept court-ordered desegregation, it nevertheless pressed vigorously its legal efforts to resist such an eventuality. In private the Board may have been willing to defy the state's authority, but in court it argued forcefully that public school segregation was a valid exercise of the state's police powers to protect its citizens. The Board also advanced the argument that it was an agency of the state and thus subject to the same privileges, protection, and immunities as the state. Further, the Board contended that the N.A.A.C.P. had filed the suit against the wrong party: technically the Board lacked the legal jurisdiction to establish and maintain a school system on its own, and merely served as advisors to the City Council, against whom the suit should have been brought. The Board's final argument, however, carried a little more weight: the court lacked jurisdiction in this dispute, it contended, since only people duly qualified for admission to the public schools and whose request for transfer between schools had been denied could legitimately prove harm (*Norfolk Virginian-Pilot* 6/22/56). This was a telling point, since, unlike the *Brown* cases, which had been brought on behalf of black children who had been denied the "equal opportunity" to attend the school of their choice, the Norfolk case had been brought by leading blacks who petitioned the court to end a perceptible public wrong; none of the petitioners could show a personal harm.

The members of the School Board knew, however, that they were merely buying time with their legal arguments, and that the N.A.A.C.P. would return to court in a few months with the right defendants and the proper mix of plaintiffs able to prove injury by rejection of their transfer applications. The Board's legal maneuvering had bought enough time to forestall school integration in Norfolk for one more school year (*Norfolk Ledger-Dispatch* 7/3/56); its members knew it would take this long for the Board to receive, deliberate, and then ultimately reject the petitions. The Board's spirited defense was enough to keep the state politicians off its back temporarily; in the meantime, it had begun to develop a plan which might take some of the pressure off of the N.A.A.C.P. desegregation suit. The School Board approached the City Council with a request for an additional $15 million building program, much of it earmarked for adding libraries, cafeterias, music centers, resource areas, multi-purpose classrooms, and other facilities to existing black schools (*Norfolk Virginian-Pilot* 10/24/56). School Board member Ben Willis was candid enough to comment on the sudden up-grading of black schools: "The better their [i.e., the black] facilities, the less pressure their argument will have (*Norfolk Virginian-Pilot* 1/26/57)." One of the schools marked for immediate construction was a combination elementary-junior high for black pupils in the Oakwood-Rosemont section, where a large number of the N.A.A.C.P. plaintiffs had been located. *Virginian-Pilot* reporter Luther Carter sensed the impact of the desegregation suit on the proposed building program:

> The School Board has indicated that when all appeals against the federal court order have been exhausted, it will attempt to minimize its effect by using a plan for gradual desegregation. [The Oakwood-Rosemont combination school] would appear to be in line with this policy. Superintendent Brewbaker also indicated that eventually a combination junior and senior high might be needed in the area [to further ease desegregation] (*Norfolk Virginian-Pilot* 3/8/57).

As part of its overall plan, the Board proposed rushing its Southside junior high school
(Campostella) to the drawing boards to accommodate the growing black population in that
portion of the city (*Norfolk Virginian-Pilot*
10/24/56).

The School Board's proposed building program was not meant as another legal gimmick to
head off desegregation; instead it indicated a
thorough acceptance of the reality that such a
court order was imminent; the Board was merely
trying to soften the impact of shattered traditions. Theirs was a moderate approach and,
as such, it put the Board in opposition to
most of the state's senior political leaders
who believed that the day of integration could
be forestalled forever. There was some hope as
well that by giving the black community their
own top-quality schools, even in the remote
areas far removed from their existing, segregated schools, the School Board would be relieving some of the pressures to integrate
from that quarter. The certain appeal of such
a sensible plan was not, however, apparent to
local politicians. Councilman Ezra Summers,
ever the most vocal of an otherwise close-
mouthed City Council, issued a strongly worded
statement supporting the Virginia's Massive
Resistance efforts and advocating a "go-slow
approach" in local school building programs
"until the integration disputes are settled."
Summers' insistence that the matter "should be
studied more carefully (*Norfolk Virginian-
Pilot* 5/11/56)" dealt a death blow to the
School Board's construction plans. The rest of
the City Council was more diplomatic in their
rejection; instead they asked the Board to
revise its plan "to what we can afford" in
light of the precipitate rise in school bond
interest rates now being extended to school
systems threatened by desegregation. Then, as
a final slap at the Board, the City Council
made preparations to go ahead and borrow money

at those same inflated interest rates to construct other capital improvements that might
attract additional state and federal funding
(*Norfolk Ledger-Dispatch* 12/19/56). Armed with
surveys indicating that 97 percent of the
city's parents and 93 percent of other adults
favored increasing school funding (*Norfolk
Ledger-Dispatch* 2/15/57), the School Board
made a strong case, but it was still rejected
outright. The inference was clear: the City
Council had higher priorities than granting
money to black schools to forestall court-
ordered desegregation.

There was nothing inherently wrong with the
school board's plan: it had been based upon
the soundest and most moderate judgement of
the time; it relied upon professional growth
surveys indicating that the schools and improvements would be needed anyway, even if the
school system was permitted to remain segregated. What was wrong was that the Board's
plan had come too late; the city had just paid
an exorbitant price to annex a large section
of Norfolk County, and the City Council could
legitimately point to the fact that it had a
pressing financial need to extend full municipal services to this area as soon as possible
(*Norfolk Ledger-Dispatch* 12/17/56). This was
reason enough to block a costly school building program that was, at best, a stopgap effort to defuse the desegregation crisis and,
at worst, a reckless gamble to lure potential
black plaintiffs away from the N.A.A.C.P. suit
with the promise of building and expanding
their own segregated neighborhood schools.
Norfolk had already made a precipitate effort
in the last decade to offer equal, although
segregated, facilities for both races, and the
city could ill afford the Schools Board's new
building proposal, the councilmen argued,
especially if integration could be averted
through other, less costly means.

Politically as well, the Board's move came too late: the calm racial attitudes that prevailed in Norfolk in the summer of 1956 had, by the winter, taken a nasty turn, and the city's white residents were giving ample evidence that they were no longer willing to buy off the black community with promises of separate but equal facilities. A shift in the stance of the city's legislative delegation was the best bellwether of this changing attitude. In the summer, the bulk of the delegation had stood behind the School Board's efforts to keep the schools open, even if desegregated. The legislators went so far as to vow to fight the governor "in opposition to any measure designed to deprive Norfolk's schools of full financial support (*Norfolk Virginian-Pilot* 7/24/56)." A year later they would back down from this moderate posture and declare that they held only minor differences with the governor; they disagreed on the tactics of how best to fight court-ordered desegregation, but the local legislators were in full accord with the governor that integration must be fought with every legal means available (*Norfolk Ledger-Dispatch* 6/8/57). In another year they would go full circle from opposition to support of Massive Resistance to integration (*Norfolk Ledger-Dispatch* 3/10/58).

One reason for this apparent shift in public opinion was the growing impact of the N.A.A.C.P. legal victories: in the spring of 1956 Norfolk's public schools were but one target in the scatter-shot legal approach of the local N.A.A.C.P. to achieve integration. By the fall, however, N.A.A.C.P. court action had forced all of the area's parks, recreation centers, and public transportation facilities to either desegregate or close indefinitely. The public school system now stood as the last bastion against a fully integrated society, and the N.A.A.C.P.'s unrelenting legal effort to crack this barrier caused increasing bit-

terness in the white community. A feeling was
growing that Norfolk needed more time to adjust to the changes that had already taken
place, and that continuing the battle to desegregate the schools only made racial moderation more difficult.

It was inevitable in the growing climate of
racial antipathy that new groups would emerge
to capitalize on this force and direct it to
serve their own needs. Although the Defenders
of State Sovereignty and Individual Liberties
had emerged first in the racially explosive
Southside as an effort by small businessmen to
combat desegregation in that area; the Defenders were gaining increasing acceptance in all
parts of the state. The Defenders were not
hood-wearing vigilantes, like their counterparts in the White Citizens' Councils further
south; instead they had made every effort to
establish in Virginia a legitimate and gentle-
manly interest group, and one that carried a
great deal of clout with the leadership of the
statewide Byrd Organization (Dabney 1971, 531-
3). Locally the Defenders had established a
storefront headquarters to test public opinion, and, having found it favorable, now
planned to mount major challenges to the
city's legislative delegation along Massive
Resistance lines (*Norfolk Virginian-Pilot*
10/25/56). One other event at the same time
indicated an escalation in both the rhetoric
and expertise of race politics. Just as the
city's business and civic elite were kicking
off their traditional fall Community Fund
drive, Norfolk was inundated with hate pamphlets aimed at one of its beneficiary organizations. After a hasty series of meetings, the
business community was forced to drop the
Urban League from the drive for its supposed
support of "race-mixing." Although the local
origin of the pamphlets was unknown (the
Defenders disavowed any responsibility), the
pamphlets were traced back to a wing of the

Christian Nationalist Party, renowned experts
on "rabble-rousing and sensational hate-mon-
gering (*Norfolk Virginian-Pilot* 10/13/56)."

The emergence of these two groups, their
apparent successes, and the mounting hostilities directed at the N.A.A.C.P. were giving
rise to a climate of political desperation.
All around, racial barriers were falling under
the onslaught of litigation; with them were
crumbling institutions of long-standing importance in the white community. The hate groups
were preparing to fan the flames of racial
unrest into a dangerous political force. The
School Board had been rebuffed in its efforts
to moderate the desegregation dispute with an
exorbitant building program aimed at lessening
the impact of desegregation. The city's legislative delegation had once stood firm in their
opposition to closing Norfolk's schools; now
they were backing away from that stance, and
instead were preparing to vote for legislation
that would turn over the control of the city's
schools to the very state politicians most
disposed to shut them down. The liberalizing
force of the People's group was nowhere to be
seen; they had been beaten back to their board
rooms and counting houses, and emerged only to
take part in lack-luster deliberations on relatively unimportant boards and advisory commissions. Even the old warhorses of the Prieur
Machine had accepted a diminished role in governmental affairs; they had been nearly crushed in the People's coup, lost interest, and
had resigned themselves to a backseat position
as the price to go along for the ride. The
entire city looked instead to the one person
who had emerged as the strong man in all municipal deliberations.

Of all the major politicians in the city,
only Mayor Duckworth had been truly silent on
the desegregation crisis. At first the public
assumed that the School Board and the Organization's legislative delegation accurately

represented his thinking, but the vacillation of the local legislators and the dispatch with which the School Board's building proposal had been dismissed gave rise to the belief that there was some middle ground between the two, and finally led to speculation that the Mayor, too, had plans to save the city from integration. By this time Duckworth was firmly in control of the city and able to direct its growth towards attainment of his own ends, and, since he had spent so much time erecting the edifices designed by C. A. Harrell and the People's administration, he was impatient to get on with the task. Like Harrell, Duckworth had a vision of a New Norfolk, but unlike Harrell and the Silkstocking crowd, Duckworth had shown little commitment to the city's past and even less compassion for its people. He saw himself as a manager, both of the city's politics and its physical plant. His attachment was thus to the city's structures, its administration, political organization, and efficiency--the bricks and mortar of growth. It was a subtle distinction, but one that would not be lost in the years ahead.

4

The Bulldozer Era

As the city's chief politician and highest elected official, Mayor W. Fred Duckworth remarkably had not yet spoken out on the subject of school integration. Most people supposed that, because of his political association with the Byrd Organization through its local affiliate, the Prieur Machine, his personal sentiments rested with those who preached resistance at all cost, yet he had endorsed none of the myriad scenarios of resistance that had already been proposed by Governor Stanley, Senator Byrd, Councilman Summers, the Defenders, the Gray Commission, James J. Kilpatrick, and others. He had never directly employed the rhetoric of interposition, and he had been strangely tolerant of others who attempted to relate the city's position. In an administration that prized closed-mouth unanimity, it was remarkable to witness the School Board left free to pursue its own moderate course while councilmen like Ezra Summers veered off in more extreme tacks. Most observers conceded that Duckworth was, at least, opposed to undertaking the School Board's building and modernization program, but even in this regard there were those who felt that his resistance was temporary, and that he was only withholding his approval as a bargaining chip in

some grander design: As yet the city lacked
the clout to force the black community into
accepting any such proposal as a token victory
short of desegregation.

By the winter of 1956, Mayor Duckworth had
achieved the promise of his 1950 Harmony
slate: He had united business acumen, professional expertise, and political astuteness into a single, concentrated focus of power that
carefully balanced the concerns of both the
business community and the Prieur Machine.
His new political force, and this was by all
rights a personal victory, was obeisant to
neither the Silkstocking Crowd nor the Organization, although it took its cues from both
camps. Duckworth had found in action and accomplishment the common ground that united
these two once opposing forces. The only real
challenges to his administration had come from
the black community: P. B. Young's councilmanic candidacy, the setback at Broad Creek
Shores, the desegregation of Coronado, the
racial unrest in Brambleton, and the court
challenges brought by the National Association for the Advancement of Colored People
(N.A.A.C.P.). The Mayor, however, had gained
the near-unanimous backing of the city's banking, business, civic, and political leaders,
and in the six years since he had come to
power, not a single effective voice had been
raised in opposition to his authority; he and
his councilmanic running mates swept to election victory year after year against only
token, gadfly resistance from the white community (*Norfolk Virginian-Pilot* 4/14/58). One
measure of the depth of Mayor Duckworth's
support may be read in the West Side voting
precincts, the traditional stronghold of the
Silkstocking establishment, where the Mayor
and his slate were now running up electoral
majorities that ran as high as ten-to-one
(*Norfolk Virginian-Pilot* 6/11/58).

A number of reasons existed to explain Duckworth's enormous personal success. Foremost among them was the fact that both time and events had been good to Norfolk, and as a result, the city was enjoying a period of unparalleled growth and prosperity. The citizens were proud of all that had been accomplished since the war, and the controversy and conflict that had characterized the planning stages under the People's government were now forgotten as the reality of annexation, redevelopment, new highways, tunnel connections, and related facilities began contributing to the city's rapid expansion. Just as the careful, cautious, consensual approach of the People's group had been perfect for the planning stage, Duckworth's forceful dominance of city policy was ideally suited to the current building phase. City government functioned smoothly, almost too smoothly, under Duckworht's firm leadership, and he seemed to control every phase of municipal operation. No longer were City Council meetings the long, drawn-out affairs that had characterized the People's sessions; instead Duckworth's Council hashed out controversies, arranged compromises, and made all the real decisions in private "presessions." Then, after all potential differences had been ironed out, the Council would emerge for its public meeting, a performance that ran as smoothly as if every member had a script: Rarely was there a dissenting vote, unnecessary discussion, or less than unanimous approval of even the most far-reaching policy decisions (Darden; Mason; Sugg).

In council-manager cities like Norfolk, the mayor is granted very few official powers beyond those of the other members of council; Duckworth, however, had added a considerable repertoire of unofficial executive and legislative authority to the traditional ribbon-cutting capacities of a weak mayor. Although lacking in official veto, budgetary, or ap-

pointment powers, Mayor Duckworth had parlayed
his position as presiding officer into un-
questioned authority over the City Council.
Both his private "presessions" and the smooth
and polished public performance of the Council
helped to heighten the sense that he alone was
firmly in control. Moreover, the city's appointed boards and commissions were no longer
functioning as a vibrant source of citizen input and participation in the city's decision-
making process; Duckworth had a strange habit
of dropping in on the boards, "suggesting" a
desired course of action, and then hanging
around until he was satisfied that his instructions had been enacted (Darden).

In a city that traditionally experienced
rapid turnover of both its top elective and
appointive officials, Mayor Duckworth quickly
emerged as one of the few stable personalities in the administration of municipal affairs. By 1956 almost all of the city's department heads, appointed board members, and
legislative delegation had been replaced since
the People's reign, and only Duckworth and
Vice-Mayor George Abbott had served more than
four years on the City Council (*Norfolk Virginian-Pilot* 9/3/56). Ironically, both the
People's group and the Organization councils
that had preceded them had shied away from
placing even the informal powers of the city's
weak mayoral position into the hands of a
single individual like Duckworth for too long:
The office had shifted from Richard Cooke to
Pretlow Darden at midpoint in the People's
tenure in order to better promote the appearance of popular democracy that they craved
(Darden). The Prieur Machine had followed a
similar practice, but political considerations
figured foremost in their decision to rotate
the seat frequently: History had shown that
the increased exposure of the office made an
incumbent mayor the most vulnerable candidate
at election time. Mayor Duckworth, however,

apparently experienced no such qualms about
either elective vulnerability or charges of
authoritarianism. By 1956 he had held the
office of Mayor longer than any other person
since the council-manager form of government
had been instituted in 1918 (*Norfolk Virginian-Pilot* 9/3/56), and he gave no indication
of a willingness to surrender his authority at
any time in the near future.

Duckworth held far more than just the policy-making functions of municipal government
within his grasp; in a very real sense he
managed the day-to-day activities of city hall
as well. Because of two resignations, an unfortunate death, and interim appointments, he
was already operating under his fifth city
manager since he had taken office six years
earlier. For this reason, the city's department heads had learned to function smoothly
under the constancy of his leadership, chan-
neling their information directly to the
Mayor's office in a route that circumvented
the authority of the city manager and the rest
of the City Council. In this skewed hierarchy,
the manager served as little more than the
Mayor's chief adviser, a role which both irri-
tated and exasperated the incumbents. In these
circumstances Norfolk was lucky to attract
Thomas F. Maxwell to the post. Even though
Maxwell possessed many talents that would ordinarily have entitled him to higher status,
he suffered one debility that would limit his
rise beyond Norfolk's functionary position:
Maxwell was a binge alcoholic who could only
survive in a closed and protective society
like Norfolk's, where the periodic abandonment
of his position made very little real difference to the operation of the city. Maxwell,
however, was a wizard with budget policy, fiscal planning, money management, and federal
grants, and this made him both invaluable to
the Mayor and an important municipal asset as

the city passed through its building phase of postwar growth (Mason; Sugg; Gregory).

Thus, in spite of the lack of official authority traditionally associated with his position, Mayor W. Fred Duckworth functioned as a strong mayor in an otherwise nonpartisan, professional, council-manager city; if all this power concentrated in one public official and a handful of advisers disturbed the citizens of Norfolk, they gave little indication of such unrest. Occasionally a newspaper editor would level a mild rebuke at the Mayor:

> The Administration in which Mayor W. Fred Duckworth has been the leading figure, has shown both good and bad points in its career. Its early weaknesses were a tendency to settle many questions at the euphemistically named "informal sessions" and a tendency to take sometimes too lightly the recommendations of qualified administrators and especially appointed commissions and agencies (*Norfolk Virginian-Pilot* 3/6/56).

Most citizens, however, apparently regarded such indelicacies as the natural consequence of having a strong-willed and effective leader at the helm. The Mayor's very personal style of leadership and his extremely hierarchical chain of command served in marked contrast to the spirited popular debate that characterized the People's regime. A surfeit of popular advice and consent had seemed to bog down the People's government in the planning process; the Mayor's "bulldozer drive and directness" (*Norfolk Virginian-Pilot* 7/23/61)--the words themselves would prove prophetic--cut quickly through the preliminaries, and the people did not appear to mind if a few of the niceties of democratic decision-making were bulldozed in the process. Indeed, the major accomplishment of the Duckworth administration to date was "its ability to undertake large programs" and bring them swiftly to their conclusion (*Nor-folk Virginian-Pilot* 3/6/56), and, as long as he continued to focus the broad powers of city government towards obtainable objectives, the citizens seemed to care little if he wielded those powers somewhat dictatorially. Although no one knew what course Duckworth proposed to follow if the city's schools really faced the threat of court-ordered integration, most as-sumed that he would act as dramatically as he had already done in almost every other field of municipal endeavor.

Two examples of the city's planning process under Mayor Duckworth help to illustrate both the enormous control of the Mayor and the shifting emphasis of developmental priorities under his administration. The primary emphasis of city planning under the People's government had been the modernization and revitalization of Norfolk's downtown commercial center--the "New Norfolk" of which they boasted. Consider-ing the size of the city, Norfolk had never had much of a real downtown business district, and even in the People's era, merchants in the area's fragile commercial strip were already feeling the press of competition from more residential shopping centers. Originally Nor-folk had been a city built around its water-front, but hard times had befallen its ship-ping-support industries since the demise of sailing ships and intra-coastal shipping, and the business quarter had shifted two blocks away from the rotting wharves and crumbling warehouses that bespoke the heyday of its seaport existence. The once prosperous and active waterfront area had fallen almost completely into disuse, and the city's remain-ing commercial strip gave ample evidence of its former residential origins: The classic lines of Georgian and Victorian houses rose above the polished marble and glass facades of first-floor businesses; narrow streets and winding alleyways were clogged with the traf-

fic they were never designed to carry; church-
spires stood in lonely vigil over neighborhoods without residents (Agle 1956, 19-20).

Because the downtown commercial center was
already struggling to overcome its competitive
handicaps, further expansion in the commercial
sector was not practical; instead the People's
planners looked to development of the downtown's noncommercial advantages as the only
hope for its crowded, misplaced businesses.
For this reason, they looked to expansion of
the city's cultural and waterfront potential
as a way to keep customers in the vicinity of
downtown shops (*Norfolk Virginian-Pilot* 5/28/
56). At the time, redevelopment laws forbade
the taking of commercial or industrial areas
(Housing and Home Finance Agency 1949), even
those that were abandoned and delinquent in
tax payments (Agle 1956, 19-20), and so the
planners were forced to seek municipal expenditures that would stimulate private construction. For this reason they turned their attention to two theme-oriented extensions to the
downtown, both of which combined a minimum of
needed public spending as an inducement to
attract private development efforts.

The first proposal focused on a Cultural
Center to be located just to the northwest of
the existing downtown commercial strip. Major
cultural attractions already existed with the
Norfolk (Chrysler) Museum at one end and the
city's Center Theater/Civic Auditorium complex
at the other end of the designated area; in
addition, the Planning Commission had convinced the Library Board to relocate its main
branch to new facilities to be built in the
center. The area already possessed an urbane
and international feeling, enhanced by the
classic lines of the Georgian and federal
architecture of the neighboring Ghent and
Freemason Street areas. The nearby Smith Creek
Marina and the Hague Yacht Basin, with its
footpaths, bridges, and waterfront park, were

popular havens both for boaters who followed the Inland Waterway and others looking for a respite from the fast pace of urban living. The Commission hoped to build on this recreational quality of the area by relocating the Confederate Monument, the city's obeisance to its Southern heritage, to a minipark to be constructed in the middle, hoping that it would serve to attract lunch-hour picnickers and pedestrian traffic to the area. A second benefit of the minipark would be that it would help to rechannel traffic into the downtown area in a more acceptable pattern; at the time, five of the city's main downtown commuter streets--Llewellyn Avenue, Olney Road, Duke, Boush, and High (now Virginia Beach Boulevard) Streets--met in the middle of the proposed Cultural Center and wound their way tortuously into the main downtown commercial district (*Norfolk Virginian-Pilot* 12/23/51).

The Planning Commission hoped to use this new Cultural Center, replete with its parks, library, museum, theater, marina, and modern traffic connectors, to attract other similar cultural enterprises to this common area. The planners hoped that trade delegations and emissaries from the North Atlantic Treaty Organization countries would relocate into a consulate's row in the area, thereby continuing the international flavor already imparted by the Hague and nearby Ghent neighborhood. The Commission was attempting to encourage some of the city's leading charities and civic organizations to seek adjacent sites, and its members were confident that once the Cultural Center began to take shape, that a major convention hotel would buy a site in the area. The Silkstocking businessmen and the various boards and commissions associated with the planning of the center were trying to use their contacts to convince the city's major enterprises to relocate their headquarters in the vicinity. The city was even reserving a site next to the museum and proposed library for an aquarium or naval museum (*Norfolk Virginian-Pilot* 12/23/51). Plans for the Cultural Center were ambitious, but they seemed realistic enough considering the constraints of the period; the planners had every reason to believe that local businesses, restaurants, specialty shops, and sidewalk cafés would be attracted by the combination of public and private construction, fleshing out a new vitality to an area just outside of the narrow confines of the existing downtown commercial strip (*Norfolk Virginian-Pilot* 7/9/52). The public funds necessary to support the undertaking were not large, and those earmarked for library construction and street improvements were necessary regardless of the success of the rest of the project. Enthusiasm for the plan was especially strong during 1951 and 1952, while C. A. Harrell was still manager, and before the People's movement had wholly lost its advisory role in municipal affairs.

At about this time, planners were also attempting to develop a parallel proposal to improve the city's deteriorating waterfront area; they knew that here, too, a similar combination of public expenditures for parks and promenades, plus the right kind of private investment, could attract a contingent of outdoor cafes and specialty shops. A number of proposals were being bandied about, including designs for a seawall, amphitheater, small boat marina, highrise luxury apartment buildings, new City Hall/Civic Center complex, naval museum, private housing developments, *cordon bleu* seafood restaurant, seafood market, and bazaar (*Norfolk Virginian-Pilot* 8/14/56). The most promising proposal for waterfront development came from the Norfolk Port Authority, a creation of the old People's City Council. Members of the Authority hoped to unite many of the aspects of earlier proposals around a single, two-staged development de-

signed both to attract new investment and to
encourage improvement of existing properties.
Phase One focused on the construction of a
huge concrete pier that would extend far
enough out into the main shipping channel to
accommodate the loading and unloading of even
the deepest draft vessels. Space along the
pier would be rented out to shipping and
freight forwarding concerns, and on the shore,
as Phase Two, a large quay would be built
broad enough to accommodate both drayage and
specialty shops, travel agents, seafood vend-
ors, a produce market, restaurants, and outdoor cafés (*Norfolk Virginian-Pilot* 5/28/56).

Plans for both these projects--the harbor
quay and the Cultural Center--advanced just as
rapidly as they would have under the People's
administration; the city's volunteer boards
and commissions proceeded in a vacuum as if
they had the same power and responsibilities
as before. The Port Authority began to buy up
property at the foot of Commercial Place and
West Main Street and to aggressively line up
prospects for space on the quay among the
local merchants and out-of-town investors
(*Norfolk Virginian-Pilot* 5/28/56). The City
Planning Commission was moving just as aggressively to line up prospects for its own
development at the other end of the downtown
area: The Salvation Army, Union Mission, IBM,
and other leading corporations and charities
were already moving into new facilities in the
Cultural Center. Thus, by the time the City
Council was approached for approval, both
projects were well off the drawing boards and
fast becoming a reality.

No official reason was ever given for the
rejection of either proposal; in fact, the
Council seems never to have docketed the items
or given them public audience. In spite of
widespread enthusiasm and the editorial en-
dorsements of the *Virginian-Pilot* and *Ledger-
Dispatch*, both projects were accorded a low

profile, back-burner status that was unusual
for such full-blown and well-planned undertakings. The only official action that was
ever taken on either project concerned the
Library Board's request to relocate the main
library to a new site in the Cultural Center:
For four years the Council delayed consideration, and then finally announced in August of
1956 that the Cultural Center was "a long-
range undertaking [that] has been accorded a
lower priority" than other city projects (*Norfolk Ledger-Dispatch* 8/22/56). It was a heavy
blow to all who had hoped for an East Ghent
commercial revival, and even though portions
of the project still survived independent of
the others, the idea for a Cultural Center in
downtown Norfolk was dead. The Port Authority,
too, was forced to abandon its plans, and
later settled for less expensive arrangements
far removed from the downtown area.

Thus, by the winter of 1956, every major
program of renewal or revitalization left over
from the People's administration had either
been fully activated or quietly put aside; the
powers that controlled city hall had shifted
dramatically in the decade since the rise of
the Silkstocking Ticket. No longer were the
city's volunteer boards and commissions, or
the business and civic elite they represented,
a power in the planning and decision-making
process; just like the Norfolk Redevelopment
and Housing Authority and the Land (Kaufman)
Commission, which were then planning the Oakwood Redevelopment Project, they were operating in a vacuum without political authority.

The appearance that the city ran so smoothly under the Mayor's direction was no acci-
dent; Duckworth had made a special point to
eliminate any opportunity for factionalism or
opposition on the City Council before it could
emerge. Councilmen and city managers came and
went at city hall so rapidly during this era
that one could easily see why Mayor Duckworth,

even if he had not been a forceful leader, would be quickly recognized as the only stable force in the city's administration. Councilmen were chosen from the broad ranks of independent but small-time business-men--insurance agents, wholesalers, real estate brokers, and shopkeepers--who were successful overachievers in their calling, but who exhibited no remarkable capacity for independent action. None came to city hall with any special following, gleaned through either prior municipal experience, volunteer service, or through leadership in the business or civic community, and each owed his advancement entirely to Duckworth and those around him.

The circumstances behind an individual's selection to elective office at this time remain clouded, partly because the unofficial nominating process was shrouded in enough secrecy to preserve both the political viability of the chosen and the continued domination of the selectors. Just as his own 1950 Harmony Ticket had been engineered by some considerable behind-the-scenes maneuvering, Duckworth and those around him apparently never trusted the election process to elevate men of good standing and high ability to the City Council. Two old standbys of the Byrd Organization were employed in Norfolk to tightly control the nominating and elective processes: first, the official slate of Duckworth-endorsed candidates was held in secrecy until its announcement at the last moment before the filing deadline, thereby eliminating those Prieur Organization hopefuls who had been passed over in the unofficial nominating process. Secondly, those who ran for elective office were not always those who served: Mayor Duckworth and those around him perfected the Organization's "planned incumbency" scheme whereby a trusted incumbent would stand for reelection and mysteriously resign so that a carefully selected successor could fill the slot without risking the perils of popular election; the newcomer would then have the advantages of an incumbent's experience and exposure when he stood for reelection in his own right two years later. Advancement by appointment had become a time-honored tradition in Virginia--most of the state's senators, congressmen, and other top office-holders had advanced at least once in this manner--and it quickly became a hallmark as well of Norfolk City government: thus in 1953, newcomer Roy B. Martin, Jr., was selected to fill the seat vacated when Councilman James M. Williams resigned; Lewis L. Layton similarly took over in 1956 when incumbent Robert F. Ripley stepped down shortly after winning re-election (*Norfolk Virginian-Pilot* 2/9/56); and Linwood F. Perkins was appointed in early 1957 when Councilman Ezra Summers died in office (*Norfolk Ledger-Dispatch* 6/26/57). Norfolk was so obviously by-passing the popular election process that the *Virginian-Pilot* targeted the Duckworth administration for their lack of political decorum:

> It is a sounder procedure to give the voters a little advance notice before selecting a successor to a man they elected to office. Settling the whole problem behind closed doors is not good procedure even if the result, in all other respects, is satisfactory (*Norfolk Virginian-Pilot* 2/9/56).

Most observers conceded that Duckworth had the final word in the unofficial nominating process that selected candidates for municipal office in Norfolk. This was no mean achievement when one considers the enormous control exerted by Billy Prieur and his Organization during their heyday, but Prieur had apparently lost interest in municipal affairs since the near demise of his political machine during

the People's administration. Instead, like
many other of his contemporaries in the statewide Byrd Organization, he had resigned himself to a lesser role. Local experts point to
Prieur's acceptance of an increasingly moderate and independent-acting, "Young Turk"
legislative delegation as a sign of his lessening involvement in the candidate selection
and election process (Mason; Sugg; Gregory).
The Young Turks were so named because they
were mostly men in their early thirties, who,
although members of the Organization, sometimes refused to back the old Byrd hierarchy.
Most were war veterans or urban legislators
like Norfolk's own Walter Paige, Theodore
Pilcher, Toy Savage, and Jack Rixey, who buck-
ed the Organization establishment to support
issues of urban concern or racial moderation.
In one sense they well represented Norfolk's
urbane constituency, and were thus good selections, but in another sense, the Billy Prieur
of the 1930s would never have brooked such independence.

All across the state the Organization was
in decline, and, especially in its urban
areas, was giving way to new leadership groups
such as the Young Turks or Mayor Duckworth's
businessmen's coalition. Billy Prieur, who had
always preferred the seclusion of the back
room to the spotlight of public recognition,
was now apparently content to accept a part-
nership role with Duckworth that placed the
Mayor in the limelight. No one is really sure
who held the upper hand, if indeed either
party dominated the arrangement, for both men
had powerful egos, and neither would have allowed himself to play a secondary role. It
seems more probable that Duckworth and Prieur,
both conservatives, were in basic agreement on
most major matters, and that each held his own
unchallengeable dominion. Prieur controlled
state and federal patronage; Duckworth, on the
other hand, controlled municipal policy with-

out interference from Prieur (Staylor; Sugg;
Mason; Gregory). The Prieur Machine seemed to
have evolved away from the corruption that
existed during the boom period of the war
years, and, once battered by the municipal
housecleaning during the People's era, now
seemed content to concentrate on the less
important "favors" of government that kept its
machinery alive: patronage, purchasing, permits, enforcement, and promotions, especially
in the more political Police and Fire Depart-
ments (Staylor; Estes). With a strongman at
the helm of government, Prieur and the Organization seemed both unable and unwilling to
challenge the authority of the Mayor, thus
giving him free reign to direct basic policy
as he wished (Mason; Sugg; Staylor).

If the people were worried that all this
power, both political and governmental, was
concentrated in the office of their Mayor,
they gave little indication of such concern.
By and large, those advanced by Duckworth and
his advisors to both political office and appointive positions were men and women of good
character who were probably more representative than the selections of the Silkstocking
crowd. If a special danger existed in so establishing Duckworth as a benevolent dictator,
it would come from one of several quarters.
First, the Mayor might lose touch with the
public will; he had made so many of the city's
decisions without public input that he might
now discover that he had lost the ability to
listen. Second, because the people had been so
silent, there was a danger that if a small and
vocal minority ever became well organized,
then the Mayor might over-react to its pronouncements. Also, the Mayor's famous temper
might intrude upon his otherwise sound judgement. Already city hall was abuzz with rumors
about individuals, even respected members of
the city's business and professional society,
who had dared to oppose the Mayor or one of

his programs, even in a minor way, only to
find their livelihood threatened (Dillon 1970,
17-19). Stories also existed about how even
senior city officials who had attempted to
question a Duckworth decision had been publicly humiliated by the Mayor in a tirade of
verbal abuse (Sugg). These, however, were only
petty examples of an even greater danger; so
far no one knew just how far the Mayor might
go in a fit of pique to destroy a political
opponent or some other, greater threat to his
administration. Earlier in the decade, blacks
had experienced a pattern of mayoral revenge
for their political deviation, and the Broad
Creek Shores controversy had shown that the
Mayor was not above employing his official
powers to punish his opposition, but these
actions only hinted at the even greater dangers that lay ahead now that Mayor Duckworth
had achieved full domination over every phase
of municipal operation.

Finally, in spite of all his power and
demonstrated skills, Mayor Duckworth had not
yet put his authority to work on any of his
own programs. The People's Council and city
manager C. A. Harrell had left behind a very
precisely planned and carefully orchestrated
program of action, and Duckworth's success in
bringing those plans to reality had brought
him much well-deserved popularity and unparalleled economic stability to the city.
Now, however, the People's program was past--
Norfolk Redevelopment and Housing Authority's
Project One was concluding, the last units of
public housing were under construction, the
bridge-tunnel connector to Portsmouth was
open, the ambitious annexation program was
complete, hundreds of new classrooms had been
added to the school system, new water and
sewer works were already on line, revamped
health, housing, sanitation, and building
codes were being enforced, and the area was
going through the greatest building boom in

its history (*Norfolk Virginian-Pilot* 3/22/56);
if the Mayor had an agenda of his own, it was
a secret as closely guarded as the names of
his running mates in the next councilmanic
election. Now that all these projects were
complete, and the People's follow-up phase of
development had been rejected, Norfolk was
about to enter a new stage of growth that
would carry Duckworth's distinctive and, as
yet, undiscernible stamp.

Now at the peak of both his political and
municipal power, Mayor Duckworth was at last
preparing to launch his own program of development, only this time there was no fanfare,
no minority advisors, no citizen involvement,
and no prior publicity. That was not his
style; Duckworth moved in a more deliberate
and purposeful manner, unhampered by either
the open accessibility or the frenzy of par-
ticipatory democracy that had seemed to bog
his predecessors down as much in the form as
in the substance of government. The Duckworth
style involved instead both the acquisition of
power and the display of its use, and he had
done well in both regards, having constructed
the base for unparalleled personal control
from the blueprints left over from the Silkstocking reformers. Now, however, the last of
the People's programs was either completed or
put away forever: The Cultural Center, harbor
quay, and Oakwood redevelopment project had
all been tabled, and the city's priorities under Duckworth would shift away from developing
its assets and turn toward destroying its liabilities. Chief among the liabilities was the
impending school desegregation crisis, now
bottled up in the federal courts on a string
of technicalities that could snap at any moment. Since Mayor Duckworth had not yet spoken
out on the desegregation issue, few residents
could have guessed that in the coming months
he would attempt to deal so directly with the
crisis, using the powers of city government to

oppose the threat of forced integration as if
it were just another political rival. The
stakes in such an undertaking were frighten-
ingly high--the desegregation controversy was
more than just a collection of human opponents; it would become the major force of
change in the nation for the next decade. At
the time, however, few people could discern
how powerful that force would become, and all
across the Commonwealth political leaders were
hastening to erect paper barriers and legal
obstacles to divert the onslaught of desegregation. Duckworth alone emerged with a plan
carefully contrived to construct more permanent breastworks, and had this effort succeed-
ed, it probably would have been imitated all
across the nation. Still, few men anywhere in
municipal government were in a better position
to hazard such a venture: Few men could match
Mayor Duckworth's record of municipal accomplishment, partisan consensus, and personal
leadership. Even so, the risk was just apparent enough that the Mayor saw fit to hedge his
bets in secrecy and couch his plan in the
guise of the priorities of the old People's
group. This was a masterful stroke: No matter
how comprehensive the endeavor, if it failed,
he would be able to step clear from its liabilities and disavow the complicity of his involvement.

   Redevelopment leaped suddenly to the forefront of municipal policy, just as it had during the heyday of the People's administration,
and events began to move rapidly--too rapidly
for the citizens to fully comprehend either
their significance or their comprehensiveness.
In December (1956), the Norfolk Redevelopment
and Housing Authority announced the commence-
ment of two new undertakings, both begun after
the Mayor had forcefully suggested their initiation (Darden). N.R.H.A. Project Two would
clear just over 37 acres of blighted housing
in the Lamberts Point section of the city

(N.R.H.A. 1974, 39), providing much-needed
growing room to the Norfolk Division of the
College of William and Mary and Virginia Polytechnic Institute (now Old Dominion University), enabling it to break out of the narrow
confines of its two-year preparatory and trade
school curriculum. The second project proposed
to bulldoze 90 acres in the Atlantic City
portion of Norfolk (*Norfolk Virginian-Pilot*
12/8/56), the chief beneficiary of which would
be Norfolk General Hospital, another popular,
landlocked public institution. Before the project could even be approved, an additional
forty-five acres were added to accommodate
long-standing plans left over from the days of
the People's administration to improve adjacent health, highway, and tunnel facilities.

In marked contrast to N.R.H.A. Project One
and the Oakwood Project proposed by the Silkstocking establishment, no housing, either
public or private, was planned in either
Atlantic City or the Old Dominion (N.R.H.A.
Project Two) Project, even though the combined
area of the two new developments was more than
twice the size of the People's N.R.H.A. Project One--the Atlantic City area alone contained close to a 1,000 dwellings. As a matter
of fact, the N.R.H.A. was just beginning to
embark upon another venture which would destroy an additional 2,600 dwellings that would
have been ideal to ease the relocation of refugees from these two new redevelopment initiatives. By annexation, Norfolk had acquired
Broad Creek Village, a 468-acre war housing
project still occupied by the families of
government and military workers. In spite of
strong protests from the navy (*Norfolk Virginian-Pilot* 6/11/54), the N.R.H.A. planned to
raze those dwellings to make room for a mammoth industrial park, thereby compounding further the relocation problem.

Bulldozers were still roaring through the
dwellings in the Atlantic City, Broad Creek,

and Old Dominion Projects when the N.R.H.A
announced a fourth venture, the Downtown Redevelopment Project. In a carefully concerted
attack, the N.R.H.A. swept bare more than 200
acres in the oldest part of the city (N.R.H.A.
1974, 39). The central focus of the assault
was Norfolk's notorious East Main Street "sin
strip," where once a vast array of bars, honky
tonks, flophouses, amusement palaces, tattoo
parlors, and burlesques had entertained the
fleet and brought disrepute to more legitimate
downtown businesses. More than 400 commercial
structures would fall in this massive attempt
to wipe out a repugnant merchandising industry, and another 485 residences would be razed
without the addition of any new public housing
units for their evacuees (*Norfolk Virginian-
Pilot* 7/26/61).

With the initiation of these four nearly
simultaneous endeavors--the Atlantic City, Old
Dominion, Broad Creek, and Downtown Projects--
the city was destroying a sizeable share of
its developed land--more than 800 acres were
scheduled for clearance--in exchange for new
opportunities for growth. This new phase of
redevelopment was unquestionably the Mayor's:
Although none of the four projects were new
ideas to his administration--all four had been
kicked around, along with numerous other proposals, among the various planning and advisory commissions--the enormous scope of this
undertaking was entirely Duckworth's invention
(Darden); the size of the projects, the coor-
dination of the endeavor, the speed with which
they were initiated, and even the rationale
for such dramatic action all derived their impetus from his character. In pure size, this
new phase in redevelopment was staggering:
The four projects encompassed an area ten
times the size of N.R.H.A. Project One, which
itself was twice the size of any development
that New York or any other city had attempted
(*Architectural Forum* 1950, 132). More than

20,000 people, almost a tenth of Norfolk's
population (based upon census tract data),
would be forced to flee the bulldozers in this
new phase of demolition. More than 4,000 residential structures, many with several apartments, and more than 500 commercial structures
would be razed in the unprecedented scope of
these combined endeavors.

The speed with which all four projects were
undertaken was almost as startling: Less than
nine months lapsed from the announcement of
the Atlantic City Project to the time that
demolition work actually began in earnest; the
N.R.H.A. began tearing down structures in
Broad Creek almost as soon as it took title to
the land from the navy. By marked contrast,
Project One had been almost three years in the
planning phase before the City Council had
made the first appropriation, and then another
full year passed before demolition work actually began. Also, by comparison, no formal
plan existed for what would be done in the
areas once they were cleared. Although the official explanation for all four projects was
that they were desperately needed to provide
room for industrial expansion, downtown development, and growth of the city's education,
transportation, and health facilities, no
blueprints or scale models of such enterprises
were put out for public display. Either the
Mayor felt no need to "sell" the projects in
this way, or else he really did not have any
firm commitments yet for new hospital wings,
educational structures, industrial firms, or
commercial ventures. N.R.H.A. Project One was
one-tenth the size of the new proposals, and
it had still taken six years to complete, even
though it was vastly overplanned in comparison.

In spite of the fact that plans for redeveloping the projects were at best only loosely formulated, the Duckworth administration
had good reason to rush them off the drawing

boards and into the demolition stage as quickly as possible. The rationale behind this apparent impulsiveness was not based upon any
immediate demand for cleared land, for, indeed, the Mayor had never placed a very high
priority upon the drudgery and precision of
community planning; his *forte* was quick and
dramatic action, and the single-mindedness
with which the N.R.H.A. pursued condemnation
in these projects was no exception. Ironically
the Mayor, who had achieved his reputation by
building to the People's specifications, would
now turn to rapid demolition of property before new plans for its use could be fully
drawn, but the simple truth remains that new
construction lagged far behind in the list of
municipal priorities. The new focus was upon
clearing land where existing uses were seriously threatening the continued prosperity of
the city. It is easy to see why the sleazy
bars and honky tonks, the festering slums, and
the seedy business houses scheduled for removal in the Downtown Project were undesirable
land uses, but why would a city suffering an
acute shortage of adequate and sanitary housing units suddenly turn to destroy more than
3,500 units with decent plumbing? Why, too,
would a city desperate for low-cost housing,
especially for its black residents, suddenly
propose to bulldoze more than 4,250 such units
without planning any additional housing, either public or private?

Each of the projects poses an interesting
contradiction to sound planning practices.
Broad Creek Village, for instance, was unquestionably ideal for future industrial development, but it would take years to fill the
468-acre site. In the meantime the area was
occupied by 2,600 individual family homes, all
less than fifteen years old and all equipped
with modern sewage and sanitation facilities.
Although the homes had been built by the navy
during the war as demountable units, prefabri-

cation was becoming more and more the rule in new home construction. Uncertainty about the future of the village had undoubtedly contributed to its decline, but the area still showed signs of health and usefulness as a solid working-class community. Broad Creek Village had served a very unique and successful purpose as a settlement of wartime government housing, but shortly after the Korean War, the navy sought to sever its relationship as landlord and turn that function over to public housing agencies like the Norfolk Redevelopment and Housing Authority. Since N.R.H.A. Executive Director Larry Cox had indicated his oppostion to operating Broad Creek Village as either low-income or public housing (*Norfolk Virginian-Pilot* 7/6/55), area residents were bitterly opposed to the N.R.H.A. takeover. Because the property was technically in a portion of Norfolk County still slated for annexation by the city, residents fought vigorously to have the navy turn it over to either the county or to some sort of tenant-sponsored mutual ownership organization. The N.R.H.A. publicly persisted in its desire to demolish the entire tract, and this bitterness between the tenants and the new landlord helped to speed the deterioration of the village once the N.R.H.A. actually took over management. Angry residents blamed deterioration upon the N.R.H.A. for its failure to perform simple maintenance duties, but the condition can just as easily be traced back to the residents themselves, who, because of uncertainty over the area's future, failed to continue the same level of upkeep as they had when the future of the project was secure under federal auspices (*Norfolk Virginian-Pilot* 4/24/55).

Hurricane Hazel struck in 1954 just as the N.R.H.A. was taking title to the property, but the debate over which agency had responsibility to repair the damage, including more than

30 carloads of missing shingles (*Norfolk Vir-ginian-Pilot* 6/19/58), soon became a moot point. Once the N.R.H.A. assumed control, it began closing off sections and preparing the houses for demolition. The sight of barricaded streets, vandalized properties, and boarded-up buildings helped to panic the residents into agreeing to rezoning the property for indus-trial use in the hope that they were buying time. They thought that once the property had been rezoned and its fate secure, the N.R.H.A. would institute a program of gradual removal as development prospects solidified (*Norfolk Virginian-Pilot* 5/21/55). Their hopes, how-ever, were short-lived; within three years most of the residents had been driven out (*Norfolk Virginian-Pilot* 6/19/58).

Regardless of which element deserves blame for the demise of Broad Creek Village, by the time the bulldozers actually began to roll through the area, blight had become rampant. What had once been valuable and relatively new housing units--all had two to three bedrooms, hardwood floors, deep sash windows, modern plumbing fixtures, and sturdy interior con-structions--had degenerated quickly into a full scale slum with vandalized and deserted buildings, piles of rubbish, and the look of despair that generally characterizes areas slated for demolition. In its heyday during the war and the years immediately following, when its survival had been certain, Broad Creek had been an ideal working-class communi-ty: It had almost no crime, the neighbors looked out for one another, shared a sense of purpose, and felt compassion and kinship with one another--in short, it exhibited a remark-able sense of community and spirit. By the end of the war it had lost its appearance as a military camp, and residents worked feverishly to tend their gardens, improve their dwelling, and save up enough to purchase their own unit. Although out in the county, Broad Creek na-

tives felt that they had their own little
city: It had its own schools, churches, parks,
playgrounds, stores, and commercial areas; for
more than 5,000 people it was "home," and for
many their first real home. No wonder that its
residents fought so bitterly against the proposal to tear the structures down; they could
not believe that with all the newly annexed
farmland, Norfolk could not find a better
place for industry than on top of their homes.

Today, more than 30 years after Broad Creek
Village was razed, many of its original "slum"
dwellings ironically remain in other parts of
the city: Some of the residents refused to
have their units torn down, bought them from
the N.R.H.A. for a couple of hundred dollars,
and then paid to have them moved to other
sites (*Norfolk Virginian-Pilot* 7/15/79).

Broad Creek Village was not, however, the
only area where residents blamed the Norfolk
Redevelopment and Housing Authority for hastening decline by spreading rumors of destruction. When Norfolk leaders first began talking
back in 1949 about large-scale renewal of the
aging neighborhoods on the fringe of the downtown area, Atlantic City was one of the few
predominantly white areas mentioned in the
early speculations (*Norfolk Virginian-Pilot*
10/4/49). Founded around the cotton mill, Fort
Norfolk, the seafood industry, and small boat
marinas, Atlantic City had been one of Norfolk's first suburbs, predating Ghent, its
richer cousin across the Hague (Smith Creek),
by almost a decade. Since Atlantic City contained the industries that supported the
carriage set who lived in Ghent, most of its
dwelling units were working-class row houses
or multi-family structures. These lent themselves easily to overcrowding and exploitation
by nonresident landlords during the critical
housing shortage that prevailed throughout
World War II and the years immediately following, but these conditions were found in even

the city's finest neighborhoods. As rumors of
its redevelopment spread, however, those same
property owners were understandably unwilling
to undertake major repairs or improvements,
and the area took on many of the appearances
of a "blighted" neighborhood (*Norfolk Virginian-Pilot* 10/11/56). Even so, however, Atlantic City should have been just the sort of
neighborhood that the newly revamped health,
housing, and building codes were supposed to
rehabilitate. Much of the housing scheduled
for removal in the Downtown Project had unquestionably deteriorated beyond repair: Census tract studies indicate that more than 80
percent of the units had inadequate plumbing
facilities, 96 percent were built before 1920,
94 percent were without any form of central
heating, and the median contract rent in 1949
had been only $14.51 per month (U.S. Census
1952 III, 38: 22). The Atlantic City Project,
however, proves a sharp contrast: In 1949, at
a time when the severe housing crisis in the
community had precipitated subdividing many
older homes into multi-unit apartments, almost
a quarter of the Atlantic City homes were
still single family, freestanding houses; another fourth were duplexes, a popular building
style in many older neighborhoods; and close
to 20% of the homes were less than thirty
years old. In addition, more than 70 percent
of the units had adequate plumbing (two apartments that shared a bathroom, a common practice in the city, were downgraded in the census as having inadequate plumbing). More than
half the units had central heating, and the
median contract rent was $34.86, twice the
value of the structures torn down in both the
Downtown Redevelopment Project or N.R.H.A.
Project One (U.S. Census 1952, III, 38: 21-2).
Undoubtedly, a number of structures had deteriorated beyond rehabilitation, even by
today's standards in which restoring older,
central-city homes has become fashionable, but

many of the deficiencies noted in the census
were not only in keeping with existing city
codes, but they were also common practices
during the local wartime and postwar housing
crises (Schlegel 1951, 20-60).

Ironically, Atlantic City was chosen by the
Norfolk Health Department for a major code-
enforcement initiative precisely because of
the overall quality of its structures and the
fact that they were so salvageable. Since federally funded redevelopment projects required
that the locality rehabilitate one living unit
for each unit torn down, Norfolk had adopted
one of the first comprehensive minimum housing
codes in the country. Because Norfolk was only
the second city in the nation (the other was
Baltimore) to attempt large scale enforcement
of its code, the Health Department was looking
for a neighborhood that was good enough to
salvage, but not so bad that code enforcement
efforts would make little difference. After
careful analysis of the 1950 census data and
preliminary field work, the Health Department
chose Atlantic City for the first concentrated
housing code enforcement effort in the nation.
When the staff of the Health Department met
with N.R.H.A. Executive Director Larry Cox,
they were told that the city had no plans to
begin any redevelopment activity in Atlantic
City for "at least five to ten years," and
that were other areas of the city rated a much
"higher priority (Monola)." According to the
former Director of Environmental Health (G. D.
Monola) who led the code enforcement project,
the only badly deteriorated section of Atlantic City lay along the site of today's
Brambleton Avenue. Because this area had mixed
commercial, industrial, and residential uses,
rental units had been allowed by absentee
landlords to degenerate. Black families displaced by Project One had begun moving in to
this section, but because it was separate from
the other residential blocks, there was none

of the violence or strong community reaction
that had occurred in Brambleton or Coronado.
In short, Atlantic City had "integrated without any difficulty . . . without any fanfare,
any publicity, or Klan activity (Monola)."
Moreover, the fact that blacks were now moving
into these units meant that they could command
higher rents, and the landlords were thus more
willing to make the investments necessary to
bring the dwellings up to code.

For this reason, the sudden announcement of
the demolition of the entire area caught both
the residents and the Health Department by
surprise. The code-enforcement project had
just been completed, and nearly every dwelling
had been brought up to the city's new minimum
housing code, some at considerable cost to the
property owners. According to Monola, the
Health Department had been meeting regularly
with the N.R.H.A. executive staff, and demolition of the neighborhood was not mentioned
until it was announced in the press. The fact
that the N.R.H.A. had used the Health Department surveys as justification for the demolition helped to deepen the rift between the two
agencies. Although there were a "surprisingly
large number of owner-occupied dwellings" in
the area and most of the buildings were well
worth saving, especially now that they had
been rehabilitated, the N.R.H.A. persisted in
its effort, against the advice of the Health
Department, to push for demolition of the
entire area. Although a building could meet
all the requirements of the city's minimum
housing code and still have major defects, the
Health Department felt that the N.R.H.A. had
gone overboard in its rush to expand the project beyond the fairly restrictive area of
blight. Block after block where only a few defects were listed were also included, but because these were lumped together with the
worst houses, the entire area was able to meet

the minimum requirement of five defects per
dwelling to qualify for federal funding.

Thus, in an ironical twist, the Atlantic
City housing units that had been rehabilitated
as a result of N.R.H.A. Project One, were then
torn down in Norfolk's second phase of redevelopment. Residents were furious with the
Health Department, especially when they learned that the appraisal of their property from
the N.R.H.A. was less than the amount they had
just spent to bring their dwellings up to the
minimum housing code. The Health Department's
code enforcement effort suffered as a result
of the uproar, and disagreements over the size
and scope of the Atlantic City project eventually led to a split between the two agencies; no longer would the Health Department
help in the housing rehabilitation efforts of
the N.R.H.A. (Monola), and even in 1992 the
city still operates two separate housing agencies with overlapping authority, mission, and
purpose.

Obviously, after eight years of rumored destruction, and the general state of despair
and disrepair that follows such rumors, portions of the Atlantic City neighborhood were
in danger of becoming a slum. The Norfolk Redevelopment and Housing Authority pointed to
the Health Department surveys as proof that it
had higher incidence of tuberculosis, venereal
disease, juvenile delinquency, dilapidated
housing, racial unrest, crimes, fires, and rat
infestation than other neighborhoods in the
city (*Norfolk Virginian-Pilot* 6/23/57), but
the residents complained that all of these had
come to the area since the talk of redevelopment:

> It seems that considerable time and ef-
> fort has gone into preparing reports by
> various functions of the city government
> to show that Atlantic City has been a
> detriment to the rest of the city. If it

was such a blight . . . and its effects
so far reaching . . . wouldn't this fact
have been so outstanding that it would
speak for itself without having to be
figured to prove it (*Norfolk Virginian-
Pilot* 7/1/57)?

Few citizens and even fewer organizations were
willing to take up these cries and oppose the
project. Only those most affected by demoli-
tion--the owners of homes, apartment buildings, or commercial properties in the area--
showed any inclination to fight. The most
vigorous opposition came not from the residents, but rather from yachting enthusiasts
and environmentalists who opposed the Brambleton Avenue bridge that would close the Smith
Creek Marina (*Norfolk Virginian-Pilot* 1/5/57).
Replacing the old two-lane drawbridge with a
broad fixed span was, however, one of the few
necessary proposals in the project: Norfolk
desperately needed another thoroughfare con-
necting the downtown area with Hampton Boulevard, and the Brambleton Avenue route offered
the best alternative (Norfolk City Planning
Commission 1950; Agle 1956). Moreover, almost
all of the deteriorated dwellings in the project area could have been demolished by careful placement of this one highway alone. The
rest not only could have been spared, they
were worth saving (Monola).
    Other aspects of the Atlantic City Project
were either too vague for thorough assessment,
too long-term in their design, too haphazard
in their application, or else so incompatible
with the other developments as to be striking-
ly ill-conceived. The project area itself was
a strange configuration that zigged and zagged
its way from Clairemont Avenue in West Ghent
to Monticello Avenue in downtown Norfolk,
never stretching more than just a few blocks
in width (see Figure 3). The lines were purposely drawn to exclude certain blocks, speci-

Figure 3
Atlantic City Redevelopment Project

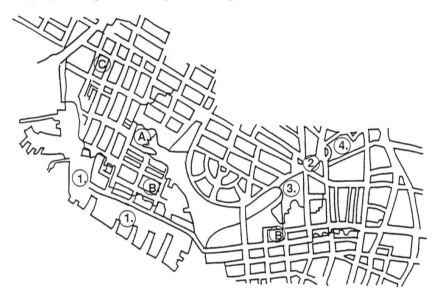

Excluded from the Project

1. Fort Norfolk and waterfront industrial area
2. Proposed Norfolk Cultural Center (never built)
3. Norfolk (now Chrysler) Museum
4. Center Theatre/Municipal Auditorium complex

Included in the Project

A. Patrick Henry Elementary School (white)
B. Mixed race areas housing 13 plaintiffs in the
   school desegregation suit
C. Norfolk General Hospital/Medical School complex

fic commercial and industrial structures, and
even single residences from demolition, while
the area around them was completely leveled.
The 700-block of Yarmouth Street, for instance, was spared by an odd gerrymandering of
the district, while the neighboring 700-blocks
of Botetourt, Dunmore, and Duke Streets were
slated for removal. All the waterfront property along the southern edge of Smith Creek
was slated for demolition while the rotting
wharves, sagging warehouses, and crumbling
storage facilities on the Elizabeth River a
block away were spared.

Outside of the close to 40 acres that would
be used for hospital, public health, highway,
and tunnel facilities, there was little reason
for including the rest of the area at this
time. Plans for their use were as yet unspeci-
fied, but the N.R.H.A. felt that the remaining
95 acres would provide a basis for industrial
sites, semiluxury apartments, and improvements
along the Hague (Smith Creek) waterfront
(N.R.H.A. 1957, 12), yet none of these uses
was fully compatible with the realities of the
site: The proposed path of Brambleton Avenue
swung too close to the southern border of the
Hague to render all but a corner on each edge
of the remaining waterfront property suitable
for these purposes. If the area was ever to
have a real future as a high-rise or luxury
housing development, the sites along the Elizabeth River should have been cleared. Similarly, the 56 acres that were set aside for light
industry had little hope of attracting prospective customers when realistically compared
to the 468 acres of prime industrial land
being opened up in Broad Creek. In addition to
major rail and highway connections, Broad
Creek Industrial Park was close to both the
central business district and the population
center of the entire region; its sheer size
meant that a number of related manufacturing,
assemblage, and storage facilities could all

be located in close proximity. The Atlantic City Project offered instead a number of smaller, oddly-shaped parcels which carried the higher taxation rate and building restrictions inherent in a downtown location.

In sharp contrast to earlier endeavors of the People's administration, planning of the public expenditure portion of the project was more than just vague, it was counterproductive. Only the proposals for highway facilities and tunnel access ramps were fully conceived before demolition began. It was true that Norfolk's hospital and public health needs would grow in coming years, but the Atlantic City Project proposed to clear in 1957 land for expansion of the medical center complex that would not be occupied for at least twenty years in the future. At the other end of the project, the N.R.H.A. was condemning the land around the Norfolk (now Chrysler) Museum upon which the People's planners had once hoped to build the Cultural Center extension of the downtown business district. Because of the city's extensive involvement with the Downtown Redevelopment Project--more than 200 acres in the heart of the city's commercial district were swept bare and "only a dozen buildings were left standing, giving the downtown the appearance of having been ravaged by a massive air raid (Schmidt 1959, 6)"--the library, monument park, civic center, and other public expenditures were needed instead to help fill in the hole left by demolitions farther downtown. The land where the People's planners once hoped to attract a convention hotel, consulate's row, charity headquarters, outdoor cafés, and specialty shops was given over instead to long-term parking lots, open fields, and misplaced convenience stores. Hopes for a Cultural Center and other orderly expansions of the central business district were decimated by the sudden oversupply of vacant land that now ringed the downtown.

Clearly, there was no immediate need for all the vacant land that had suddenly been made available through the enormous scope of this new redevelopment activity. Although each of the four projects had a noble purpose at its heart--expansion of industrial, highway, tunnel, education, or medical facilities--none evidenced any of the signs of precision and clarity of purpose that so completely characterized the endeavors of the People's administration. When one considers the tremendous destructive force unleashed upon the city in these four new enterprises, the more than 800 acres scheduled for clearance, the 20,000 individuals uprooted, the demolition of whole communities, the heavy financial burden that would be carried even far into the future, and the tremendous urgency with which the whole affair was undertaken, it becomes obvious that some underlying ulterior motive knit these projects together into a unified plan, and that, whatever the objective, immediate demolition of properties that had somehow become offensive was a far higher priority than rebuilding. Duckworth had proven himself to be too skillful at administration during the "Building Phase" to so lose control during the "Bulldozer Era"; he had shown too great a mastery of power politics not to be brokering some sort of deal with these developments.

5

Redevelopment Rationales

The process of planning and redevelopment had come full circle in Norfolk: What had begun under the People's administration as a noble attempt to build the great city of the future had become corrupted by more pressing political and social concerns. Thus Norfolk, because it was the very first city in the nation to attempt redevelopment and among the earliest to initiate urban renewal on any large scale, also became one of the early leaders at manipulating its exemplary purposes to serve a more personal, partisan end. Redevelopment in Norfolk had fallen from its position as part of an overall program of community improvement, and had instead become but one weapon in the arsenal of a powerful political leader, one who was willing to employ this new tool to chastise his enemies, reward his supporters, and otherwise strengthen his grasp on municipal government. Mayor Duckworth was not so much trying to rebuild Norfolk as attempting to redesign it in a more personally acceptable form; in so doing he was guided as much by the vagaries of redevelopment law as he was by more salient considerations.

Although Norfolk's four redevelopment projects proposed massive new public and quasi-governmental facilities--new hospital, public

health, educational, highway, tunnel, and
municipal structures--all of these, and in
fact most of the other elements associated
with the renewal plans, could have been
achieved without subjecting the city to the
tremendous destruction necessitated by redevelopment. Norfolk already had the power under
its grant of *eminent domain* to acquire private
land for just such public uses, but the city
was attracted by the additional grant of
authority offered by redevelopment. Under
redevelopment, a city could legally acquire
private property, clear it, and then resell it
to new and different private owners. This was
supposed to correct the misuse of valuable
urban land, but, instead, it encouraged cities
like Norfolk to acquire more land than they
could ever use. Redeveloping areas, as opposed to just condemning the land necessary
for public facilities, actually rewarded
cities for expanding the scope of their public
works proposals: First, it allowed them to acquire huge tracts of valuable private property
that they could never have otherwise obtained;
second, the cities were paid by the federal
government in matching funds to clear the land
for reuse; finally, redevelopment cost no more
than the cities would have spent anyway on
smaller scale public works projects. Thus,
although it had plans to use less than a third
of the acreage in the Downtown and Atlantic
City Projects for public facilities, Norfolk,
because it could qualify the entire area as
redevelopment projects, was able to acquire
close to 200 acres of additional land on the
edge of the central business district, including some of the most potentially valuable
commercial and waterfront sites in the city.
In addition, in purchasing, clearing, and
redeveloping this land, the city did not have
to put up a penny more than it would have had
to spend anyway on the necessary public facilities (Darden; Martin; Crenshaw).

Thus redevelopment, because it gave Norfolk these vast tracts of highly valuable land, was a boon to both the business leaders who sought to reuse the properties and the power brokers who controlled their eventual disposition. The Atlantic City and Downtown Projects were an immediate hit with the remnants of Norfolk's Silkstocking establishment for a number of other reasons. Just as in N.R.H.A. Project One, redevelopment destroyed unwanted uses of land, and it was easy to see why the old People's planners would have dreamed of wiping out parts of the two project areas. The Downtown Project contained some of the city's worst slums that, because of their close proximity to the central business district, would forever impede further commercial expansion in the downtown area; in addition, the city's notorious East Main Street "sin strip" and red-light district, Norfolk's most repugnant reminder of the shady days of its wartime past, were likewise targeted for demolition. By contrast, the housing and small commercial establishments in the Atlantic City area were not nearly as deteriorated or as offensive as those downtown, but the Silkstocking crowd had never been happy with having this deteriorating working-class community so close to Ghent, one of Norfolk's most prestigious neighborhoods, and home to most of its Silkstocking establishment. The declining fortunes of Atlantic City were a great concern to homeowners in nearby Ghent, and the N.R.H.A., one of the last bastions of the People's rule, felt that the demolition slated for the area was the only way to save that neighborhood from similar deterioration (Darden). The Old Dominion Project also helped to create a convenient buffer zone between the working-class community of Lamberts Point and the wealthier (white) subdivisions nearby.

Some of the members of the old People's coalition had undoubtedly been in on planning

a portion of Norfolk's new endeavors: Since
1950 the City Planning Commission had been
proposing an additional access route to the
downtown area by extending Hampton Boulevard;
the Elizabeth River Tunnel Commission had been
lobbying almost as long for another underwater
link to Portsmouth in the area (Norfolk City
Planning Commission 1950); the city's Health
Department, so much a part of the People's
cleanup and code enforcement campaigns, had
been in desperate need of expanded facilities
for some time. For more than a decade a general consensus had prevailed among the business community that the fate of any New Norfolk would be invariably linked to proposals
to expand the Norfolk's two-year college and
its general hospital into vast urban educational and medical centers. Indeed, the list
of those who served on the governing bodies of
Norfolk General Hospital and the local division of William and Mary/Virginia Polytechnic
Institute during these planning years very
nearly matches any comparable listing of Norfolk's power elite during the People's administration. Not even the United Fund, the
major civic endeavor of the People's group,
could match the drawing power of these two
popular institutions: At least five of the
seven people who had served as commissioners
of the N.R.H.A. had served on the hospital's
board. Two city managers, two judges, one
state senator, one city councilman, the school
superintendent, three N.R.H.A. commissioners,
two Planning commissioners, two newspaper publishers, and a former governor had served in a
similar capacity for the fledgling precursor
to today's Old Dominion University.

Redevelopment, and especially these four
new endeavors, involved a number of other
factors that were immediately attractive to
large segments of the business community.
Especially when it was attempted on such a
grand scale, redevelopment was good for busi-

ness because it brought an infusion of new
jobs, revenues, developmental opportunities,
and numerous other spin-off and multiplier
effects to the local economy. Some businessmen
would obviously profit directly from the initiatives, either because they owned property
affected by the projects or because their own
enterprise would participate in some stage of
the work. Those firms directly involved in
demolition, construction, contracting, building supply, and related activities, including
many enterprises owned by the power elite of
the People's era, favored these new redevelopment proposals; so did the lawyers who would
handle the condemnation proceedings, the realtors who would appraise the properties, and a
host of bankers, building and loan executives,
real estate brokers, and others who stood to
gain by having so many new people suddenly on
the move. Others looked forward to unloading
failing properties that might otherwise have
been difficult to sell: slum housing faced
with major renovations under the beefed-up
health and housing codes, landlords in the
fading red-light district, expanding industries and commercial enterprises that needed
to unload outmoded and obsolete facilities,
and sagging retail establishments faced with
heavy competition from suburban shopping centers. Others saw the massive clearance operation as a way to preserve the value of their
investment by placing open-space barriers
between their own property and deteriorated
areas. Some would gain by new development
possibilities already under consideration--the
medical center complex, for instance, would
enhance the practice of every local physician,
attracting many of them to new office facilities within close proximity--while others felt
they would gain by participating in planning
the use of massive tracts of cleared acreage
that were still uncommitted.

The myriad economic benefits of redevelopment were readily apparent to all who had par-
ticipated in N.R.H.A. Project One, which had
provided an unparalleled economic boost to the
area, and its well-conceived Tidewater Drive
industrial minipark was filled almost before
it opened (*Norfolk Virginian-Pilot* 3/22/56).
No one doubted that Norfolk would continue
with new redevelopment proposals, and a number
of plans were eagerly bandied about in the
business community--some of that speculation
may have made new projects necessary by hastening the decline of neighborhoods under consideration. There were also, however, some
very solid reasons why no individual businessman or corporate entity would want to oppose
the projects under consideration, no matter
how far-fetched or ill-conceived they might
be. Mayor Duckworth had never been an easy man
to confront, and now, with the very special
powers inherent to redevelopment, any person
who openly sought to oppose the Mayor, his
programs, or his policies would be committing
an act tantamount to social and financial
suicide. With so much of the downtown and
neighboring Atlantic City residential and commercial properties scheduled for clearance--
326 acres with more than 500 commercial and
700 residential structures--four powerful new
economic weapons fell to those who controlled
the city.

Foremost among these was the power to determine the exact boundary lines of the projects, and, by inference, to decide which
structures would be exempt. Since few solid
commitments for either public or private development existed at the time of demolition,
the N.R.H.A. had tremendous leeway in determining which structures would fall and which
would be spared. Initial plans showed that
only 90 acres in the Atlantic City area would
be cleared (*Norfolk Virginian-Pilot* 12/8/56),
but it was quickly expanded (*Norfolk Ledger-*

Dispatch 2/17/57), and then enlarged again (N.R.H.A. 1974, 39) to include an another fifty acres of commercial properties. The final shape of the project zigged and zagged its way across a wide expanse, purposely avoiding a few commercial structures, such as the newly built Greyhound garage facilities on Colley and Brambleton Avenues, and just as randomly including others for demolition (*Norfolk Virginian-Pilot* 1/5/57).

Second, the city had considerable leeway in determining the acquisition value of land scheduled for demolition. In most cases a flat fee, without regard for the actual value or condition of the structure, was offered for all buildings in a certain class. Those with buildings equal to or below the value offered were obviously satisfied; those with more valuable properties faced the costly prospect of hiring an attorney and additional appraisers in order to undergo a prolonged legal battle. One local attorney, a member of an old-line family with solid connections in the Silkstocking establishment, was willing to fight condemnation and appraisals of business properties, but in case after case he found local appraisers unwilling to buck the city: They knew that if they attested to the true value of the properties in question they would never get appraisal work from the city again (Dillon 1970). Corollary to the ability to fix the value of the building was the power to actually drive down the worth of property under consideration, a not uncommon complaint from Broad Creek (*Norfolk Virginian-Pilot* 4/24/55) and Atlantic City residents (*Norfolk Virginian-Pilot* 7/1/57). Robert A. Caro tells in *The Power Broker* how New York City handled recalcitrant land owners who attempted to appeal low appraisals: Bulldozers moved in to demolish uncontested properties, leaving the holdouts stranded in a vast wasteland of rubble, debris, swirling dust storms, and unguarded

excavations. Electric, sewer, gas, and water
lines to the remaining homes were cut by city
workers. Hordes of scavengers and looters descended upon the area to pick the remaining
buildings clean, and each day the holdouts had
to fight their way through this tortured
course of rubble, muggers, and derelicts. One
resident still tried to hold out until an
adjoining building with a common wall was torn
down: He dropped the appeal and packed his
family before his own home collapsed (Caro
1975, 880-4).

Additionally, redevelopment gave the city
considerable leverage with the local banks and
lending institutions. The National Bank of
Commerce (later Virginia National Bank, Sovran
Bank, and now NationsBank) was the locus of
power for the Silkstocking crowd: Its officers
and board of directors included two former
People's Ticket councilmen, two N.R.H.A commissioners, three Planning commissioners, and
numerous other bluebloods of the Silkstocking
crowd that had once backed the People's revo-
lution (*Norfolk Virginian-Pilot* 8/9/57); a
year later Mayor Duckworth was added to the
board. Not surprisingly the bank kept a sizeable portion of both the city and N.R.H.A.
funds, which ran somewhere between four and
five million dollars at this time (Conrad;
Smith). In 1970, the first year that such
reports were made available to the public, the
N.R.H.A. kept more than a million dollars in
that bank, while most of the other banks had
less than a tenth that amount. One establishment lawyer willing to oppose the N.R.H.A.
soon found that his business clients were
refused bank loans because "they had the wrong
lawyer (Dillon 1970, 18)." For most other
attorneys, realtors, appraisers, contractors,
and building supply houses, the lure of fat
fees, healthy commissions, and the purchasing
power of the N.R.H.A. and the city was enough
to assure support.

Finally, the city had considerable leeway over the disposition of land once it had been cleared. Redevelopment land suitable for business use was considerably cheaper than competitive sites that would still have to be cleared; thus the power to establish a pecking order to decide which business or corporate entity would be rewarded with prime building sites was an important motivator in the effort to drum up support. Whether or not the city actually ever used its considerable powers over commercial properties, finances, and land disposition on any grand scale to force compliance and cooperation really makes very little difference; there were those, like the establishment lawyer mentioned earlier, who suffered for their token opposition to the Mayor's redevelopment programs, and their example was evident to all other members of the city's commercial and professional establishment. The fact that those powers, containing both awards for cooperation and punishments for opposition, lay in hands that were not above using them to excise whatever was deemed objectionable, was enough of an incentive for at least tacit support in these undertakings. Businessmen, especially those with influence that stretched beyond the realm which the Mayor could ordinarily reach, soon found that cooperation with Mayor Duckworth's redevelopment proposals could be a mutually profitable agreement; those who opposed the city or its agencies for whatever reason, faced the prospect of certain defeat anyway and probably considerable needless hardship. Those who might have spoken out to oppose plans so loosely formulated and so obviously capricious needed no other incentive to remain silent.

Thus, when the Mayor ran into heavy opposition from Atlantic City residents, he quickly scheduled a second public hearing, which was packed, as one reporter described it, with members of "the leading business and financial

interests representing organizations who [*sic*]
foster the overall needs of the city (N.R.H.A.
1974, 47)." With the backing of the Silkstocking establishment assured, the project was
pushed through over the anguished cries of its
residents. Similar support enabled the Mayor
to crush opposition to both the Downtown (*Norfolk Virginian-Pilot* 9/11/56) and Broad Creek
Projects (*Norfolk Virginian-Pilot* 6/11/54).
The earlier warnings of Norfolk's newspapers--
"the powers of a housing authority should be
zealously guarded and used only in proven
cases as a last resort (*Norfolk Virginian-
Pilot* 5/20/53)"--the traditional spokesmen of
the business community, were now hushed. Neither paper spoke to the vast uncertainties or
incongruities in the projects; instead, the
Ledger-Dispatch praised the vision of the proposals:

> This will be a dramatic second stage in
> a process that is giving much of Norfolk
> a splendid new look. But the really
> important factor--and the one which is
> encompassed in the very phrase *slum
> clearance*--is the ugly <u>old look</u> which the
> city is casting off (*Norfolk Ledger-
> Dispatch* 7/23/57).

Even in its saddest editorial lament, a poig-
nant piece that bemoaned the passing of a
portion of Atlantic City that had "a Greenwich
Village flavor" and a "Bohemian and cosmopolitan character," the *Virginian-Pilot* added:
"Change must come and better things for the
whole downtown area will be wrought through
the Atlantic City Redevelopment Project (*Norfolk Virginian-Pilot* 7/23/57).
No where did either paper question why so
many acres had to be leveled so quickly, especially when few solid commitments for construction were evident. Perhaps access to information was really limited to the official

press releases; maybe the editors were afraid
to undertake an exposé when so much of the
city lay in ruins and so much of the city's
future was tied to the success of the projects, or else, as one editor later revealed,
a reporter really was measured by what he knew
but couldn't write (Mason). The sad truth is
that a local newspaper would never want to
reveal the compelling motivation behind these
four new redevelopment endeavors, nor would
any scion of the business establishment seek
to oppose the urgency of the projects. More
was involved than a pressing need for new
public service facilities, more than a desire
to provide growing room for popular institutions, more than a longing to destroy deteriorated or unwanted properties, and more than
just a desire to build a new and exciting
city. The actual size and shape of the Downtown and Atlantic City Projects were in part
dictated by the requirements of the controlling federal legislation. Title I of the Housing Act of 1949 forbade the taking of land for
nonresidential uses, unless the area was: "(a)
a slum, deteriorated or deteriorating area,
and (b) is predominantly residential in character (H.H.F.A. 1950, 7)."

In order to acquire the vast areas of light
industries, warehouses, flophouses, commercial
properties, and honky tonks proposed, the project borders were made to zig and zag their
way through just enough slum housing to qualify the entire area as both "deteriorating" and
"predominantly residential in character." The
Broad Creek development, since it was not
technically a redevelopment project at all,
but rather a gift from the navy, was not bound
by the same restrictions. The housing included
in the Downtown Project undoubtedly composed
one of the worst slums in the city: More than
85 percent was badly deteriorated by census
estimates. But Atlantic City was no slum--in
spite of massive efforts by the N.R.H.A to

prove otherwise. The Atlantic City neighborhood may have been in danger of becoming a
slum, and it might thereby legally qualify for
clearance under the U.S. Housing Act, but
Norfolk still had a number of other *bona fide*
slums, like Oakwood, that should have merited
first consideration for clearance long before
Atlantic City; indeed, that was why the area
was the prime contender for a neighborhood
rehabilitation and restoration project, and
not demolition. Premature talk of redevelopment and overhasty speculation about clearance
had produced a dramatic change in the neigh-
borhood--not a shift in the housing or the
living conditions, but nevertheless enough of
a modification of the character of its residents to vault the neighborhood to the top of
the list of priorities for clearance under the
political conditions of the era. This same
change in the character of population, not so
much the need for space or the condition of
the buildings, was what doomed Broad Creek
Village and the Lamberts Point neighborhood in
the Old Dominion Project as well. In spite of
the fact that these three projects meant the
almost simultaneous uprooting of more than
4,000 families and the destruction of a large
percent of the city's lower- and middle-income
housing stock, the simple truth is that the
city's political leaders had no interest in
preserving these neighborhoods in their existing character, regardless of the condition of
the structures--in fact, they were in a hurry
to demolish the homes as quickly as possible.

A similar situation existed with Norfolk's
schools (see Figure 4). Although the city had
at least three schools still in service that
were built before the Civil War (i.e., J. C.
Smythe, Lott Carey, and John B. Goode), these
buildings would see almost two more decades of
service. Instead, Norfolk was proposing to
tear down Broad Creek (*Norfolk Ledger-Dispatch*
12/21/57) and Benmoreell (Brewbaker 5/7/56)

Figure 4
Norfolk's Dual School System, *circa* 1954

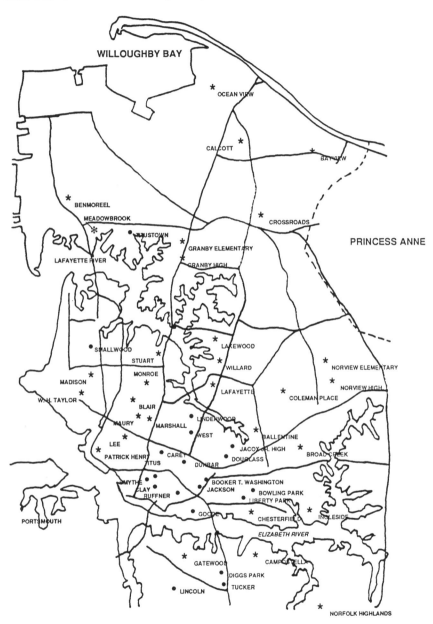

* White School
• Black School

Source: *Norfolk Ledger-Dispatch*, May 18, 1954, back page.

elementary schools, both barely more than a
dozen years old; close the even newer Pineridge Elementary (*Norfolk Virginian-Pilot*
2/10/56) for a few years; and convert Patrick
Henry Elementary for use as administrative
offices (*Norfolk Virginian-Pilot* 8/19/60).
Although Benmoreell and Broad Creek were wood
frame buildings that were erected as "temporary" structures during World War II, they
were still serviceable, especially if funds
were invested in upkeep. Pineridge, a con-
crete-block structure built in 1947 on a ten-
acre site at Sewells Point and Progress Roads,
was one of the newest elementary schools.
Moreover, both Broad Creek and Pineridge were
in the rapidly expanding Tanners Creek district just annexed from Norfolk County, where
the School Board had just been told it needed
to add four new schools a year for the next
ten years (*Norfolk Virginian-Pilot* 9/19/55).
Patrick Henry, built in 1892 and expanded in
1920 (*Norfolk Virginian-Pilot* 8/9/57), was
being converted to office use even though the
school administration had been saying for
years that it wanted to move out of the downtown area to a site closer to the center of
the city (Brewbaker 8/8/55). Why would it now
acquiesce to such a drastic plan of school
closings, demolition, and altered use?

The reason why may best be seen in the
Atlantic City neighborhood: The 1950 census
revealed that it was the only predominantly
white area in the city where black families
comprised more than ten percent of the population (U.S. Census 1952 III, 38; Norfolk
Chamber of Commerce 1954, 10-20); since that
time the newspapers reported "the changing
character of the neighborhood from white to
Negro." Premature talk of redevelopment had
helped to break down the already tenuous color
barrier, and landlords who were reluctant to
make major improvements to properties threatened by demolition found they could still

charge higher rent to black families because
of the housing crisis in the black community.
One contemporary news account described the
situation this way:

> The talk in Atlantic City is that prop-
> erty owners are realizing higher rentals
> from Negros than they had in the past
> from whites. "A lot of them are parti-
> tioning the interiors (into additional
> units) to get a lot more money," one
> resident says.

The fact that Atlantic City was a transition
neighborhood going through a change in its
racial makeup was underscored in a caption to
a newspaper photograph: "I've no idea where I
would go . . . but I won't live with Negroes
all around me (*Norfolk Virginian-Pilot*
3/10/57)."

Similarly, Lamberts Point, a predominantly
white neighborhood, showed, even in 1950, a
small concentration of blacks in the vicinity
of the college (Norfolk Chamber of Commerce
1954); by 1957, this small black community had
expanded, due in part to the squeeze put on
the housing market by redevelopment, the
city's population explosion, and the lack of
homes built especially for the black community. Broad Creek Village, on the other hand,
had begun its existence in 1943 as a navy
housing project for whites only, but when the
armed forces were integrated after World War
II, a number of black families began to appear. As uncertainty about the project's
future increased in the 1950s, so also did the
small percentage of black population, isolated
at first in one corner of the community (*Norfolk Virginian-Pilot* 1/3/58). A similar situation existed in the Benmoreell Navy Housing
Complex just outside the base: Although only a
few blacks lived there in 1950 (U.S. Census
1952 III, 38, tracts 9 and 11), their numbers

had grown as whites gained other housing opportunities in the increasing number of private, whites only, developments which ringed
the base. Blacks had cracked the previous
racial barriers in the Berkley area, and the
School Board noted with dismay "the pronounced
tendency for whites to leave Berkley, and for
Negroes to move in (*Norfolk Virginian-Pilot*
10/24/56)". The Downtown Project areas, which
had been predominantly black for several decades, still housed at least 19 white families
(*Norfolk Virginian-Pilot* 1/3/58).

Thus, one of the major reasons for Mayor
Duckworth's sudden and massive reliance upon
the powers inherent in redevelopment was to
accomplish the one thing that neither the
courts nor the legislature, nor any political
leader, local or national, could promise:
Mayor Duckworth was attempting to replace *de
jure* segregation (i.e., mandated by "Jim Crow"
laws) with *de facto* (i.e., the separation
resulting from one's choice of residence in a
predominantly black or white neighborhood)
segregation. The Duckworth Plan proposed to do
more than just control urban blight, it aimed
to wipe out all of the city's transition
neighborhoods where indistinct color lines had
failed to produce two distinct neighborhood
school communities, one black and the other
white (See Figure 5). The concept of geographic proximity and neighborhood schools is
essential to understanding the mastery of the
Mayor's approach. The U.S. Supreme Court had
been carefully led to its finding that separate schools were inherently unequal by metic-
ulous documentation of unequal treatment: The
Brown case involved the child of a black minister who was living in an otherwise all-white
neighborhood. Because Linda Brown was forced
by state law to go to an all-black school farther from her home than the all-white school
attended by her neighbors, the Court ruled
that this separate treatment of black students

Figure 5
Norfolk's Racial Patterns and Redevelopment Areas, *circa* **1958**

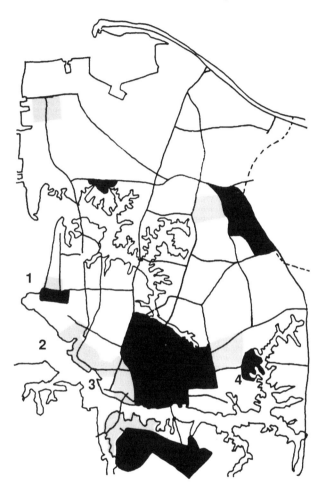

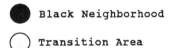

● Black Neighborhood

○ Transition Area

1. Old Dominion Project
2. Atlantic City Project
3. Downtown Redevelopment Project
4. Broad Creek Park Project

living in white neighborhoods was unequal, and
therefore unconstitutional. Other companion
cases involved school systems where there was
no comparable school for blacks or where lawyers could show by a preponderance of statis-
tical evidence--differences in teacher salaries, per-pupil expenditures, quality of textbooks, age of physical plant, lack of support
facilities, and the like--that proved that the
black schools were clearly inferior to those
operated for whites only. In such instances,
the Court ruled, where separate schools are
demonstrably unequal, then the laws requiring
such separation are unconstitutional (Leflar
1957; Stephan 1980, 11-7). Thus, a careful
reading of the legal situation at the time
revealed that segregation was safe from attack
as long as all of the city's black residents
could be served by a black school closer than
a white institution; if blacks lived closer to
a white school, then either the school would
have to be closed or torn down or the neighborhood demolished.

     Norfolk was no longer worried that its
black schools would be found inherently inferior to its white: The city had made great
strides at improving and upgrading its black
schools, even to the point where black teachers were better paid, better educated, and
more experienced than whites (*Norfolk Ledger-
Dispatch* 12/13/51). Indeed, writing in February 1957, District Court Judge Walter Hoffman
commented on Norfolk's success in achieving a
"separate but equal" dual system of education:

     The sum and substance of the School Su-
     perintendent's evidence is that the City
     of Norfolk has substantially complied
     with the "separate but equal" doctrine,
     which was applicable prior to the deci-
     sion in *Brown v. Board of Education*. The
     City of Norfolk is to be commended for
     its rapid strides in bringing about an

equalization in physical equipment, curriculum, teacher load, and teachers' salaries. If the "separate but equal" doctrine were now in existence, there would
be no grounds for relief to be afforded
these [black] plaintiffs (*Beckett v.
Norfolk* 1957, 338).

Mayor Duckworth was worried, however, that
a close scrutiny of the city's neighborhoods
would reveal several areas where color lines
were indistinct or where black students actually lived closer to the all-white school
than the black school they were attending.
His plan aimed at stamping out any potential
variance to the *de facto* segregated school
concept still tentatively approved by the U.S.
Supreme Court because it was based upon geographic proximity, rather than state law. Top
priority among those schools that would have
been forced to integrate on the basis of
neighborhood proximity was Patrick Henry
Elementary in Atlantic City. The *Virginian-
Pilot* underscored this concern:

The increase of Negro population in Atlantic City in recent years is reflected
in Patrick Henry School, which would feel
the highest proportionate integration of
the thirteen Norfolk white schools in
"fringe" districts. Recent figures indicated that there would be 50 Negro pupils
to 300 white pupils at Patrick Henry in
the event of desegregation (*Norfolk Virginian-Pilot* 3/10/57).

Thirteen of the plaintiffs in the school
integration suit filed by the N.A.A.C.P. lived
closer to Patrick Henry Elementary than to the
black institution they were attending when the
suit was filed in May of 1956 (*Norfolk Virginian-Pilot* 5/21/58). When the Atlantic City
Project was first announced, the case had just

finished its discovery phase, and Judge Hoffman was about to order the integration of Patrick Henry Elementary, which had previously served just the white students in the area. Judge Hoffman apparently realized that the N.R.H.A. was rushing to reduce the impact of his decision: "As to the Patrick Henry School, there is a redevelopment and housing plan now in its early stages which, if carried through to its completion, will substantially reduce the number of colored children who would ordinarily be assigned to [the] Patrick Henry School (*Beckett v. Norfolk* 1957, 339)." Not even Judge Hoffman realized the speed with which the N.R.H.A. would undertake demolition of the project area. Although the project was not announced until December (1956), its boundaries were not set until late May (1957); even so, by the start of the 1957-1958 school year, demolition had been extensive enough to close more than two-thirds of the Patrick Henry classrooms (*Norfolk Virginian-Pilot* 8/9/57). By the start of the crucial 1958-1959 school year, the school had closed entirely (*Norfolk Virginian-Pilot* 5/21/58).

Five other plaintiffs in the suit lived closer to the all-white Gatewood School in the Berkley section of the city than to one of the black schools there; by the time the 1958-1959 school year was about to begin, the Gatewood School, the other school that Judge Hoffman had indicated would experience extensive integration, had been shifted to the black system, thereby relieving that threat as well. The political powers that governed Norfolk at the time were well aware, as was the *Virginian-Pilot*, that such actions dissipated the force of the N.A.A.C.P.'s argument:

The significance of a plaintiff's proximity to a school has been pointed up repeatedly in other places where desegregation was ordered. . . . Two elementary

schools that formerly faced the prospect
of desegregation apparently don't any
longer. Gatewood School, now white, will
become a Negro school next fall. For five
plaintiffs, it was the closest school.
Patrick Henry School is nearest for thirteen plaintiffs, but this school will be
converted to administrative uses (*Norfolk
Virginian-Pilot* 3/10/57).

The other nine plaintiffs in the suit lived
closer to a black school than a white one
(*Norfolk Virginian-Pilot* 3/10/57), thereby
giving the School Board "legitimate" reasons
for denying their transfer applications. The
N.A.A.C.P. had filed the action in May 1956,
and only the city's headlong rush into redevelopment in Atlantic City had averted the
immediate threat; bulldozer diplomacy achieved
the desired result in less than two years'
time from conception to completion.
    The Mayor and his advisors knew that under
current state law, if even one of Norfolk's 46
elementary schools were forced to open with
mixed classes, then state funds, which then
accounted for one-fourth of the local school
budget, would be cut off to all 46 schools
(*Norfolk Virginian-Pilot* 5/21/58). Although
their precipitate actions in the case of
Patrick Henry and Gatewood Elementary Schools
had temporarily "saved" the elementary school
system, they were not disposed to take any
chances: For this reason Pineridge Elementary
in the Broad Creek section was closed (*Norfolk
Virginian-Pilot* 2/10/56), and Henry Clay Elementary in the Downtown area (*Norfolk Virginian-Pilot* 1/3/58) and the Broad Creek Village
School (*Norfolk Virginian-Pilot* 12/21/57) were
torn down as a result of the other redevelopment projects. The School Board, whose earlier
$15 million school building program had been
rejected because of past differences with the
City Council, was now sent scurrying back to

the drawing boards for a quick, and less costly, revision. An amended $5.5-million proposal
included an immediate go-ahead on the combined
elementary, junior, and senior high school for
blacks in the Oakwood-Rosemont area and a cut
back of 40 percent of the improvements earlier
proposed for existing black schools (*Norfolk
Virginian-Pilot* 3/28/58). The Oakwood-Rosemont
combination school was designed to alleviate
the triple threat of integration to Norview
Elementary, Junior, and Senior High schools in
the newly annexed area. The Mayor was anxious
to dis-pense with the preliminaries and break
ground as rapidly as possible. A *Virginian-
Pilot* reporter quoted his rationale: "This is
the school that the School Board promised the
court it would build by this fall. Let's go
ahead with it as rapidly as we can (*Norfolk
Virginian-Pilot* 1/14/59)."

The only other area that might possibly be
effected immediately by court-ordered integration lay in the Lamberts Point section of
the city. Although six of the plaintiffs in
the N.A.A.C.P.'s suit attended the Smallwood
Elementary School (black), all lived closer to
that school than to nearby Madison or Larchmont (white) elementary schools (*Norfolk Virginian-Pilot* 5/21/58). Nevertheless, the Old
Dominion Redevelopment Project (N.R.H.A. Project Two) would bulldoze 40 acres in the area,
wipe out the transition neighborhoods, and
reestablish readily identifiable color lines
in that community. Thus, of the more than 500
blacks who were determined to "threaten" the
sanctity of the white segregated school system
in the winter of 1956 (*Norfolk Virginian-Pilot*
2/13/57), fast action towards redevelopment
and school construction had alleviated the
legal standing based upon geographic proximity
of all but about 40 of the potential plaintiffs, and none of these as yet posed any
immediate threat in current litigation. The
Mayor's plan to make *de facto* segregation a

permanent substitute for *de jure* segregation appeared to be a masterful success: Only black students in the tiny Bollingbrook community (near Suburban Park Elementary School) in the Granby district and secondary students in the Titustown and Benmoreell areas remained as yet unaffected by changes already instituted. Of the fifteen schools potentially threatened by a court order to integrate upon the doctrine of geographic proximity, two (Patrick Henry and Broad Creek Village) were in the path of the redevelopment bulldozer, another (Benmoreell) was to be torn down for a park, two (Gatewood and John Marshall) had been transferred from the white to the black school system, one (Pineridge Elementary) had been closed, three others (Norview Elementary, Junior, and Senior High) had been spared by the Rosemont combination school then under construction, and four others (Taylor Elementary, Blair Junior High, Maury High School, and Madison Elementary) had been rescued from much of their potential threat by the aggressive redevelopment program (see Figures 6 and 7).

Mayor Duckworth's plan to achieve total *de facto* segregation was in full keeping with the political realities that then existed in Virginia. The School Board, the City Council, the city's legislative delegation, and other astute political leaders knew that if Norfolk took any steps to comply with the impending desegregation litigation, then such action would "provoke" the rest of the state into a "Stop Norfolk" movement that could have dire consequences for the city (*Norfolk Virginian-Pilot* 3/16/57). They knew that the city's best hope lay in delaying the eventuality of such a decision long enough so that a number of other areas would be forced into the "same boat" as Norfolk, and thereby form the impetus for a more realistic approach by the rest of the state. A crisis hitting several localities

Figure 6
From *De Jure* to *De Facto*: School Resegregation in Norfolk, 1956-1958

SCHOOL	BLACK STUDENTS	ACTION	DISPOSITION	DATE
Patrick Henry Elem.	50	Atlantic City Project	Closed	7/10/57
Robert Gatewood Elem.	50 - 60	Transferred to Blacks	Transferred	5/20/58
James Madison Elem.	25 - 30	Old Dominion Project	Rezoned	7/10/57
Norview Elementary	35	Construct Rosemont	Rezoned	3/27/58
James Monroe Elem.	1 - 3	Not Available	--	--
W. H. Taylor Elem.	1 - 3	Atlantic City Project	Rezoned	7/10/57
Pineridge Elem.	Navy Housing	Broad Creek Project	Closed	2/09/57
Broad Creek Elem.	Navy Housing	Broad Creek Project	Torn Down	12/20/57
Benmoreell Elem.	Navy Housing	Closed the School	Torn Down	5/7/56
John Marshall Elem.	extensive	Transferred to Blacks	Transferred	3/21/57
Norview Junior High	200 - 225	Build Rosemont/Coronado	Rezoned	3/27/58
Blair Junior High	some	Atlantic City Project	Rezoned	7/10/57
Granby High School	some	Not Available	--	--
Maury High School	some	Atlantic City Project	Rezoned	7/10/57
Norview High School	75	Build Rosemont/Coronado	Rezoned	3/27/58

(*Norfolk Virginian-Pilot* 2/13/57)

Figure 7
Impact of *De Facto* Segregation on School Locations

█ **Black Housing Area**

▦ **Mixed Race/Transition Housing**

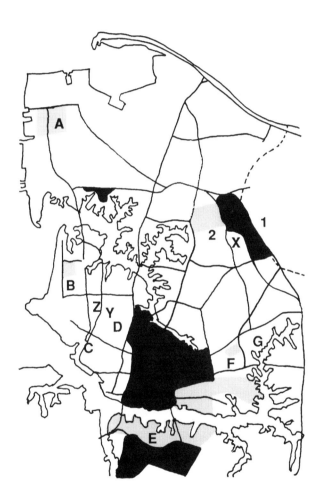

A Benmorell	E Gatewood	Y Maury High
B Madison	F Broadcreek	Z Blair Junior
C Patrick Henry	G Pineridge	1 Rosemont Elementary/Junior
D Marshall	X Norview Junior, Senior and Elementary	2 Coronado Elementary

simultaneously, most political leaders felt,
would increase the pressure on the governor to
convene a special session of the legislature
to enact some "reasonable" plan for gradual
desegregation. Thus the city's best hope in
the winter of 1956-1957 was to hold out long
enough for cases already pending against Newport News, Arlington, Charlottesville, Prince
Edward County, and, hopefully, other localities to achieve a simultaneous decision (*Norfolk Virginian-Pilot* 3/26/57). The Norfolk
case, which was decided by Judge Hoffman on
February 12, 1957 (*Norfolk Virginian-Pilot*
2/13/57)·, was by then winding its way through
the appeals process to the Supreme Court, but
local legal experts privately doubted that
legal maneuvering could stall desegregation
for the one more year it would take the cases
in other cities to catch up (*Norfolk Virginian-Pilot* 3/26/57). The emergency state laws
that established the state pupil placement
board had already been declared unconstitutional in the Norfolk case, and that decision
had been upheld by the U.S. Supreme Court
(*Norfolk Virginian-Pilot* 10/22/57). In the
winter of 1956-1957 there seemed little the
city could do to forestall desegregation of
its white public schools in the fall (1957)--
at least a full year before any other locality
would be faced with a similar crisis--except
sit back and accept the calumny of the rest of
the state.

Thus, the Duckworth Plan, although no such
proposal was ever publicized, was introduced
within this atmosphere of political panic;
there was no announcement of any concerted
program to achieve anything other than the
publicly espoused goals of the redevelopment
and school building projects, nor was there
any widespread understanding of just why the
city was taking these particular steps; nevertheless, a certain calm prevailed among the
citizenry that "something" either would be or

was being done to avert the crisis, regardless of the cost of such a diversion. The
immediate action--the time between the first
public hearing to the first demolition was
less than six months--on the Atlantic City
Project, and the transfer of the Gatewood
Elementary School to the black system solved
the crises at hand by frustrating the 14 litigants who would probably have been assigned to
white schools during the 1957-1958 school
term. With the state pupil-placement legislation declared unconstitutional, a local-board
policy of denying transfer, regardless of the
race of the applicant, to a school at a greater geographic proximity was just enough of a
legal loophole to delay speedy enactment of
Judge Hoffman's order. It was a brilliant
ploy, and one that won an additional one year
reprieve for the school system (*Norfolk Virginian-Pilot* 10/22/57). That extra year gave
the city time to plan for additional delays by
using the powers of redevelopment and the
policy of school construction to forestall
additional transfer requests based upon geographic proximity; until this was achieved,
the School Board was apparently instructed to
deny all requests for transfer from a black to
a white school, even if it was faced with
court order to do so (*Norfolk Virginian-Pilot*
8/19/58).

At its very least, the Mayor Duckworth's
program of concerted redevelopment and school
construction helped to buy time before the
city had to face the eventuality of school
desegregation; at its very best, the plan
lessened the impact of school desegregation
upon specific areas targeted by the N.A.A.C.P.
suit, and thus made it possible for the court
to diffuse that impact as thinly as possible
among all the schools in the city--a step that
was crucial in leading to eventual compliance
and acceptance of desegregation. In all likelihood, the city's white voters, given the

political climate and emotional conditions of
the day, would probably have concurred with
his program had they been given a chance. The
important thing from the point of view of history, however, is that the public was never
given an opportunity to approve or disapprove
the overall program; neither were the people
given a chance to understand either its ramifications or political consequences. Mayor
Duckworth's Plan had been carefully handmade
in a political vacuum of his own construction,
one that maximized his personal powers and
control of the decision-making process. Redevelopment projects, especially, had to fulfill federal requirements that the affected
individuals had been provided a full opportunity to be involved in the planning, design,
and implementation of the program. Norfolk,
however, was extremely remiss in this regard,
and its officials preferred to run the city as
much like a company as they could--as if they
were the board of directors, major decisions
could be made in secrecy, and no one else
mattered much (Carter). The people, however,
seemed to care very little one way or another
about the decisions that faced the city; so
long as they were spared the gory details of
complicated policy, they would approve by in-
ertia whatever actions, no matter how drastic,
were undertaken to preserve the *status quo*.

As for the business community, their consent was assured from the outset. Redevelopment was too good for business in general and
too important an economic boost for the Tidewater area as a whole to be opposed. The Mayor
was simply enacting their most far-fetched
dreams, although with a speed, scope, and
urgency they may not have understood. Surely
there were those among the business community
who fathomed the true motivation behind the
redevelopment proposals, but these same leaders knew how disastrous a school confrontation
would be for the city. The state had backed

the city against the wall on desegregation:
The federal courts would not allow it to
continue public education as before, and yet
the state would not let it retreat towards
token integration. Credit is due Mayor Duckworth because he at least found a way to break
out of that corner. Probably no one, not even
the Mayor, expected redevelopment to provide a
permanent solution to the problem, but it did
supply the city with a grant of additional
powers that might help him negotiate some sort
of settlement short of desegregation with the
black community. At the very least, the Duckworth Plan answered the court directives,
bought additional time for the city to work
out a more permanent solution, and gave the
Mayor flexibility to deal with both the crisis
at hand and the rebuilding of the city. No one
in the city's business or political leadership
really expected that black children would ever
attend white schools in Norfolk (Mason), and
so nobody suspected how much the city had
traded for what would turn out to be a temporary fix. Ironically, by advancing such a far-
reaching program under these less than honor-
able motivations, Mayor Duckworth had finally
achieved the promise of his 1950 Harmony
Ticket: The city's business establishment and
its political organization were at last joined
together in a consensus on municipal direc-
tions--more united than they had been at any
time since Duckworth had assumed control of
its destiny.

6

Prelude to Confrontation

Norfolk and especially its established business and political leaders began to harden into a stronghold of Massive Resistance for a number of reasons--in spite of the apparent success of the Mayor's redevelopment program in preventing school desegregation. For several years since the *Brown* decision, the local chapter of the statewide Massive Resistance support group--the Defenders of State Sovereignty and Individual Liberties--had labored to establish a respected political force that could be counted on to endorse the Byrd Organization when it advanced ardent segregationists, but also to oppose it when it backed more moderate local-option resisters. In spite of its penchant for lost causes, such as support for the Separatist Party candidate for President in 1956, the local Defenders had carved for themselves a minor following among the city's small businessmen, the major component of their statewide effort. In the past it had been pushed dangerously close to the fringe of accepted political behavior, but it had always fought its way back to the core of this small constituency.

The logic of the Defenders' argument was powerfully convincing for most of Norfolk's white citizens: They felt that the Supreme

Court had made an "unconstitutional" decision in the *Brown* case, and, because it substituted its own "judicial legislation" for the more legal process of constitutional amendment, the decision posed a grave threat to the powers of the states, the time-honored tradition of state control of public education, and the rule of the majority. Since most of the people in the country seemed to favor a continuation of segregated schools, they argued, the *Brown* decision really worked to undermine rule by the majority in favor of the interests of a few. The Defenders backed their claim of an "unconstitutional" court decision with a supporting document signed by three-fourths of the nation's state supreme court justices. Most of Norfolk's white voters apparently agreed with the Defenders' unconstitutional-court-order sentiment; it was the second part of their logic they resisted: The Defenders felt that closing public schools in defiance of court orders to integrate was the only way to show opposition against such dangerously political decisions (White 1959).

Partly to test the depth of Massive Resistance feeling in Norfolk, the Defenders fielded a three-man slate in the June (1957) Democratic Primary to challenge the local Byrd Organization and its more moderate legislative delegation. The race provided a classic confrontation between the progressivism of the incumbents and the more extreme approach of the Defenders. In spite of the considerable strength of the Organization and the backing of the business community, the Defenders' Ticket of Colonel J. Addison Hagan (U.S.M.C., Retired), jeweler Frank R. Ford, and attorney Harvey E. White, Jr. waged such a vigorous campaign that the outcome hinged on late returns from a few critical voting precincts; Colonel Hagan later claimed that Billy Prieur stole the election by stuffing the ballot boxes to insure victory (Hagan).

The attitude of Norfolk's voters was hard-
ening against moderation, and a position of
defiance that included the sacrifice of closed
schools was gaining in popularity. When the
issue emerged five months later in the gubernatorial race, it pitted Democrat J. Lindsay
Almond, widely seen as the legal brains behind
Massive Resistance, against the more moderate
Republican challenge of Ted Dalton. Although
four years earlier Dalton had come within just
a few percentage points of winning, Almond
swept to easy victory by calling for hardline
defiance all the way to the school house door.
In spite of his appeal, Dalton was swamped by
events beyond his control: When federal troops
were sent to Little Rock, Arkansas, to enforce
court-ordered desegregation, all hope of a
Dalton victory faded forever. Although no one
in Virginia really wanted to close schools,
Almond's promise of Massive Resistance provided a way to prevent integration without
having to face a similar threat of armed
troops in Virginia (Dabney 1971, 538-40).

The intervention of federal troops in
Little Rock had a profound effect upon local
residents as well. Whereas only a few months
earlier most citizens seemed prepared to accept a minimum of desegregation in order to
keep the schools open, now a majority appeared
to prefer closing the schools to accepting
even token integration. The sight of rifles,
bayonets, and uniforms had seemed to underscore the resisters' argument that the South
was at war with the federal courts, and that
any tactic which bypassed or postponed a similar confrontation in Norfolk was acceptable.
The shift became most evident when the local
legislators began to back away from their own
earlier position of moderation in favor of
Almond's hardline posture (*Norfolk Ledger-
Dispatch* 3/10/58). They were obviously aware
that not even ballot box finagling could have
saved them if Little Rock had occurred just

before their own primary race against the Defenders' slate. As a result of the strength of
the Defenders' challenge, the events in Little
Rock, Almonond's impressive showing in the
city, and an emerging sense of defiance on the
part of the citizenry, Norfolk's legislators
now found themselves supporting a Massive
Resistance stance that every one of them would
have found repugnant only a year earlier.
Events were moving rapidly to a showdown. No
wonder that, in this context of defiance, the
Mayor's plan of immediate and selective redevelopment was accepted by all those in a position to guess its true intent.

One other factor contributed to the shift
shown by the local legislators: the unrelenting legal pressure still being applied by the
N.A.A.C.P.'s attorneys (*Norfolk Ledger-Dispatch* 3/10/58). Any thought of congratulatory
action on the Mayor's part for avoiding a
Little Rock in Norfolk in 1957 quickly faded;
the N.A.A.C.P. refused to back down. Mayor
Duckworth's plan and his willingness to employ
the myriad powers of redevelopment against the
homes of black litigants had bought time, but
had not intimidated the N.A.A.C.P. into withdrawing its case. Instead, they forced a re-
thinking of the strategy, and the N.A.A.C.P.
went ahead with plans to enlist new plaintiffs
in order to continue the challenge. If the
N.A.A.C.P. had erred it was because it had
followed the *Brown* precedent too closely, and
sought elementary students who lived in similar mixed-race areas as plaintiffs. The Mayor
had won the first round because he was willing
to demolish both the threatened areas and
their neighborhood schools.

The N.A.A.C.P. was determined to win this
next round, and decided to aim its second
legal assault at Norfolk's white junior and
senior high schools. This tactic seemed appropriate for a number of reasons. First, the
assault seemed to block the Mayor's use of the

redevelopment weapon: each secondary institution served too many students and too wide a
geographic area to make it a target for either
closing or urban renewal. Second, the attack
on secondary schools meant that there were
potentially hundreds of litigants for whom the
argument of geographic proximity could be
made. Third, the new approach would involve
older students who could more easily be prepared physically and mentally for the personal
hardships, isolation, and even dangers inherent in integration. Finally, the N.A.A.C.P.
hoped that the white community might be more
sympathetic to breaking down the doors of
segregated secondary institutions rather than
an assault on the city's primary schools: Older students might be more open to new ideas,
their parents less protective, and the bastion
of the neighborhood school, so important to
both the black and white communities, would be
protected by expanding the concept to include
racial as well as geographic neighbors. There
was only one high school and two junior highs
in the black system, and to many, the most
insidious form of racial discrimination was
evident in the lines of black youths forced to
queue up at an early hour for long bus rides
across town to these institutions (Hoffman;
Mason).

The shift in strategy was a brilliant legal
maneuver, and one which the N.A.A.C.P. sensed
would ultimately prove successful. Duckworth,
however, was not disposed to give up so easily; he could foresee doom if the N.A.A.C.P.
won, and so, with the powers of redevelopment
useless against this new threat, he began to
seek other means to intimidate the black community into withdrawing its litigation. By
late spring of 1958, the pressure upon him had
become so intense that he became embroiled in
a prolonged name-calling battle with the black
community. The opening shots in the verbal
battle were fired by the Mayor when a group of

traditional black leaders approached the City
Council with a request to establish a biracial
advisory commission to address the deterioration in race relations that had taken place.
It was a simple request, and one with which
the old People's aministration would have com-
plied forthrightly. Dr. Lyman Brooks, the
president of Norfolk's black state college,
and a figure of gentility highly regarded by
both the black and white communities, rose to
present the request (*Norfolk Virginian-Pilot*
6/11/58). Before Dr. Brooks could get through
reading the first lines of the entreaty, however, the Mayor felt prompted to utter a prolonged racial slur which included the comment
that there were "too d--n many blacks behind
bars and not enough at the tax counters." The
Mayor's off-color remark at the usually staid
and highly predictable City Council session
caught the press and spectators off guard.
Most, including the news reporters present,
pretended not to hear the invective, and Dr.
Brooks, much to his credit, did not argue the
point, but the affront came in for some mild
criticism at the hands of the editorial writers as "an unwelcome and irrelevant note that
is not a politically sound one (*Norfolk Virginian-Pilot* 6/12/58)."

If Mayor Duckworth had hoped to provoke an
outburst from the black leadership, and so
turn public reaction against them, he was sad-
ly mistaken. Instead, his off-color invective
only served to strengthen their resolve to air
their grievances before a broader representation of the white citizenry. Newspaper reporters who sought a response from Dr. Brooks,
found only this staid assessment:

> There really are no relations between the
> races in Norfolk. . . . Richmond is con-
> sidered to be a more conservative city,
> yet Negroes are on all the important com-
> missions in Richmond. . . . Norfolk has

no police officer above the rank of pa-
trolman, and there are no Negroes on any
policy-making commission under city government (*Norfolk Virginian-Pilot* 6/12/
58).

Dr. Brooks, a powerful force in arranging con-
ciliation between the races, was attempting to
point the way towards several symbolic shifts
that would help to placate the black community
and resolve the current impasse. Indirectly,
by pointing the finger at city hiring and appointment practices, he was laying the blame
for nonexistent racial communications at the
feet of the Mayor and his political organization. P. B. Young, who had served on a number
of advisory boards and biracial special commissions during the People's reign, indicated
that:

> The deterioration in race relations--in
> business, government, welfare agencies,
> the Community Fund, school administra-
> tion--has been noticeable since the
> Supreme Court decisions began banning
> segregation in public schools and public
> parks.

He also listed several other reasons why the
city's blacks were agitated:

> The current housing shortage, difficul-
> ties in obtaining credit for [black]
> construction, and the activities of the
> Defenders of State Sovereignty and In-
> dividual Liberties (*Norfolk Virginian-
> Pilot* 6/12/58).

The uproar caused by the Mayor's prejudicial remark only served to unite the black
leadership more closely than ever before behind the goal of attaining desegregated public
schools. In the absence of other symbolic

goals befitting their rank and standing in the
community, the desegregation of Norfolk's all-
white schools in direct defiance of the wishes
of the Mayor and the Prieur Organization that
had fought so hard against them, took on new
meaning for the city's black leaders. A group
of prominent black ministers responded to
Duckworth's retort by opposing his desire to
have blacks "waive their civil rights" as a
condition to restoring racial harmony; other
black leaders joined them in repudiating the
Mayor's attempts at "biracial bargaining (*Norfolk Virginian-Pilot* 6/19/58)." The N.A.A.C.P.
declined comment in the white press, and, instead, redoubled its efforts to attain black
plaintiffs for its litigation. Before the
Mayor's remarks, 44 black students had requested a transfer (*Norfolk Virginian-Pilot*
6/13/58); after the imbroglio, more than 100
new plaintiffs joined the effort (*Norfolk
Virginian-Pilot* 8/19/58), in spite of the fact
that the School Board was releasing their
names for publication (*Norfolk Virginian-Pilot*
6/13/58)--an action that subjected them to the
dangers of verbal abuse, intimidation, and the
possibility of physical assault.

By the summer of 1958, the black and white
communities were thus locked in a head-to-head
struggle over school desegregation from which
there could be no retreat. The effects of racial intimidation, both official and unofficial, had failed to force the N.A.A.C.P. into
withdrawing its suit from the courts. As a
final attempt at intimidation, the School
Board delayed the reappointment of the black
teachers (*Norfolk Virginian-Pilot* 6/13/58),
but this action also failed to produce the
desired panic. The black community rallied
around the N.A.A.C.P. and its efforts to
desegregate the city's secondary schools; the
harshness of the Mayor's attitude and the
viciousness of these tactics precluded any
hope of an out-of-court appeasement with

symbolic gestures--something that might have
worked earlier. Far from discouraging new
litigants, however, these actions produced
151 plaintiffs, only one of which lived closer
to the white secondary school to which he had
applied than the black school he currently
attended (*Norfolk Virginian-Pilot* 8/30/58).

Now that the integration of at least some
of Norfolk's secondary schools seemed assured,
public opinion began to coalesce around three
separate philosophical responses. The Defenders firmly believed that closing the public
schools in defiance of a court order to integrate was necessary to show united opposition
to the Supreme Court's political decisions. If
the South held solid in its efforts to resist
the Court's encroachment upon state's rights
and individual liberties, then, they argued,
the federal government would be forced to back
down. There were not enough troops, the Defenders argued, to force integration in every
Southern community; they did not want trouble
here in Virginia, and that was why the state's
political leaders had endorsed their idea to
close the threatened public schools rather
than invite the type of conflict that had
occurred in Little Rock. As one of the first
communities in the South to be faced with of
court-ordered integration, Norfolk stood at
the brink of a historic moment. If Massive
Resistance worked here, the Defenders argued,
every other Southern city would be heartened.
In light of the prominence of the city's position, the closing of the school house doors
was a "small sacrifice" to pay for the free-
doms of the majority.

> Maybe the schools will be closed for a
> time, maybe for a whole year. But it's a
> mighty small sacrifice to pay to prevent
> integration and discourage the federal
> courts from further encroachments on
> state's rights. We can teach them [the

white students] just as well in private
schools; maybe better, because we'll have
a little more control over what they're
going to learn. . . . When we close the
schools in September, I say to mothers,
don't start squawking (*Norfolk Virginian-
Pilot* 7/25/58).

In order to provide a "temporary" substitute
for the public schools that might be forced to
close in September, the Defenders had formed
the Tidewater Education Foundation (T.E.F.) to
operate segregated alternative schools for
students locked out of public classrooms. To
help defray the cost, the state was willing to
provide substantial "tuition grants" to pupils
who chose private or parochial schools over
integration (Muse 1961). Thus, the T.E.F. offered parents a way to have segregated schools
with public support, without sacrificing the
schooling of their children. In addition, the
T.E.F. would be able to make its pitch free
from the political connotation of the Defender's name. If the "small sacrifice" the public
was expected to bear grew into more than a
year's duration, as most Defenders believed it
would, the T.E.F. was ready to buy the closed
buildings for a nominal fee and reopen them as
segregated private schools.
    The great majority of Norfolk citizens, ho-
wever, did not yet seem ready to accept the
separate system of private schools proposed by
the Defenders and the T.E.F. The epitome of
the city's moderate opinion even as late as
the summer of 1958 was expressed by School
Board Chairman Paul Schweitzer, who, when he
contemplated the possibility of closing all of
Norfolk's white public schools, proclaimed: "I
just can't imagine 36,000 children out on the
streets. . . . Let's don't lose our faith yet
(*Norfolk Virginian-Pilot* 6/13/58)." There were
two scenarios of how a school lockout could be
prevented: The first was the rather Pollyanna

belief that "it couldn't happen here"--that either some event or, as before, some means would be found to further delay or defer the imminence of the legal challenge. Nothing as dramatic as the plan of selective redevelopment was envisioned in this scenario, but the full appeals process had not yet been exhausted, the court order was not yet absolute, and some legal gimmickry was still possible. Others believed, as did Joseph Leslie, editor of the *Norfolk Ledger-Dispatch*, that the public schools would have to be closed, but only for a brief period of time (Mason). These individuals held that the decision to close public schools in defiance of court orders to desegregate was a powerful political weapon that, once wielded with resolve, would force both the courts and the black community to withdraw and accept some other symbolic victory short of desegregation. This was the essence of the Massive Resistance theory: Once the white community stood solidly against integration, even going so far as to accept private school alternatives, the crisis could not continue, and Congress, the courts, the President or the state authorities would seek a settlement. Local Byrd Organization chieftain Billy Prieur, the bulk of the state's political leaders, and the majority of Norfolk's business community apparently held this belief (Mason).

There were others who felt that a school crisis was both more imminent and more long lasting than most suspected, and could not be as easily resolved as the Organization promised. Foremost among them was Lenoir Chambers and his editorial staff at the *Virginian-Pilot*. Once schools were closed, they argued, Norfolk faced a more difficult confrontation than it might otherwise have experienced: The black community would not back down, the courts would not relent, and the city would be forced to submit to an even greater federal

authority over its public schools once they
reopened. The greatest effect of closing the
schools, they argued, would be the calumny
Norfolk would face as the scapegoat for 300
years of Southern culture:

> If our schools are closed, not only our
> children suffer, but the entire city will
> be severely damaged economically. Nor-
> folk's black eye on the national scene as
> a result of closed schools would be one
> of the most disastrous effects. Norfolk
> is in the market for industry . . . but
> industry would not likely come to a city
> with a closed school reputation. . . .
> The closing of any schools, and the dis-
> organization of the school program might
> have a disastrous effect on the Community
> Chest . . . naval facilities . . . ef-
> forts to attract industry . . . and every
> aspect of the economic well-being of our
> city (*Norfolk Virginian-Pilot* 6/20/58).

The only hope that the anti-resistance forces
could offer was that the public schools could
survive a minimum of integration: Accepting a
few black students would neither dilute nor
destroy the education program of the white
majority. Only in this way, they argued, could
the city take its school system out from under
the authority of the federal courts and continue economic growth undeterred. The most
important action the people could take, the
anti-resisters argued, would be an outpouring
of public support for the school system regardless of its racial purity (*Norfolk Virginian-Pilot* 8/19/58). The School Board had
labored for almost four years to achieve this
end, but as yet had been unable to build much
of a constituency for keeping the schools open
in the face of desegregation. In spite of the
fact that they owed their advancement to a
political organization advocating Massive Re-

sistance, the Board members were each deeply committed to continuing quality public education, part of the rationale for their appointment. Board members were quickly becoming aware that at least some of the N.A.A.C.P.'s 151 litigants would slip through whatever screening criteria they could legally impose, thereby closing all the (white) schools at that level (*Norfolk Virginian-Pilot* 5/14/56). Chairman Paul Schweitzer summed up the situation the Board faced that summer: "It is obvious that this irresistible force of [a] court order is about to collide with this immovable object, the state (*Norfolk Virginian-Pilot* 6/13/58)."

If differences between the School Board and the more conservative City Council existed, they were not made public, and, in general, the school program progressed with the solid backing of the Council. In July, Chairman Paul Schweitzer was cordially reappointed without any indication of differences with the Mayor or the Prieur Organization (*Norfolk Virginian-Pilot* 1/25/59); the City Council apparently felt that the Board's willingness to close threatened schools, transfer facilities, redraw district lines, and carefully target its construction plans were all supportive of Massive Resistance, even if their intent was "to minimize the effect of integration by using a plan for gradual desegregation (*Norfolk Virginian-Pilot* 3/8/57)." Even the Board's earlier posture of moderate compliance seemed to have been forgiven as the work of the Silkstocking holdovers then on the Board; since that time a majority of the Board had been replaced with Duckworth appointees. Subsequent statements by the School Board had been issued jointly with the Council and the city's legislative delegation, both of whom had at one time similarly vowed to keep Norfolk's schools open at all cost (*Norfolk Virginian-Pilot* 1/25/59). Up until then, the

Board had cooperated in every way with the
Council and its efforts to delay, avert, and
even sabotage the eventuality of school desegregation. Its actions that summer (1958)
were no different: The Board waited until
mid-August to render its decision on the
N.A.A.C.P.'s transfer applicants, and even
then, it resisted the pressure from the court
to make a determination. Finally, the Board
rejected all 151, using both rational logic
and subterfuge to do so: Sixty-two applicants
were denied because they had failed to submit
to follow-up interviews or the testing program
required to support their transfer request;
another 60 were found unsuited for transfer
because of low test scores, poor grades, or a
record of "too frequent transfers;" 34 applicants who applied to schools in the Norview
area were denied because of the district's
past history of racial disturbance. Four other
applicants were denied admission to Maury
High, Granby High, or Blair Junior High
Schools because: "The isolation which would be
caused by such an assignment would be detri-
mental to educational progress and may well
cause emotional instability and even detriment
to health (*Norfolk Virginian-Pilot* 8/19/58)."
Only one of the potential transfers was rejected because it came from a black living
closer to a black school than a white one
(*Norfolk Virginian-Pilot* 8/30/58).

The Board's denial did not, however, last
very long; in less than two weeks Judge Walter
Hoffman rejected the rationale of "potential
racial tension" and "probable isolation," and
the folders of the 38 applicants in these two
categories were returned to the School Board
for appropriate assignment. A slight modification in the district lines for the projected
Rosemont School, the black combination elementary and junior high school (earlier it was
referred to it as a combination elementary,
junior and senior high) that was part of the

Mayor's *de facto* segregation plan, brought
most of the 38 applicants within the school's
boundaries. Although School Superintendent
Brewbaker admitted that the district lines for
Rosemont were hastily redrawn only "after he
had learned the addresses of the applicants
involved [in the litigation]," Judge Hoffman
allowed the Board to deny the transfer requests of these petitioners. The School Board
was also able to manipulate district lines to
accommodate all the remaining litigants challenging the city's elementary schools, but
when every possible readjustment had been
made, 17 black secondary students still re-
tained an unquestionable right to legally
transfer to the white school which was closer
to their homes than the black school they
presently attended.

Ironically, the most important decision
ever made by the Norfolk School Board took
place not in a public meeting, but rather in a
private home. Because board member Francis
Crenshaw had just undergone an emergency ap-
pendectomy, the rest of the Board gathered
around the bedside of his West Ghent home to
discuss their options. Meeting without legal
counsel, except for Crenshaw, who specialized
in maritime and redevelopment law, the Board
faced the grim prospect that they might have
to go to federal prison if they defied Judge
Hoffman's orders. Slowly they came to the
conclusion that, in the long run, integration
would be easier to accept if the assignment of
black pupils to white schools came from fellow
Virginians and not an officer of the federal
court (Crenshaw). Finally, acting "against the
Board's better judgement, but pursuant to the
law as interpreted by the court (*Norfolk Virginian-Pilot* 8/30/58)," the School Board,
under threat of legal duress, was forced to
accept these final 17 applicants just days
before the 1958-1959 school year was scheduled
to begin.

By dragging the decision out over as long a
period as possible, the Board was hoping to
delay even further the implementation of the
assignments. It immediately filed a motion
asking for a postponement on the grounds that
it was "wholly unprepared at this time for immediate compliance," and that the Board needed
additional time to arrange for the security of
the transferees and otherwise "prepare" school
officials, patrons, teachers and students for
"the sudden shift" in the traditional pattern
of Southern education (Crenshaw). Their plea
was based on the hope that the violence and
uproar that followed similar court action in
Little Rock would be reason enough to dissuade
the local court from imposing its will upon a
community still not ready to accept integration. Even though Judge Hoffman would not
accept the argument at this late date, the
Board postponed the opening for two more weeks
while the Supreme Court pondered their appeal
for further delay (*Norfolk Virginian-Pilot*
9/3/58).

When seen against this backdrop of legal
stall, foot-dragging, and delay, the statewide
vilification of the School Board is hard to
comprehend. Only after every conceivable legal
maneuver had been exhausted and its members
seriously threatened with criminal contempt
citations, had the Norfolk School Board voted
to assign black students to a white Virginia
school. Even so, the state's political leaders
rushed to heap abuse on the Board for making
the assignment "voluntarily"; their objection
was that the Board, itself--a group of Virginia citizens empowered by state and local
laws--had accepted the transfers, rather than
leaving the task to the court, which they
viewed as an illegal usurper of the state's
authority. This was a crucial distinction in
Virginia's interposition argument: Governor
Almond, the Byrd Organization's calmest and
most reasoned spokesman, stated that the

courts had the "power" to make such assignments, but lacked the "constitutional authority" to do so. Local school boards, he continued, were restrained by the state's Massive
Resistance statutes from making such assignments (*Norfolk Virginian-Pilot* 9/5/58). In
Almond's scenario, the Organization had every
right to curse the Board because, when given
the chance to obey one governmental authority
and defy the other, Norfolk school authorities
had chosen to follow the dictates of the federal court, and ignored the sovereignty of the
state. More than that, the Board's action
threatened to undo the tenuous interposition
logic of Massive Resistance.

It seems improbable that the Board had made
this very deliberate decision without some
degree of calculation on the part of its best-
informed members. There was one major difference between the Norfolk School Board and the
posture of the Byrd Organization, both the
statewide leadership and its local affiliate:
The appointed members of the Board were willing to operate the city's schools even if
integrated, and the elected politicians were
adamantly opposed to such a course. To the
Board, the assignment of 17 black students to
six previously all-white junior and senior
high schools was the type of "minimum of integration" that both the City Council and the
city's legislative delegation had once said
they could abide. The political climate had
changed drastically since the Council had
assented to such moderation, and the Council
was now committed to closing the schools in
defiance of the court's authority; the Board,
however, felt that this course would be highly
destructive, both to public education and to
the Southern culture in general. For this
reason, the Board purposely acted to undermine
the state's intention to interpose its authority in a show of Massive Resistance. The Norfolk School Board was composed entirely of

individuals who personally preferred segregation; they had made every effort to resist
assigning blacks to previously all-white public schools until forced to do so by the
courts, but once having done so, they were
determined to abide by that ruling in order to
preserve the public educational system they
held more important than segregation. This was
the basis for the underlying disagreement that
existed from this point onward between the
individual members on the School Board and the
City Council.

The Norfolk School Board represented an
unlikely pairing of individuals destined for
such heroics, and considering the climate of
casual malaise that then characterized the
majority of the population, their action in
defense of public education could well be
termed "heroic." It was not a blueblood Silkstocking group, although most of its members
bordered on the periphery of the city's business and financial establishment. There were
no First Citizens, bank presidents, major
industrialists or corporate entrepreneurs on
the Board; only one had achieved any renown
for charity work, and only one was even active
in the Chamber of Commerce. Just like the
other independent boards and commissions, the
appointees of the People's era had long ago
been replaced by respectable, but politically
unknown, small business leaders and professional people who owed their advance entirely
to Duckworth and the Prieur Organization. An
examination of its membership revealed a group
of prosperous individuals striving for re-
spectability in a city which, in spite of its
size, still carried much of the atmosphere of
a small town: Chairman Paul Schweitzer ran an
industrial pump manufacturing firm; Benjamin
Willis managed the plush carpet and salon
furniture establishment started by his father;
W. Farley Powers was an executive with one of
Tidewater's few large industrial concerns;

Francis N. Crenshaw practiced maritime and redevelopment law; William P. Ballard managed the family seafood business; and Mildred J. Dallas, although retired, had started her own private kindergarten in the prestigious Loch Haven neighborhood (*Norfolk Ledger-Dispatch* 2/16/60; *Norfolk Ledger-Dispatch* 5/29/61; *Norfolk Ledger-Star* 12/22/72; *Ricmond Times-Dispatch* 2/3/63). They were just the sort of small business and professional leaders who had the most to lose by provoking an open confrontation with the dominant political forces of the state and city government: They depended too heavily upon government contracts, professional fees, inspections, and favorable regulation to lightly defy such authority. On the integration question in particular, they had the most to lose if they or their businesses became the target for boycott or vigilante activity. In short, they were not the sort of individuals who ordinarily defy such authority, especially when it is backed by strong, effective leaders and a highly passionate cheering section.

The School Board's singular act of courage set in motion a variety of forces which now vied for public acceptance; at the same time, because it held out the hope of yet one more reprieve from the courts, its action made it difficult for any other coherent plan of action to win that endorsement. For the Mayor, the two week delay in the scheduled opening of the schools provided one more opportunity to pressure Norfolk's black leadership into withdrawing the final 17 litigants. Both publicly and privately, the City Council used every resource at its disposal to force some sort of compromise from the black community (*Norfolk Ledger-Dispatch* 5/19/60), but racial antipathies had progressed too far in the last few months for the city's black leadership to accept any sort of token remuneration now that victory appeared so close at hand. Although

this time many Norfolk newspapers, fearing
reprisals against the individuals involved,
declined to print the names and addresses of
the 17 approved transferees. The *Journal and
Guide* suffered no such qualms: All 17 were
featured in a photo-essay that praised their
courage and pioneering spirit, even though it
recognized that, under Virginia's school-
closing laws, they "may not gain their goal
immediately (*Norfolk Journal and Guide*
8/30/58)."

In the weeks leading up to the School
Board's defiant action, the organizers of a
fledgling pro-school lobby, the Norfolk
Committee for Public Schools, had begun to
move into a more public posture. Earlier that
summer a small group had approached the Mayor
about the need for such a support group. Duckworth was not opposed to the idea; he even
thought it might be helpful if the schools
actually closed (Stern). Quietly the group had
begun the task of contacting the city's respected and conservative citizens--the cream
of the city's business and civic elite--asking
them to join, or even form themselves, a pressure group that would work to keep the schools
open in the face of court-ordered integration.
The Committee organizers were convinced that
the Governor would have a hard time closing
the schools in any community where he felt
strong opposition from the conservative business establishment, and this thought gave new
impetus to their push for membership. Although
most of those approached were sympathetic to
the cause, they were nevertheless unwilling to
come forward publicly at this time. Typical
was the reaction of one well-known civic
leader: "I'm with you one-hundred percent;
however, you know my position. If I place myself in the forefront of your movement, it
might harm my organization. Come back when you
get your first hundred business leaders, and
I'll be glad to join (White 1959b, 3)."

Other community stalwarts found similar reasons for refusing to join the Committee: Businessmen were worried about possible economic reprisals; executives did not want to face loss of position or prestige; municipal and state employees feared pressure from the Byrd Organization; doctors, lawyers, realtors, and other professionals worried about losing clients; ministers did not want to face divided congregations; civic workers wanted to avoid pressure from their governing boards; naval officers were concerned about the effect upon their careers; federal workers were specifically instructed by Washington authorities that this was a "local affair," and that they should not play a public role (Reif 1959, 9); and everybody was concerned about the subtle social pressures and ostracism that might be applied against anyone who deviated from the silent norm and took a vocal stand one way or the other. Many of the community leaders approached by the Committee urged the group to wait longer before making any public move; they might help once the schools were actually closed and the hardships were real, but the time was not yet right, they felt, for going public with such an organization (*Norfolk Virginian-Pilot* 9/19/58).

The Committee, however, was in a hurry to publicly launch a legitimate pressure group before the schools were actually closed. They saw that, in spite of the atmosphere of acquiescent hesitancy that blocked their movement, the Defender-backed Tidewater Education Foundation could boast a membership that had passed the 2,500 mark, including several attorneys and prominent small business leaders. The organizers of the Norfolk Committee for Public Schools surveyed this roster and decided that the public had to be offered a calm and rational choice that stood in opposition to closed schools and Defender-sponsored private education. Most of those business and

civic leaders who had earlier indicated support for such a group were invited to attend
an organizational meeting at the residence of
Professor Robert L. Stern, a native New Yorker
who embodied the predicament faced by the
organizers of a group that was too Northern,
too liberal, and too Jewish to compel much
community support. The meeting was a dismal
failure to all those who had worked to establish the group: The few citizens who had any
claim to the city's social and financial elite
stood on the front porch of the residence,
showing their private sympathy for the cause,
but also indicating their reluctance to join
the proceedings inside. There were no bank
directors, attorneys, corporate executives,
leading merchants, elected officials, naval
officers, government officials, or major religious leaders present; only a handful of
Parent Teacher Association (P.T.A.) activists,
interested professionals, and small businessmen were in attendance. Even so, the Committee
felt that the issue was so great and the demands so pressing that they must push ahead
and expose themselves to the risks involved in
taking a stance of public advocacy (Stern;
White 1959b, 4). Since the Norfolk Committee
for Public Schools lacked any ties to the
city's business and financial leaders, the
Committee announced instead its intent to form
a parent's lobby in support of public education, and to finance legal efforts to block
the closing of the schools. The organizers
chose as their leader Reverend James Brewer,
pastor of the Norfolk Unitarian Church, hoping
that having a minister at the head would lend
credence to their appeal, even if the Unitarian Church was held in less esteem than the
Baptist, Methodist, Episcopalian, Presbyteri-
an, and Lutheran congregations that dominated
the city. Other officers included Irving F.
(Buddy) Truitt, the head of a small real estate and insurance firm, P.T.A. activist Mary

Kidd, civic leader Mary Thrasher, pediatrician
Dr. Forrest P. White, real estate broker Ellis
James, Professor Robert L. Stern, high school
government teacher Margaret White, and "another member who requested that his name not be
disclosed (*Norfolk Virginian-Pilot* 9/19/58)."
It was not a prestigious assemblage--reporter
Luther Carter once referred to the organization as "mostly a grouping of little people
(*Norfolk Virginian-Pilot* 10/25/59)," an assessment that was true even by the Committee's
own standards. The unnamed board member, gyne-
cologist Mason C. Andrews, the only person
with any real standing in the Silkstocking
community that had backed the People's revo-
lution, felt that he could best serve the
Committee in attracting people of equal prominence if his name was not released to the
press. The group was so desperate for such a
link that it grudgingly accepted this unusual
arrangement, even though others on the board
were not told that Dr. Andrews had removed his
name before publication (Stern; White 1959b,
4-5).

The Norfolk Committee for Public Schools,
just like the School Board and the editors of
the *Virginian-Pilot*, had overestimated the
public's capacity to either comprehend the
gravity of the situation or to resist the
scapegoat fate to which Norfolk had been
condemned by the state's political leaders.
Events proceeded at such a rapid pace that
these desperate pleas for support were rendered moot. The final legal hurdles were quickly
overcome, the last-ditch appeals for one more
delay denied, and on September 22, 1958, in
accordance with Virginia's Massive Resistance
laws, the doors of the city's six previously
all-white junior and senior high schools remained locked, while those of its segregated
elementary schools opened for the fall semester. There were no closings in the city's
parallel black school system, where all twelve

grades opened as usual. Thus, nearly 10,000
students were locked out of their classrooms,
and neither the Governor nor the President
could offer much hope for an early resumption
of classes (*Norfolk Virginian-Pilot* 9/26/58).

Even with the school doors actually pad-
locked, however, few citizens were willing to
discuss the implications or project the consequences of such drastic measures; even fewer
seemed willing to gather to talk about what
should be done. The majority of the city's
leaders apparently still dismissed the idea of
a prolonged school closing as "scare talk,"
and promptly banished these thoughts from
polite conversation. Most appeared to cling to
the belief that the Byrd Organization had out-
smarted the federal authorities by daring to
close the schools, and that soon either the
courts or the black community--they did not
really care which--would back down (Mason).
The realities of the confrontation that had
taken place the year before in Little Rock, or
the relative success of school integration in
cities such as Charlotte, St. Louis, Nash-
ville, and Washington, remained far from their
thoughts. "The best of the Southern leadership" and "the majority of Southerners" that
the *Virginian-Pilot* had earlier predicted
would rise up to abide by the authority of the
courts (*Norfolk Virginian-Pilot* 5/18/54) were
nowhere in evidence. The cream of the city's
civic and business elite, at one time so vocal
in determining the course of the Norfolk's
direction, remained completely silent, abandoning the stage to the Mayor, the Organization, and others who shouted encouragement
from the periphery. Instead, prejudice--the
unreasonable adherence to the conventions,
traditions, and mores of the past--reigned
supreme, replacing civic pride and boosterism
as the underlying force behind every phase of
municipal policy.

7

In Pursuit of a Mandate

Norfolk's was not the only educational system effected by Virginia's school closing laws: Schools in Prince Edward County, Charlottesville, and, to a lesser extent, Arlington and Front Royal were closed as well. But Norfolk was by far the largest scale test of the state's Massive Resistance plan to replace integrated public institutions with a system of private, segregated academies, financed in part by public funds (for details about Massive Resistance elsewhere in Virginia see Muse 1961; Smith 1965; Eley 1976). There was never any question that Prince Edward County, the birthplace of the Defenders of State Sovereignty and Individual Liberties, would prove how well Massive Resistance could work on a small scale. There the Defenders were a well organized and respectable segment of the community; when Blacks moved to desegregate the only public high school in the county, Prince Edward Academy opened its doors to most of the county's white secondary students. Even when the public school was finally reopened after years of litigation (the Prince Edward suit had been a part of the *Brown v. Board of Education* decision), most of the county's white students continued on at the Academy.

Of all Virginia's small cities, Charlottesville was perhaps the poorest choice from a
political perspective for the Organization
showdown over school integration: Because of
the strong influence of the University of Virginia, education was too highly prized and its
citizens too independent for Massive Resistance to succeed there. Under ordinary circumstances, Norfolk, with all its liberalizing
influences, would have been an equally poor
choice for a Massive Resistance showdown.
Richmond, with its close ties to the Southside
and its capital-of-the-Confederacy heritage,
would have provided a more malleable citizenry. The leadership dynamics in Norfolk, however, gave Massive Resistance a far greater
opportunity for success than most would have
thought possible: In spite of its size, the
city had a generally small and in-bred leadership that was usually united in its aversion
to outside authority--a fact that had made
Norfolk unpopular with both the Organization
and the State Legislature. W. Fred Duckworth,
one of the few outsiders to be truly accepted
by all levels of Norfolk's society, had come
to occupy a unique place of leadership in the
city. In the years since he had come to power,
Duckworth had employed his consummate political, financial, and managerial powers with
such success that he had become not just the
leader, but the true focal point of the community. In short, Norfolk was far from typical
for cities its size: Few other municipalities
were so completely dominated by a single per-
sonality or had dissent so thoroughly silenced
by his restraints.

Public education in Virginia was under attack in the Norfolk crisis at its weakest link
--the secondary school. Historically, since
little more than basic skills was all that was
necessary for comfortable survival in the a-
grarian economy of the Old Dominion, Virginia
was among the last states in the nation to

support universal public education, and certainly among the most reluctant to fund any
more than a program of minimum competency.
Alongside its impoverished system of public
education, however, was a highly structured
system of private preparatory schools and
semipublic universities, such as the College
of William and Mary and the University of Virginia, to which the average graduate of the
state's public schools could hardly aspire.
These public institutions helped to reinforce
a sort of social caste system that allowed the
state's leading citizens to follow this parallel education tract, in part underwritten by
scarce public funds, and often at the expense
of the more universal, public school system.
The growth of secondary schools in the state
can be traced back to the appearance of an
urban middle class just before the turn of the
century, but even as late as 1958, several
rural counties still lacked their own public
high school and others did not go beyond the
eleventh-grade--major reasons why Virginia
consistently ranked near the bottom of any
measurement of education quality in the
country. Even in urban areas, secondary education was not universal, and was still the
property of the middle class. Mandatory school
attendance laws did not apply beyond the age
of 14, and because wartime and Depression era
drop-out levels had run unusually high, even a
significant percentage of the middle class had
been forced to forego secondary schooling. The
median education level for adults in Norfolk,
with one of the finest school systems in ths
South, was still less than tenth-grade, and
more than one-fifth of the teenage population
over fourteen had already dropped out of
school (U.S. Census 1952 II 46 B, 46-7).

It is against this backdrop of closed leadership, oneman politics, and spotty support
for public education in general and secondary
schools in particular that the concept of

Massive Resistance faced its most important test in Norfolk. In one sense the Defenders' plea had a great deal of validity: If Massive Resistance could be made to work here, it might be successful all across the South. Norfolk was not just their first large scale test--the time, the circumstances, and the leadership dynamics of the city offered the Byrd Organization a reasonable chance to score a major victory for their cause. Since public schools were still open for elementary students, only a small percentage of the city's white pupils would actually be locked out of public classrooms. Of these, perhaps as many as one-fifth would drop out of high school anyway. Another group could successfully make the shift to one of the city's private preparatory schools, all of which were then undergoing an unprecedented building boom, prompted in part by the school desegregation crisis (*Norfolk Virginian-Pilot* 12/5/58). The navy was concerned enough about the permanency of the crisis that it, too, was drawing up plans to expand to a series of off-base institutions for military dependents (*Norfolk Ledger-Dispatch* 1/22/59). Another group of secondary students, perhaps as many as 500, could be expected to transfer to segregated public schools in nearby communities (*Norfolk Virginian-Pilot* 10/19/58) or leave the area to live with friends or relatives in other parts of the country.

Thus, although almost ten thousand students would actually be locked out of public classrooms, the maximum load to be carried by the Tidewater Educational Foundation and its substitute system of private schooling would actually be less than 5,000 pupils. The T.E.F. hoped that the enhanced status of private schooling and the chance to strike a blow at outside intervention would provide a strong incentive to prospective patrons. For the first time many of the city's middle-class

residents would be able to afford the luxury
of private schooling for their children now
that the state provided tuition grants to students in communities with integrated public
schools--one of the hallmarks of Massive Resistance. The group's major effort, however,
focused upon a day school operated at Bayview
Baptist Church, and the T.E.F. began to make
ambitious plans to use other buildings if the
need for more facilities arose. In addition,
the T.E.F. arranged to rent the public schools
in nearby South Norfolk for less than three
dollars a month per student. It found a powerful ally in William J. Story, Jr., Superintendent of schools in South Norfolk and a
member of the State Board of Education, who
agreed to start his city's schools one hour
earlier so that the buildings could be cleared
by 2 p.m. for the T.E.F. (*Norfolk Virginian-
Pilot* 9/12/58). In spite of its optimism, the
T.E.F. faced enormous logistical problems in
its effort to provide private replacements for
even half of the city's closed secondary
schools. Norfolk employed a whole staff of
administrators, supervisors, principals, and
teachers to struggle with the sort of text-
book, personnel, curriculum, transportation,
guidance, accounting, and maintenance problems
that awaited the handful of staff members and
volunteers at the T.E.F. Lenoir Chamber and
the editorial staff of the *Virginian-Pilot*
hammered away at this shortcoming:

> Substitute private schools are by their
> very nature "inferior education.". .
> [They would] be hurriedly makeshift, even
> if adequate teachers, adequate facili-
> ties, or accreditation could be found.
> Providing public education is the duty of
> the American government (*Norfolk Vir-
> ginian-Pilot* 9/25/58).

Mayor Duckworth, however, was not willing to risk the entire fate of Massive Resistance on the T.E.F.'s plans alone, and a few days after the schools were closed, he proposed to Governor Almond an elaborate scheme to close only those grades actually under court orders to integrate; students in the grades unaffected by desegregation could then be reassigned to other public schools in the city. Because Norfolk was then operating on a split-year system, with graduations in both January and May, Duckworth felt that the city could open the second semester (the "H" sections) of the eighth, ninth, tenth, and eleventh grades. Since blacks had not been assigned to the twelfth grade, schools could have opened for seniors and the "H" sections--roughly 40 percent of the white students locked out of classes. Governor Almond and the state superintendent of schools quickly lined up the schools in South Norfolk, Norfolk County, Portsmouth, and Princess Anne County to accommodate the remaining students in the "L" sections of each grade (Duckworth 10/6/58). Although it is unclear whether their opposition was based upon operational considerations, conscientious objections, or, as one newspaper report indicated, legal grounds (*Christian Science Monitor* 10/8/ 58), the Norfolk School Board apparently refused to participate, and the plan died without implementation. Regardless of its reason, the Board's rejection helped to increase the level of conflict with the Mayor and City Council.

Even if the public had been willing to overlook the administrative shortcomings of the T.E.F., its ambitious plan to replace the closed, integrated public schools with a private system of segregated academies was crushed by forces that had been up to now only incidental to the struggle. Many of the churches that could have provided a power base and alternative source of educational facilities in-

stead refused to support the T.E.F.'s schools.
The Catholic Church was among the first to
speak out at the national level in urging
compliance with the *Brown* decision; locally,
Norfolk Catholic High and its feeder parochial
elementary schools had been successfully integrated since 1955. Although the historically
strong Jewish belief in the importance of
education was a sustaining force behind the
Committee for Public Schools and other efforts
to oppose Massive Resistance (Reif 1960, 1,
9), the Jewish community was so intimidated by
the possibility of reprisals that it never
took a united action to support public education. The big break in the battle against Massive Resistance came when the Protestant de-
nominations began openly to align their forces
against the T.E.F. Even before the schools
were closed, the Norfolk Presbytery voted
nearly unanimously to support the dictates of
the federal courts, and cautioned member
churches against allowing their facilities to
be used as alternative private schools (*Norfolk Virginian-Pilot* 8/7/58). Lutherans and
Episcopalians soon followed with similar
instructions for their congregations. Methodist and Baptist churches had a more difficult
time following this lead: Bayview Baptist and
a number of other Southern Baptist facilities
already figured strongly in the T.E.F.'s plan
of resistance. The Norfolk Ministerial Association, however, a Protestant organization
largely in the control of Methodist and Baptist clergymen, took a united stand when they
requested that Duckworth and the City Council
reopen the schools on a local-option integrated basis (*Norfolk Ledger-Dispatch* 10/1/58).

The ministers soon found themselves aligned
with an even more vocal professional group in
their effort to reopen the public schools. Although several teachers were active in the
formation of the Committee for Public Schools,
as a group Norfolk educators resisted efforts

to take a stand early in the crisis; once the schools closed, the Norfolk Education Association voted overwhelmingly to petition the City Council to reopen the closed schools under local authority (i.e., without state funding) on an integrated basis (*Norfolk Ledger-Dispatch* 10/3/58). Individual teachers then joined with the more active of the city's ministers to establish tutoring groups for almost 3,500 students in a number of private homes, storefronts, and in 23 churches across the city (*Norfolk Ledger-Dispatch* 10/13/58), not as substitutes for public schools, but rather to prepare pupils to resume classes once the schools reopened. School authorities and Education Association officials soon became concerned that these "parlor schools" were degenerating into replacements for public schools, and were thus accomplishing the same end as the T.E.F. Also, they feared that support for public school teachers, who were still receiving full pay at state expense (*Norfolk Virginian-Pilot* 10/2/58), would wane if educators were discovered making money as a result of the school crisis. The N.E.A. thus adopted a resolution that recommended a salary of only $50 a month, about what teachers were spending out of their own pocket for books and supplies (*Norfolk Virginian-Pilot* 11/6/58). In addition, the N.E.A., in an effort to put pressure on the city's elected officials, voted to withdraw from the stopgap schools at the end of the semester, even if the public schools were not yet open; it feared that its members' efforts to continue teaching might make parents complacent and less prone to push for quick reopening of schools (*Norfolk Virginian-Pilot* 10/26/58).

Individually the teachers struck an even more direct blow at the forces of Massive Resistance. Efforts by the Tidewater Education Foundation to informally recruit public school teachers for its private facilities were continually rebuffed by the School Board, the school administration, and the teachers themselves. Out of desperation, T.E.F. President James G. Martin, IV, went to the Mayor for assistance. Duckworth intervened, and assured the T.E.F. an audience with the teachers (*Norfolk Virginian-Pilot* 1/25/59). Even though they could still draw full state pay while teaching private school classes (*Norfolk Virginian-Pilot* 10/12/58), the out-of-work educators listened quietly while Martin made his pitch. Then, one by one, they got up and left the auditorium; not a single one of the city's professional educators was willing to support an effort that might undermine public schools (Reif 1960, 6). The teachers' unanimous rejection of the T.E.F. was a bitter defeat for the Defenders, the Mayor (*Norfolk Virginian-Pilot* 1/25/59), and all the state politicians who favored Massive Resistance.

In spite of this setback, the T.E.F. hoped to go forward with its plans anyhow, resolving to start small but pick up teacher support as the crisis continued. A handful of retired school teachers, fundamentalist ministers, and housewives were recruited to serve as their temporary educational staff, and late in October (1958) the T.E.F. finally opened Tidewater Academy with only six instructors and fewer than 60 students; plans for expansion of its facilities at Bayview Baptist Church were contingent only upon its ability to find additional qualified teachers (*Norfolk Virginian-Pilot* 10/26/58). Thus, Norfolk's teachers, by unanimously rejecting the financial rewards that would accompany a defection to the T.E.F., had almost single-handedly destroyed any chance that the Defenders, Mayor Duckworth, or the Byrd Organization had to make Massive Resistance work in the city (Mason).

Even though they had unanimously rejected the T.E.F.'s offer, Norfolk's teachers, by setting up their own private tutoring groups,

were accomplishing what the Defenders had
sought to establish: a segregated alternative
to integrated public schools. The tutoring
groups that had sprung up in private homes,
church buildings, and empty store fronts were
actually contributing in a large part to the
apathy of the parents and the students themselves. The public tended to overlook the
crowded quarters and the lack of textbooks,
library, laboratory, and support facilities,
and saw instead the makings of an even finer
education for their children: classrooms with
only a small number of motivated students,
dedicated teachers, and a high degree of individual attention. Although these were educational commodities that could be found only
among the most expensive and exclusive private
preparatory schools, they were now almost uni-
versally available for less than $50 a month.
Parents began to see how much their children
were learning in spite of the make-shift
quality of the tutoring groups, and a danger
existed that they would eventually shift their
support to private schools after all. Leaders
of parent and student groups who wished to
rally support for public education found that
they could not be heard as long as the tutoring groups remained in operation; their
best efforts to create a pro-school sentiment
produced only hollow resolutions that lacked
the backing of their full membership--the
individuals with the greatest stake in continuing universal public education.
    In Norfolk, no one had as yet been forced
to pay the price for closing public schools.
The *Virginian-Pilot* continued to hammer away
editorially at the long-term economic disaster
that awaited the city--naval ship reassign-
ments and loss of industry, ship-repair contracts, business prospects, and the like--but
these were intangible expenses that had not
yet hit home for the average citizen. The
Pilot went on to estimate that the cost of

operating a public school system in the city
without state funding and control would mean
at least a one-third rise in real estate taxes
and a concomitant drop in federal impact aid
funds (*Norfolk Virginian-Pilot* 10/16/58),
which were still channeled through the state.
While tutoring groups continued, however, with
their primary form of subsidy coming from the
state's obligation to honor the teaching contracts of the instructors in the closed
schools, the more direct costs of rising taxes
and increased local support seemed distant and
unreal. As long as no one had to pay directly
for Massive Resistance, the great majority of
citizens remained silent and aloof from the
struggle, preferring instead to allow others
to incur the risks of active participation.

In this atmosphere of public malaise, the
Norfolk Committee for Public Schools saw
little hope for success if it operated as just
another local pressure group; after more than
a month of frantic activity, it could only
boast 6,000 members (*Norfolk Ledger-Dispatch*
10/22/58), large enough to rival the Defenders, but still too small to dodge the "inte-
grationist" label that destroyed its political
effectiveness. Instead, the Committee vowed to
seek other means to reopen the schools, and
turned its attention toward convincing state
and national leaders. A delegation from the
Committee talked with Governor Almond, and
urged him to return the closed schools to
local control. The Governor's response that
only the courts could reopen the closed
schools (*Norfolk Virginian-Pilot* 10/23/58),
strengthened the Committee's resolve to add
class action litigation to its rapidly diminishing arsenal. On October 27 (1958), a class
action suit was filed in federal court on behalf of the Committee for Public Schools; the
suit named Governor Almond, the School Board,
and others as defendants, and was filed on
behalf of 33 white parents and their children.

Although 89 individuals were listed as plaintiffs (*Norfolk Virginian-Pilot* 1/16/59), real-
tor Ellis James took the biggest risk by lending his name to the proceedings. The state was
already testing the legality of the school
closing in *Harrison v. Day*, a "friendly" suit
filed in the Virginia Supreme Court (*Norfolk
Virginian-Pilot* 10/24/58), but *James v. Almond*, the Committee suit, went far beyond this
rather limited action. *James v. Almond* claimed
that the closing of Norfolk's six previously
all-white secondary schools had deprived their
students of equal protection of the laws guaranteed under the Fourteenth Amendment (Campbell and Boswell 1959).

The sudden shift of the Norfolk Committee
for Public Schools into the field of litigation caught the N.A.A.C.P. off guard; it was,
however, quick to realize the historic significance of the action: *James v. Almond* was
the first lawsuit of its kind filed by white
litigants in the South. When its own suit was
filed a few days later, the N.A.A.C.P. took a
secondary position, and entered it only as
companion litigation to the Committee's action
(Reif 1960, 6). The N.A.A.C.P. was unwilling,
however, to back away in its quest to enlist
new transfer applicants for the next (1959-
1960) school year, thereby signaling both its
intention to keep up the long-term legal pressure to desegregate schools and its refusal to
negotiate the issue. Even so, Duckworth and
the City Council redoubled their own efforts
to force the black community to withdraw the
17 pending transfer applicants. At one Council
session Duckworth turned to a group seeking to
reopen the schools and stated, "If you gentle-
men want to help, you could talk to the families of the seventeen Negro children and get
them to withdraw. . . . Then we could open
these schools tomorrow (*Norfolk Ledger-Dispatch* 10/1/58)." Councilman Abbott repeated
the Organization's position, "We've got seven-

teen Negro children who are keeping 10,000
white children out of school." Mayor Duckworth
followed by laying most of the blame on the
N.A.A.C.P., saying that they

> Did not truly represent Norfolk's colored
> population. The city has demonstrated
> what Norfolk's colored people mean to it
> by spending millions on slum clearance
> and schools, yet Negroes here pay less
> than five per cent of the taxes and make
> up seventy-five per cent of the jail pop-
> ulation (*Norfolk Ledger-Dispatch* 10/1/
> 58).

His unfortunate repetition of these inflammatory sentiments--an earlier remark had rallied
the black community behind its more extreme
leadership in the N.A.A.C.P.--reveals a lot
about both his famed intemperance and the
helplessness he felt in the crisis. It also
demonstrates a fatal flaw in the Mayor's
thinking that tended to reduce complex issues
to simplistic terms, especially casting the
people behind those issues in roles as either
supporters or detractors. For Duckworth there
was no middle ground--no way to be both independent on principal, but supportive on the
issues--and this made it difficult for the
School Board and others to take a stand before
the Mayor had publicly committed himself.
Duckworth, although an excellent leader, was a
poor coalition builder, and the fact that he
had achieved a broad base of support in the
white community was more a result of force-
fulness than any diplomatic bent.
      For their own part, the black community
refused to be goaded by his remarks; the
city's black leadership did not want to challenge the Mayor in a name-calling contest that
might make them a target for the frustrations
of whites faced with school closings. The
Mayor probably would have been delighted to

have had such sharply defined antagonists, but
except for the N.A.A.C.P.'s new litigation,
the city's black leadership seemed perfectly
content to pull back from the struggle in the
white community and let the Committee for Public Schools take the lead. One of their most
promising behind-the-scenes efforts was an
attempt to prepare the 17 black transfer students for the hardships they would face in integrated classrooms. Black leaders started a
separate tutoring group for these "pioneers,"
and coached them in both the academic subjects
and the fine points of dress, poise, and eti-
quette, as well as to provide them with the
psychological preparation and self-defense
skills they would need to make integration
work. Mrs. W. T. Mason, chairwoman of the
project, told the students, "When you sought
entrance to white schools, you left your
childhood behind (Reif 1960, 25)."

Mayor Duckworth was too pragmatic to think
that those 17 black students would somehow
taint the education of the ten thousand whites
locked out of their classes, but he was also
too astute to attempt to oppose the Organization on its best issue in decades. The Mayor
was faced, however, with the first real conflict within his Harmony coalition since its
formation eight years earlier. The majority of
the city's business community was not yet
ready to abandon public education, and the
School Board and the editorial writers of the
Virginian-Pilot in all likelihood represented
the still-private concerns of the Silkstocking
crowd, more than even Duckworth would have
cared to admit. Although he had shown a great
deal of racial intolerance in his remarks and
policies, Duckworth was above all else a sharp
politician, and the Organization had always
found that race-baiting was good politics. He
had not so far overtly committed himself to
promoting Massive Resistance, only to giving
the Defenders a fair hearing before Norfolk's

teachers; to do otherwise, in light of the
Defender's powerful electoral appeal, would
have been bad politics.

The public was probably unaware of the ramifications of Duckworth's involvement up to
this point, but they were knowledgeable enough
to know that the Mayor was the key to any resolution of the current crisis: Both the School
Board and the Massive Resisters needed his
support to prevail. Duckworth was not the type
of leader who could sit by while such a momen-
tous crisis ran its course; with the prospect
of Massive Resistance failing, he needed a
quick and dramatic political maneuver that
would shore up his constituency and give new
impetus to the drive to retain segregated
schools. The School Board's request that the
Council join it in petitioning the Governor to
return the schools to local control--the one
loop-hole in the state's Massive Resistance
plan whereby a closed public school could reopen, albeit on an integrated basis--brought
this behind-the-scenes conflict into the open.
Local control meant opening the schools, but
it also meant integration; rejecting the
Board's request would prolong the school
closing and promote Massive Resistance. The
political risks of joining the Board in its
petition were enormous: It meant bowing to the
N.A.A.C.P., the federal courts, and the Committee for Public Schools--all enemies in the
Mayor's eyes. Moreover, it meant forfeiting
forever the support of both the Defenders and
the Old Guard of the Byrd/Prieur Organization,
Duckwoth's natural supporters. If the appeal
was successful and schools were reopened without state funding, the Mayor would be personally responsible for an increase in local
taxes; and finally, such an act would place
the Mayor far beyond any course of action that
the public had as yet indicated it would approve. Denying the Board's request, however,
would risk provoking the ire of the School

Board, school patrons, editors of the *Virginian-Pilot*, and probably the Silkstocking
element of the business community, still a
powerful, yet strangely silent, force in the
community. Seen in this context, the Mayor's
attempt to avoid the question by calling upon
the Governor to reopen the closed schools on a
segregated basis--something he could not legally do--comes as no surprise. The controversy would not go away; the School Board and
the editors of the *Virginian-Pilot* continued
to press for petitioning the Governor, firm in
their resolve to use every opportunity to witness for public education. The issue, however,
was not as clear-cut as the Board made it
appear: Once the Council asked the Governor to
return the schools to local control, nothing
guaranteed that the Governor would then honor
their request. State law was just vague enough
on the point that the Governor was under no
obligation to make any response at all. If
this were so, then the School Board was urging
a course that might potentially isolate the
Mayor from his supporters, divide the community, and then make him appear ineffective for
attempting such a futile gesture. The simplest
solution to the dilemma would be for the Governor to indicate ahead of time how he would
respond to a request for local control, but
when a Norfolk delegation sought a preliminary
indication of his stance, the Governor "just
grinned (*Norfolk Virginian-Pilot* 10/23/58)":
Almond was too good a politician to commit
himself and risk alienating his own supporters.

Duckworth, however, had discovered another
solution, and one that would not only legitimately stall the issue for another month, it
would also take him permanently off the hook:
He would let the people decide the question in
an informational referendum. The Mayor, in announcing the Council's intent to delay action
until after the referendum, explained his

rationale: "Governor Almond was elected by an overwhelming majority to do exactly what he has done. I think the only way to impress the Governor is to let the same voters show him what they want done now (*Norfolk Virginian-Pilot* 10/19/58)." His emphasis on "the same voters" was part of the brilliance of this tactical ploy: Since this was an offyear for elections, the referendum would come at a time when less than a fourth of the city's voters had paid their poll taxes; nor was there any time either to register new voters or to allow delinquent accounts to be brought up to date. The question was thus to be put to the same conservative and established electorate that had given a two-to-one mandate to Governor Almond and Massive Resistance the year before. Second, since the referendum "was purely informational in nature," the vote would not decide anything; the City Council would be free at any time to disregard the outcome if it felt so inclined (*Norfolk Virginian-Pilot* 10/19/58).

The Organization was the clear beneficiary of the Mayor's decision: Their constituency would be the ones who would decide the issue; less than a sixth of the voters would be black (*Norfolk Virginian-Pilot* 10/19/58); navy personnel and others new to the area would be disenfranchised by the poll tax and preregistration requirements, and the shortened time frame would not allow the pro-school forces an opportunity to mount much of a campaign of opposition. Further, it put the School Board, the Committee for Public Schools, the editors of the *Virginian-Pilot*, and school patrons in the unenviable position of having to oppose both the Mayor and the concept of popular democracy. In an editorial titled "In Principle, Wrong; In Practice, Confusing," the *Pilot* castigated the Mayor for his lack of leadership, courage, and statesmanship. The editorial warned that: "It runs directly

counter to the views and formal recommendations of the Norfolk School Board, [and]
thereby digs a deep and ominous chasm between
these two bodies (Reif 1960, 17)."

The vote and the closed electorate were
only part of the overall plan: Duckworth
wanted to make sure that the voters--his con-
stituency--would have to face the same tough
decision that the School Board demanded. Just
to underscore this point, the actual question
was weighted with code words and catch phrases
that would make a clear-cut decision difficult: "Shall the Council of the City of Norfolk, pursuant to State Law, petition the
Governor to return to the City control of
schools, now closed, to be opened by the City
on an Integrated Basis as required by the
Federal Court?" Voters were to check "For" or
"Against Petitioning the Governor." Another
section, labeled "For Information Only, Not To
Be Voted On," made the decision even harder:

> In the event the closed schools are re-
> turned to the City of Norfolk, and are
> reopened Integrated by the City, it will
> be necessary, because of the loss of
> State Funds, for every family having a
> child or children in Public Schools. . .
> to pay the City a substantial Tuition
> (*Norfolk Virginian-Pilot* 11/6/58)."

The pro-school advocates who had hoped to
rally voter support in favor of opening the
schools now found that task impossible: There
was not enough time to mount an effective campaign; the electorate was too closely allied
with the Byrd/Prieur Organization; and the
question was both too confusing and too emo-
tionally charged for voters to make a meaningful choice. The loaded ballot meant that
the pro-school forces would first have to
undertake a highly organized and well financed
effort to reeducate the populace before they

could tackle the issue in the referendum. The
teachers, the ministers, the Committee for
Public Schools, the School Board, and even the
editorial staff of the *Virginian-Pilot* were
incapable of such a monumental undertaking.
The Committee for Public Schools saw how
hopeless its task had become, and turned its
efforts instead to legal actions to block the
referendum. Two suits were filed--one challenged the legality of an informational action
where no binding decision would be rendered;
the other hoped to strike the "For Information
Only" portion off the ballot on the grounds
that charging tuition fees for public schools
was contrary to state law--but both efforts
were quickly struck down by the local and
state supreme court justices (*Norfolk Virginian-Pilot* 11/15/58).

The School Board, realizing that it had
been outflanked by the maneuver, attempted to
pull back from a clash over the referendum,
and instead chose only to complain about the
additional delay; later its members apparently
considered campaigning in favor of petitioning
the Governor. Mayor Duckworth got word of the
Board's intent, and publicly lectured them on
the virtues of neutrality on the issue: "The
Council is maintaining a 'hands off' policy on
the referendum. We don't have any idea of
politicking one way or the other. I would like
to suggest that the School Board do the same
(*Norfolk Ledger-Dispatch* 10/22/58)." School
Board Chairman Paul Schweitzer tried to respond that "politics has never entered into
the Board's decisions," but both of the city's
newspapers picked up the tone of the exchange
as an attempt to rebuke the Board and get them
back into line (*Norfolk Virginian-Pilot* 10/22/
58). Even though it backed down on this score,
the Board still chose a course that was independent from the Mayor: Instead, it put itself
on record as opposed to charging any form of
tuition. Public schools are an essential

community service, members reasoned, the cost of which must necessarily be borne by the entire public, and not just those who benefit directly. To the Mayor's charge that he was "politicking" even with this stance, Board Chairman Schweitzer answered, "I don't intend to be involved in politics. I intend to inform the public of the facts and let them make up their minds (Reif 1960, 19)." Ben Willis, a Duckworth appointee and the most conservative member, was even more contemptuous of the attempt to silence the Board; "I'll wear no man's muzzle. . . . It is the School Board's duty to inject itself into the controversy (*Norfolk Ledger-Dispatch* 3/30/60)."

The referendum issue had left the members of the Board more isolated than ever before: They were not quite at war with the Council and the city's political leaders, but they were certainly further out on the limb of opposition than any other group of successful businessmen had been in almost a decade. They were cut off as well from the rest of the business community: Not a single civic or financial leader of any note had been willing to join them, the teachers, the Ministerial Association, or the Committee for Public Schools in any action which might threaten the Organization's Massive Resistance program. Norfolk under Duckworth had always prided itself on the unanimity of its business and political leaders, and now the School Board threatened to disrupt that hard fought harmony in the middle of the most intense crisis the coalition had ever faced. The pressure on its members to remain quiet was intense (*Norfolk Ledger-Dispatch* 3/30/60), but unanimously they rejected this course as a matter of conscience. They knew that the referendum would be a disaster for the closed schools; not because the concept of public education would be rejected, but rather because the election would only further delay the inevitable deci-

sion to comply. In the meantime the forces of
Massive Resistance would have a chance to
claim some sort of mandate--a unanimity of
popular defiance that the Council hoped would
impress the federal court and force it to
retreat. Instead the Board saw it as a futile
gesture: The lesson of Little Rock was that
the federal government had no intention of
withdrawing. Still, the Board hoped that by
opposing only the references to tuition payments, they had chosen a moderate position
somewhere between the two competing demands:
they were not instructing the voters to vote
"For" integrated schools; neither were they
advocating a decision "Against" public education. In reality they were attempting to be
moderates on an issue in which there could be
no moderation, and each step brought them
closer to a choice between further confrontation or compliance. Board member Ben Willis
thought that they should resign and abandon
this collision course--"I feel the School
Board has served its usefulness," he said--but
Chairman Schweitzer was more philosophic: "You
follow the detour, take the bumps, and hope
that you'll soon be back on the good road
again (*Norfolk Virginian-Pilot* 1/25/59)."

At any rate, the six individual members of
the Norfolk School Board seemed willing to
risk both their political futures and their
business ventures over what each must have
felt was a matter of conscience. Each had
personal reasons for choosing this independent
course, but all six were obviously sustained
by a common and overriding belief in the
merits of public education, and in a way each
provided a powerful, living testimony to that
ideal. Paul Schweitzer, the chairman and most
visible spokesman for the Board, had grown up
on a ranch in Arizona, where he had experienced an "integrated" education: "My sister
and I were the only gringos in that little
one-room schoolhouse . . . it was a lonely

experience (*Norfolk Ledger-Dispatch* 2/16/60)."
Francis Crenshaw, the son of a navy captain,
had lived all over the country, and had also
attended integrated schools in New England
(Crenshaw; *Norfolk Ledger-Dispatch* 5/29/61).
Board member W. Farley Powers was born and
raised in a log house in the impoverished coal
mining counties of Virginia's Southwest; hard
work and a solid devotion to learning had been
his only escape from the deprivation that
surrounded him (*Norfolk Ledger-Star* 12/22/72).
William Ballard had grown up in the equally
poor Eastern Shore region, where he was employed by his family fish and oyster packing-
house. After working his way through high
school and then college, he returned to raise
the family seafood business into one of the
area's leading employers (*Norfolk Ledger-Star*
9/1/64). Although heir to his father's posh
furniture salon, an upbringing that was more
typical of the rest of the business elite, Ben
Willis owed his fortitude to something his
father had taught him: "There are two things
you cannot compromise--principle and equality
(*Richmond Times-Dispatch* 2/3/63)." Mildred
Dallas, the only woman on any of the city's
major boards and commissions, brought a minority prospective of her own.

Thus, although on paper they were similar
to many of the city's civic and business leaders, the members of the School Board had a
profound commitment to the concepts of equality and public education--a conviction strong
enough to endure the sense of helplessness and
isolation they now faced. Although publicly in
favor of petitioning the Governor and privately opposed to even putting the decision to a
vote, the School Board still backed away from
openly campaigning on the issue--Mayor Duckworth's scolding had produced at least that
much compliance--instead abandoning that cause
to the Committee for Public Schools and the
other zealots of the pro-school movement. In

spite of the fact that the odds were heavily stacked against them, the Committee still nursed vague hopes that Duckworth and the Organization had blundered by putting the issue to a vote. It was a remote possibility, but the Committee nevertheless prepared guide ballots, handbills, and a massive newspaper advertising campaign to promote a vote "for" public schools. The Defenders of State Sovereignty and Individual Liberties led the forces that urged a vote "against" the resolution-- the Council remained true to its pledge to stay out of the contest once it had drawn up the ballot (*Norfolk Virginian-Pilot* 11/15/58). In one sense it was a classic struggle between the liberal Committee and the ultra-conservative Defenders, but the odds were too heavily stacked against the resolution to make it a fair fight. The wording on the ballot, the nature of the electorate, the short duration of the contest, and the tacit opposition of the Organization all doomed the Committee's efforts to failure before they had even begun. The only surprise in the results was the paucity of the turnout: Only 21,000 people-- less than half of those eligible, and only a tenth of the city's adult population--showed up to cast a ballot in the most important election in a decade. The referendum to petition the Governor to reopen the closed schools lost by a healthy three-to-two margin, the same figure by which Senator Harry Byrd and Governor Almond had defeated their recent opponents. Only 3,600 black voters--still less than half of those eligible--turned out to help the pro-school forces; their presence, however, helped to dilute the harshness of the two-and-a-half-to-1 rout that the Committee suffered in the white precincts (*Norfolk Ledger-Dispatch* 11/19/58). Even so, the vote was much closer in the Silkstocking precincts on the West Side than in the largely blue collar neighborhoods in the northern, eastern, and central portions of the city (*Norfolk Virginian-Pilot* 11/19/58).

8

A Very Massive Resister

The people had spoken, or so it seemed; the message of their mandate was, however, indistinct. On the one hand, they appeared to endorse a continuation of the school-closing strategy to avoid court-ordered integration; on the other hand, they gave no indication of just how long they would support this tactic. The message was clouded by the fact that as yet no one had really suffered greatly from the closings: Tutoring groups and the heightened sense of shared emergency had helped to mask the fact that the burden of Massive Resistance had fallen disproportionately upon the young, poor, and transient populations not represented in the established electorate. The people had not, as spokesmen for the Defenders claimed, endorsed Massive Resistance: The tutoring groups and the dismal patronage drawn to the Tidewater Education Foundation's segregated private academies gave substantial testimony to the fact that Norfolk parents wanted the education of their children to continue in the public realm. If there was any significance at all to the election, and any meaning to the events that fall that preceded the contest, it was that most citizens were still waiting for some sort of dramatic action that would resolve the crisis--the scenarios pro-

posed by the T.E.F. and the Committee for Public Schools were both unacceptable--and most
were hoping for a return to segregated public
schools--the one option not available. Thus,
the people were not ready, as the Governor
surmised, to reject racially mixed schools
(*Norfolk Virginian-Pilot* 11/20/58); they were
just not prepared to accept them yet.

The one man who bore the heaviest responsibility for reading these auguries was Mayor
Duckworth, but both time and events were con-
spiring in such a way as to cloud his judgment
of the referendum's relative importance with
other, largely political, considerations. Far
from lessening the pressures upon him to act,
however, the referendum had served instead to
focus new attention upon his response. The
referendum and rebuke of the pro-schools advocates had won him new found respect among
the state's conservatives:

A gleam has replaced the old suspicious
look when you mention Norfolk in the
politically potent domain called the
Virginia Southside. It's because of a new
feeling that Norfolk is not going to bow
easily to school integration. And that
gleam shows when the name of Norfolk's
frank-talking mayor comes up. The word
most often heard in describing his
actions is that he has "guts (*Norfolk
Virginian-Pilot* 1/11/59)."

Increasingly, the eyes of the state's political leaders began to turn away from the
staid and passive elegance of the Governor to
the energy and dynamism of Norfolk's Mayor;
there was no question that they liked what
they saw. Almond had won office by portraying
himself as the brains behind Massive Resistance, but now it was Duckworth who was seen as
the guts, and his blunt, out-spoken "go-
getter" image proved a sharp contrast to the

rolling rhetorical rodomontade that characterized Almond's style. Almond appeared to be
the consummate silver-haired patrician, the
type Virginians had always sought for higher
office. Thus, it was ironic that now, in
crisis, they should turn instead to Duckworth,
the epitome in appearance of the urban political boss with his stocky, even pudgy, five-
foot, ten-and-a-half-inch frame, and jowly
visage. Even his trademark, the ever-present
cigar and cigar holder, was more a big-city
stogie than the plantation Havana of the gen-
teel; he smoked three a day, but unlit, all
three did double duty as the maestro's baton
of his furious pace of action: "He thinks fast
and calls the shots quickly--sometimes with a
suddenness that is startling"--is how one
reporter described him, going on to add that
he "can snap with a voice which is some where
[sic] between a bark and a bite." It was this
very openness--"he's no diplomat, but he lays
his cards on the table face up (Norfolk Virginian-Pilot 9/5/60)"--that was attracting the
attention of the most ardent segregationists;
they sensed a steely harshness in his opposition to federal authorities that seemed lacking in Almond's calm demeanor. In short, Duckworth, not Almond, appeared to be the emerging
hero of Massive Resistance, and already his
name was being bandied about by political insiders across the state as a gubernatorial
contender (Norfolk Virginian-Pilot 1/11/59).
Local Byrd Organization chieftain Billy Prieur
had begun to take him to Skyland, Harry Byrd's
mountain retreat, for regular sessions with
the Senator, both to underscore the importance
of continued resistance and to explore the
possibilities of advancing the Mayor's political career. For the first time, Duckworth was
entertaining ambitions that stretched beyond
municipal service, and he was eager to parlay
this new statewide following into the Organization's nod for governor (Darden; Mason).

All of this political speculation--as yet
only the talk of insiders who thrive on such
badinage--led Duckworth to misinterpret the
results of the referendum as both a personal
endorsement of his policies and a call to arms
for further resistance. For the time being,
however, the vote seemed to both solve all his
present problems and to promote new opportunities: First, it relieved the City Council of
having to make any decision on the Norfolk
School Board's appeal for action from the Governor; second, it seemed to mend a potential
rift in his business/organization constituency
by allowing the people, not the politicians,
to rebuke the School Board for entertaining
thoughts of surrender; it had bought him time
to establish that cool and rational citizen
response to the crisis was possible; and
finally, and most important, it had convinced
the rest of the state of the solidarity of
Norfolk's resistance to school integration,
relieved the pressure from the Southside to
overreact, and bought time in which to effect
a purely local decision. Unfortunately personal ambitions and political pressures blinded
the Mayor to the beneficial escape-valve qual-
ities of the referendum, and led him instead
to overreact in favor of Massive Resistance.
Duckworth possessed a marvelously analytical
mind that was well suited to the rough and
tumble realm of urban politics; he now sized
up the situation in terms of potential obstacles, options, and sources of opposition,
and then proceeded one by one to clear the
obstacles and opposition from the path that
blocked his choice of options.

Chief among those obstacles was the threat
still posed by actions before the courts. It
was not the *Harrison v. Day* "friendly" suit
brought to test the legality of the state's
Massive Resistance laws, nor even a continuation of the N.A.A.C.P.'s integration litigation, that most observers feared; instead, the

Committee For Public Schools' *James v. Almond*
action was the challenge upon which the fate
of Massive Resistance hinged; this entreaty,
wholly unexpected by both Duckworth and the
Organization, had Governor Almond and the legal experts concerned. Almond knew that the
state could not continue to offer public secondary schools for black students, but not to
whites, and that this challenge by white parents would ultimately sink the interposition
logic of Massive Resistance. Duckworth, however, was not inclined to accept defeat so
easily, and instead began to lay the ground-
work for a plan that would undermine the
Committee's action. At the first City Council
meeting after the referendum Duckworth proposed a "cut off of funds" clause in the
School Board budget slated to begin January 1
(1959), thereby reserving for the City Council
the right to "change or cancel the unexpended
portion" of school funds at any time during
the year, even prohibiting specific expenditures if it wished. There were several reasons
for such a ploy: First, it brought the more
moderate School Board more directly under his
control by giving the City Council the power
of month-to-month approval of every facet of
the Board's budget (*Norfolk Virginian-Pilot*
11/26/58)--a potent check on the independence
of the Board. Second, the measure was partly
designed to retaliate against the errant
teachers who had undermined the Organization's
Massive Resistance strategy. According to reports, the Mayor had personally intervened to
set up the meeting, and was still smarting
from the teachers' rejection of the T.E.F.'s
offer. When Superintendent J. J. Brewbaker
expressed his concern, "I hope we don't do
anything to encourage teachers to look for
other jobs--we have good teachers," Mayor
Duckworth snapped, "With what some of them
have done . . . I would have to disagree with
you (*Norfolk Virginian-Pilot* 1/25/59)."

These two retaliatory aspects of the funds cut-off measure were, however, only secondary to other more pressing considerations. With the added power, City Council now directly controlled a potential solution to its legal dilemmas. In the event that the ruling in the Committee For Public Schools' *James v. Almond* suit went against the city, the Council could close the remaining white junior high as well as the city's black junior and senior high schools, a move that would put Norfolk's case in uncharted legal waters. No court had yet ruled that a municipality was required to offer secondary education to its citizens; in fact, Virginia Attorney General Albertis S. Harrison had already indicated that the U.S. Supreme Court's *Brown* decision had struck down the entire state constitutional mandate to provide public schools at all, because the establishment of a public educational system in Virginia was entirely conditional upon the schools being segregated (*Norfolk Virginian-Pilot* 11/8/58). The legal arguments in the *James v. Almond* case turned upon the fact that Norfolk was providing public secondary schools for some and not all its patrons; if the remaining secondary institutions were closed, the ploy would at the very least tie up the legal efforts to integrate the schools for several more years, perhaps giving the Organization enough time to permanently salvage its Massive Resistance plan to substitute private, segregated academies for integrated public schools. In fact, a similar maneuver in Prince Edward County was not definitively broken by the courts until 1963 (Smith 1965).

Closing the city's black junior and senior high schools was at this time, at least, a last resort and only an ancillary aspect of the proposal. The major purpose of the clause was not to serve as a legal dodge, but rather to stand as the most formidable in a series of power plays to pressure the black community

into finally withdrawing their integration
efforts. Up to now the School Board had been
able to serve as a buffer between the Mayor
and the black community, insulating the black
educational system from political reprisals.
Now that the School Board had been short-
circuited out of direct control of any portion
of its funding, the entire black educational
system was dangerously exposed to reprisals.
Councilman Lewis Layton renewed the Mayor's
call for a black withdrawal from integration
efforts, and dangled the potent threat of the
funds cut-off as the cutting edge of that demand. Duckworth, too, wanted the black community to know that this time he meant business:
"The only way schools can reopen now is by
getting the cooperation of the colored citizens (*Norfolk Virginian-Pilot* 11/26/58)." The
black community knew that the Mayor's threat
was no idle bluff: He had both the inclination
and the capacity to carry it out. "We could do
nothing less in the light of the school referendum (*Norfolk Virginian-Pilot* 1/14/59)," was
the Mayor's carefully worded counter to those
who challenged the cutoff. The threat was real
enough: Unless the N.A.A.C.P. withdrew its
efforts to integrate the city's schools, the
black community would be faced with at best a
prolonged shutdown and, at worst, a permanent
closing of its secondary school system and
additional retaliatory encroachments upon its
elementary schools. The enormous progress in
black education that had taken place in the
twelve years since the People's group first
took over the city government would now come
to an abrupt halt, and was even in danger of
retrogressing. Was the black community willing
to trade the future of an entire generation of
its young people for the expanded educational
opportunities of seventeen youths? The Mayor
was betting that they would not.

    The Mayor's funds-cutoff proposal was a
direct result of the lopsided referendum vic-

tory, a growing awareness of his aspirations
for higher office, and an increase in the hostile attitudes of a few of the state's most
powerful and most ardent segregationists. The
referendum had helped to quiet much of the
rabid rhetoric coming from Virginia's Southside counties, but some highly visible step to
preserve the legal facade of Massive Resistance still seemed necessary to appease former
Governor Bill Tuck and others who had been
roused by the *Virginian-Pilot*'s editorial policy and its continued coverage of the pro-
school advocates. Mayor Duckworth had come
under increasing pressure, in spite of his own
growing personal popularity with these resisters, to prove that Norfolk was not a "hotbed
of integrationists" as Tuck and his cohorts
were charging. The funds-cutoff measure was
designed in part to appease these sympathies,
as well as to buy the city enough time to
negotiate some sort of out-of-court settlement
of the issue. Tuck and the rest of the Southside's Massive Resisters represented a powerful political force in the Organization--one
with which even a Mayor lacking in ambition
for advancement would have to deal in order to
secure continued state funding for the highways, bridges, tunnels, institutions, and
other projects that were so crucial to Duckworth's development desires--and they were not
above threatening to cut off state funds earmarked for any political jurisdiction which
bowed to court-ordered school integration: "If
Norfolk won't stand with us, I say let them
stand alone" was Tuck's philosophy (*Norfolk
Virginian-Pilot* 11/13/58).

Duckworth's quick action on the funds-cutoff measure--so soon after the referendum--
earned him accolades of praise from the Byrd
Organization hierarchy and the Southside
cheering section. Even so, no immediate end to
the crisis was possible until January, when
the Council assumed control of the School

Board's funding, the court cases were slated for resolution, the black community would have to respond, the tutoring groups were scheduled to cease (*Norfolk Virginian-Pilot* 10/26/58), and the School Board threatened to resign if the Mayor's funds cut-off proposal went into effect (*Norfolk Virginian-Pilot* 1/25/59). Norfolk was thus stuck in a holding pattern: The flurry of activity that followed the first weeks of closed schools had all but died away; the doors had now been locked for more than three months; and the federal government showed no signs of quick surrender. Onlookers could not agree whether the citizens were "complacent" or just "frustrated" by their inability to influence the crisis (*Norfolk Virginian-Pilot* 10/19/58); even so, Norfolk was remarkably quiet for a city with 10,000 students out on the streets, and the future of both its public educational system and continued racial harmony at stake.

In the air of official calm that prevailed, Norfolk's rumor mills worked overtime, helping to shift the focus of attention away from the political arena. Increasingly the attention of parents and civic leaders began to turn away from the student leaders towards a different type of pupil--not the ones who attended the tutoring groups, lead protests, or were active in school clubs and organizations. More and more there was concern that the effect of the closings would be tallied as well in the sudden upsurge of teenage unemployment, hostility, delinquency, crime, pregnancy, forced marriages, dropouts, and the like--the kind of effects that have a lasting impact upon the future of the community. Lenoir Chambers and the editorial staff of the *Virginian-Pilot* hammered away at this theme as well as the long-term economic ruin that lay ahead. Washington continued to sound ominous notes about the crisis' potential impact upon naval contracts, ship assignments, and billeting ar-

rangements--the navy was reluctant to make
assignments to a community that lacked public
schools--but these warnings seemed to go un-
heeded. Rumors spread about officers who had
requested transfers, ships that had been reassigned, new business prospects frightened
away, and the likelihood of congressional
retaliation (Reif 1960, 11-22).

In spite of these dire warnings that the
underpinnings of Norfolk's economy were severely threatened, the full impact of the
crisis had not yet hit the business community.
Local business leaders and economic trends
were still pointing as late as January (1959)
to a bright outlook and a rapid recovery from
the national slump that occurred in the last
years of the Eisenhower administration (*Norfolk Virginian-Pilot* 1/1/59; 1/4/59). Even so,
elements within the business community never
gave up their attempt to attract the remnants
of the People's group to the pro-school camp.
To no avail, School Board Chairman Schweitzer,
businessman Sam Barfield, psychiatrist William
F. Blair, Committee for Public Schools' lawyer
Archie Boswell, and Lewis W. Webb, Jr., pro-
vost of the junior college that was the precursor to Old Dominion University, pleaded
with the Chamber of Commerce to take a stand
in defense of reopening the closed schools
(*Norfolk Virginian-Pilot* 10/13/58; 1/17/59).
Over and over again Lenoir Chambers and the
editorial pages of the *Virginian-Pilot* echoed
the theme that the business leaders must put a
stop to the school crisis, and that the city's
future as a major naval base was threatened
(*Norfolk Virginian-Pilot* 1/1/59; 1/17/59); in
spite of this, not a single leader of the old
People's group, not one major corporate executive or civic leader, dared to take up the
challenge. The only corporate voices that were
heard came from outside the city, although
some, like John Fishwick, the president of the
Norfolk and Western Railroad, former governor

Colgate Darden, brother of Norfolk's former
Mayor and now president of the University of
Virginia, political leader Francis Pickens
Miller, and other statewide industrialists
(*Norfolk Virginian-Pilot* 12/7/59; Dabney 1971,
537), had a special relationship with the
city. Only Frank Batten, publisher of the *Virginian-Pilot* and *Ledger-Dispatch* newspapers,
was willing to join with three dozen business
leaders from across the state who were urging
Governor Almond to reopen the closed schools
(*Norfolk Virginian-Pilot* 9/3/ 90). Most of the
rest of Norfolk's business and civic establishment remained quiet on the issue, giving
Duckworth a free hand to negotiate with the
black community.

The black community refused to back down
from their efforts, in spite of the fact that
almost every element of the white populace
stood poised against them--or at least seemed
prepared to silently assent to the closing of
their schools, too, in retaliation. Norfolk's
blacks gave every indication that they were
prepared to choose closed schools rather than
give up on integration (*Norfolk Virginian-
Pilot* 12/11/58). Their defiance led Duckworth
to announce on January 13, 1959, the intention
of the Council to close down after February 1,
all grades above the sixth--an additional
1,914 white pupils and 5,259 black students
would be locked out. A small band of pro-
school advocates made an emotional plea at the
session for Council to "think it over" before
taking this drastic step, and once more appealed to the business community to end the
crisis (*Norfolk Virginian-Pilot* 1/14/59).

Ironically the first crack in the Mayor's
coalition came not from any of these sources,
but rather from within the Council itself.
For the first time in the history of the
crisis, a single councilman split from the
pack and voted "No" to a Duckworth proposal.
Councilman Roy B. Martin, Jr., a Duckworth

appointee, caused a ripple of surprise and
then applause from the pro-school advocates.
Martin listed the reasons for his opposition:

> I sincerely feel we are headed for a def-
> inite backward step economically if we do
> not straighten out our school situation,
> not further impair it. My strong appre-
> hension about the economic future of Nor-
> folk impels me to vote "No (*Norfolk Vir-
> ginian-Pilot* 1/14/59)."

Years later Martin would indicate that it was
the punitive nature of the measure, as much as
the economic considerations, that made it objectionable: "It was stupid to enlarge the
problem by closing more schools (Martin)."

Instead of serving as the rallying point
for business opposition to the Mayor's retaliatory tack, Martin was left to stand alone in
moderation; the Silkstocking crowd remained as
silent as before, failing even in this eleventh hour opportunity to back one of its own in
an act of raw political courage. Roy Martin's
vote, although a seemingly useless act of defiance, was not as suicidal as it may have
first appeared. Thirty-seven years old and the
youngest member of the Council, Martin was
fast emerging as the one member of the Duckworth coalition closest to both the people and
the business community. The editors of the
Virginian-Pilot were determined that his action not seem an isolated incident, and therefore promoted the split with unprecedented
news and editorial coverage for a single
council vote. The pro-school advocates--the
teachers, ministers, Committee For Public
Schools, P.T.A.'s and their sympathizers--who
up to that point had carried the banner of
opposition to Massive Resistance alone, took
heart. If Roy Martin was willing to risk his
political career on a single vote, they figured, he must have sensed some new surge of

sentiment stirring. For this reason, they planned a flurry of activity, unmatched since the first week of closings, to probe this new development. The *Virginian-Pilot* sensed the change in the city:

> At present Norfolk may be likened to a bus coming down a narrow mountain road in the command of drivers who have misread the road map, neglected to read the warning signs, and who are cheered on by a group of front-seat passengers who don't know what they are doing. . . . Norfolk's task would be difficult under any leadership . . . but the difficult task is horribly compounded when the leadership acts on vain and dangerous assumptions. There will be hope only when--a lot of silent, unhappy people screw their courage to the sticking point and speak and act (*Norfolk Virginian-Pilot* 1/16/59).

The first shots in the new barrage were fired at a meeting of the Granby High School P.T.A. Granby had been closed four months, but suddenly 450 people jammed a standing-room-only meeting to demand a more vocal opposition to the school closing plan. The most telling fusillade in the new barrage came not from the closed secondary schools, but rather from the Bay View Elementary P.T.A., long a stronghold of Defender sentiment. Even though only 26 Bay View seventh-graders would be effected by the cut off, a crowd of angry parents at a packed meeting of the P.T.A. shouted down the objections of William I. McKendree, president of both the T.E.F. and the Bay View P.T.A., and voted unanimously to pass a resolution opposing the closing of any more schools (*Norfolk Virginian-Pilot* 1/16/59). The editors of the *Virginian-Pilot* were shocked: "In these dark days, the action of the Bay View P.T.A. lights a candle of hope." Five more P.T.A.'s followed their lead, and the *Virginian-Pilot* took these actions as a cue to ask, "Has the Counter-Revolution Begun (*Norfolk Virginian-Pilot* 1/18/59)?"

The next salvo was fired by the School Board, a group that had been relatively silent since it had been stripped so unceremoniously of its financial power. In an action of silent defiance, Board members served as the star witnesses for the Committee for Public Schools in its *James v. Almond* suit. Even though the School Board had been named as a codefendant along with the Mayor, it supported each of the Committee's claims of economic and educational hardship. Moreover, the School Board now took two remarkable actions that brought it dangerously close to direct confrontation with the Council. First, Chairman Paul Schweitzer issued a carefully worded statement that skirted the edge of defiance by indicating the Board's displeasure with the new closings tactic (*Norfolk Virginian-Pilot* 1/20/59). Next, the Board gave every indication that it would like to lose this new suit, and when City Attorney Leonard Davis joined them in withdrawing from the case, the Council was left alone to face the court (*Norfolk Virginian-Pilot* 1/25/59).

A new harshness in the Mayor's attitude had brought about the situation where the School Board, his City Attorney, and one of his Council members were willing to risk open disagreement; for the first time they understood just how far Duckworth was willing to go to make Massive Resistance work, and the prospect frightened them. At the very time most Norfolk residents were beginning to entertain thoughts of reopening the schools, Duckworth was calling selected members of the School Board and the City Council to a secret strategy session at his home. There, Mayor Duckworth, Vice-Mayor George Abbott, and Organization head Billy Prieur--Martin was not invited --indicated both their willingness and their

intention to close every school in the city,
if necessary, in order to prevent integration
(*Norfolk Virginian-Pilot* 1/25/59). Since they
knew that this was no idle threat, the prospect of even more closed schools and a continuation of hardline resistance frightened
the Board members present almost as much as
Duckworth's next announcement: The Council was
considering an offer by the T.E.F. to buy up
the closed schools and operate them on a private, segregated basis (*Norfolk Virginian-
Pilot* 1/28/59). This was the final step in the
total abandonment of public education: With
the schools closed, buildings sold, teacher
salaries cut off, and low-cost tutoring groups
phased out, the teachers and students would be
forced to accept Massive Resistance, and the
schools would be reopened on a private, segregated basis with the help of the state's
generous tuition grants. Mayor Duckworth and
the Organization had at last the machinery
that would make Massive Resistance work, and
the fact that they were willing to use it, was
enough to make both the School Board and Councilman Martin revolt in spite of the risks of
defying the Mayor.

Events began to proceed at such a rapid
pace that they quickly outstripped these hopeful signs of protest. On the same day that the
School Board was announcing its opposition to
the funds-cutoff plan, the entire legal structure of the school-closing maneuver was being
struck down in both the state's "friendly"
Harrison v. *Day* action before the Virginia
Supreme Court and the Committee For Public
Schools' *James* v. *Almond* suit in federal court
(*Norfolk Virginian-Pilot* 1/20/59). The court
decisions, however, spoke only to the issues
presented in the fall, and failed to address
the new obstacles presented by the Mayor's
funds-cutoff plan. Although they could prevent
any scheme to keep the desegregated schools
closed, the courts could not stop further

closings, thus leaving Duckworth free to enact
the next phase of Massive Resistance (*Norfolk
Virginian-Pilot* 1/24/59).

The fact that both the federal court and
the Virginia Supreme Court handed down their
decision on exactly the same day was no acci-
dent. In early December (1958) when U. S.
District Judge Walter Hoffman ran across Chief
Justice Eggleston of the Virginia Supreme
Court on a golf outing, Eggleston drew Hoffman
aside and inquired as to whether the three-
judge federal court had reached a decision in
the *James v. Almond* case. Hoffman replied that
it had, and that he was writing the opinion
for release on December 22 (1958). Eggleston
indicated that the Virginia Supreme Court had
reached a conclusion in *Harrison v. Day*, but
the dissenters would not be ready with their
opinion until January 19 (1959). Hoffman took
the hint, and signaled that he would delay his
opinion until then. Judge Eggleston nodded,
and departed with a smile.

> We both knew it was better for Virginians
> to hear it [the death of the state's
> Massive Resistance plan] from their own
> court. Judge Eggleston never said which
> way his court had decided, but I knew
> what he wanted, and which way the [state]
> court was leaning when he said he was
> writing the majority opinion (Hoffman).

Now that the courts had finally acted, the
issue of more school closings came in for a
new round of response. In a fiery speech to a
statewide radio and television audience, Governor Almond referred in lurid terms to the:

> Livid stench of sadism, sex immorality,
> and juvenile pregnancy infesting mixed
> schools. . . . Let me make it abundantly
> clear for the record now and hereafter,
> I will not yield to that which I know to

be wrong . . . we have just begun to
fight (Dabney 1971, 542)!

Congratulations poured in from Senator Byrd,
legislative leaders, and hardcore resisters
all across the Commonwealth, all expressing
their desire to lead Norfolk into another
round of school closings, legal obfuscation,
and delay.

Public reaction in Norfolk to the fast-
breaking chain of events was loud and angry,
even if its message was unclear. At a stormy
session of the Council following the courts'
pronouncements, Mayor Duckworth found for the
first time that he was unable to conduct the
city's business. In a city inured to years of
meaningless Council sessions that only rein-
forced the actions of private presessions, a
strange event took place: An angry crowd,
three-fourths of whom were women, was determined to prevent the Council from enacting its
usual show of empty democratic pageantry. The
entire meeting was repeatedly interrupted by
clapping, catcalls, boos, and laughter from a
rowdy crowd of onlookers; finally, after
thirty-five minutes of this verbal assault,
Duckworth adjourned the meeting in disgust
(*Norfolk Virginian-Pilot* 1/21/59).

The Norfolk school crisis had long been the
focus of national media attention--Governor
Almond's picture adorned the cover of *Time*
magazine (22 September 1958) in an issue that
featured the Norfolk crisis as its lead story
--but now an event took place on prime time
national television that helped to crystallize
both local attitudes and national opinion. At
the height of the turmoil and just two days
after the court rulings, CBS television ran an
Edward R. Morrow/Ed Friendly production titled
"The Lost Class of '59: The Norfolk Story" at
8 p.m. Wednesday, January 21. The production
was remarkably objective (*Norfolk Ledger-Dispatch* 1/22/59), and sought to portray opinions

from both sides of the issue. It also featured
a segment that brought the viewers up to date
on the recent legal developments, including a
telling interview with a resolute Governor
Almond. In spite of the factual documentary
presentation of the hour-long program, the
chief impact for local residents was emotional. Parts of the program that focused poig-
nantly on the hardships of the locked-out
students--how the closing had fragmented the
goals and dreams of the best and the brightest
and doomed their less achievement-oriented
classmates to the dismal prospects of teenage
unemployment and listlessness--were instrumental in shaping half-formed local opinions: For
the first time Norfolk really saw the crisis
as it was viewed by the rest of the world
(Reif 1960, 22). For businessmen who had up to
now been relatively unconcerned about the
city's loss of national reputation, the prime
time exposure, the documentary objectivity,
the emotional impact, and Edward R. Murrow's
reputation for honesty helped to project an
urgency to the crisis that was not present
before: Slowly the realization dawned that the
Organization had brought the city to the brink
of a municipal disaster unlike any it had
faced since the postwar People's revolt, and
that if the gimmickry of closed schools continued, a decade of municipal reform, national
leadership, social concern, and vital fence-
building with the navy would be destroyed,
along with the city's reputation and its hopes
for a secure future.

Events had moved so rapidly that week of
January 19-23, 1959--first, the advancement of
the funds-cutoff measure; next, the two simultaneous court orders striking down the legal
framework of Massive Resistance; followed by
the sight of both the Governor and the Mayor
vowing further resistance; and finally, the
prime-time appeal of the Edward R. Murrow/Ed
Friendly production--that the state's politi-

cal leaders, including Mayor Duckworth, apparently lost touch with the changing mood of
the people. The politicians were still preparing to take their cue from the November
referendum and a quiet December of public ac-
quiescence--they assumed that the people still
wanted to fight integration to the bitter end,
even if it meant more school closings along
the way. Something, however, had happened to
the public mood, and more and more individuals
were apparently now ready to quit the fight.
No one is really sure which event, or even
which combination of events, triggered the
shift, but for the first time a massive change
was evident. To many of the city's business
leaders it was the finality of the state supreme court--a Virginia, and not a federal
court--decision. "My own court had spoken--I
had divorced myself from the U. S. Supreme
Court and I had given up any allegiance I had
to it--that's when I was willing to lay down
the fight (Darden)." For others, it was the
spectacle of the Governor in full red-faced
harangue in spite of the personal tragedies
portrayed by "The Lost Class of '59" that
finally brought home the realization of how
Norfolk must appear to the rest of the nation
(Reif 1960, 21-2).

Even though a surface tranquility had descended upon the city that weekend, a strange
hubbub of activity was taking place in a number of subterranean circles. Mayor Duckworth
was plugged into a statewide hookup of frantic
political leaders scurrying to help plot the
Organization's next step. A bloc of Southside
legislators headed by Mills Godwin (later Governor) was attempting to devise a series of
desperation measures that would block the
reopening of the desegregated schools. Among
the plans under consideration was a ten-day
school holiday, a proposition to close every
school in the state until each could be selec-
tively recertified by a safety inspector, a

statute that would make it a felony for courts
to assign pupils to any school without the
backing of the state's pupil placement board,
a repeal of the state's compulsory attendance
laws, and an amendment to the Virginia Consti-
tution that would allow local jurisdictions to
close down their own schools. There was even a
proposal that paralleled Duckworth's funds-
cutoff plan, only reaching out to a statewide
application (*Norfolk Virginian-Pilot* 1/30/59).
It was just this sort of frantic activity--the
high-level phone calls, the hurried confer-
ences, the official entreaties, and the specu-
lative nature of the schemes being advanced--
that deafened Duckworth and the Byrd Organization leadership to more subtle murmurs in the
rest of the community. Another factor seemed
to influence the Mayor in his deliberations:
Duckworth reported receiving between 50 and
100 phone calls that weekend threatening to
"blow up the schools" if they reopened integrated. Whether the calls were local or part
of some Southside effort to stiffen his resistance makes very little difference: By the
close of the weekend, Duckworth was committed
to another round of closings, intimidation,
and legal obfuscation. The specter of violence
and the fear of reduced state funding if Norfolk bowed to integration were the reasons he
publicly cited for that commitment (*Norfolk
Virginian-Pilot* 1/27/59).

The rumor mills worked overtime that weekend with reports of political intrigue, specu-
lative legislation, and a buzz of excitement
that something big was going on in the business community. The grapevine had it that a
downtown meeting had been held between the
navy's top brass and some gilt-edged Norfolkians, the remnants of the Silkstocking crowd;
in it, supposedly, the navy issued an ulti-
matum: Either open the schools or lose the
fleet. Other rumors had it that two local financial leaders were called to an urgent con-

ference in Richmond with representatives of the state's largest banking and mortgage interests; they were reportedly told that the school situation had to be cleared up before serious economic repercussions were felt (Reif 1960, 21-2). Regardless of the veracity of these rumors, they express some very real fears that were circulating among the city's civic and financial elite: Now that the courts had finally spoken, business leaders were afraid that the navy and the federal government might take some retaliatory action if the city continued its posture of defiance; others could see that efforts to attract new industry were already falling apart; and financial experts had their eye on the collapse of local bond issues in the northern mortgage markets. The substance of these realizations lent credence to the rumors, and may well have formed the basis for what followed.

The Tuesday editions of the *Virginian-Pilot* and Ledger-Dispatch carried the most dramatic evidence of the shift in public opinion that had taken place that weekend: a full-page advertisement, really an appeal to reopen the schools now and avoid further resistance, that by itself was the most important single event in the 141 days of the Norfolk school crisis. The advertisement carried the following message signed by one hundred of the city's most prominent business, financial, civic, and industrial leaders:

> While we would strongly prefer to have segregated schools, it is evident from the recent court decisions that our public schools must either be integrated to the extent fully required or must be abandoned. The abandonment of our public schools system is, in our opinion, unthinkable, as it would mean the denial of an adequate education to a majority of our children. Moreover, the consequences

would be most damaging to our community.
We, therefore, urge the Norfolk City
Council to do everything within its power
to open all public schools as promptly as
possible.

A front page, banner headline and the accom-
panying story proclaimed the appeal to be "the
first time a large segment of the Norfolk
business community has taken a public stand in
the city's school crisis." The editors hailed
it as "a new clear voice . . . a striking and
welcome change . . . a striking new development (*Norfolk Virginian-Pilot* 1/27/59)."

In spite of disclaimers to the contrary,
the public viewed the document as a personal
affront to Mayor Duckworth, his power, and the
course of action he had chosen. This was the
first time in Duckworth's eight-and-a-half
year tenure of office that any concerted group
of businessmen had ever publicly tried to influence a City Council decision, much less
move so forcefully and so openly to oppose its
authority. As a further sign of the intended
insult, the signers had handed over the petition to attorneys for the Norfolk Committee
For Public Schools so that it could be introduced that day as evidence in the Committee's
new *James v. Duckworth* effort to block the
Mayor's plan to implement further closings
(*Norfolk Virginian-Pilot* 1/27/59). Even so,
former People's Mayor Pretlow Darden and a
representative group of the signers had gone
to see Mayor Duckworth on Monday to soften the
blow before the appeal was made public. Mr.
Darden's recollection of the conversation only
underscores the Mayor's anger at having been
double-crossed:

Darden: We're doing something good for
the city and good for you . . . it gets
you off the hook because these schools
have got to be opened.

Duckworth: You've stabbed me in the back!

Darden: Well, you can always say . . . that a bunch of these--whatever you want to call us--got this thing up without your knowledge. Would you like to see it?

Duckworth: Hell, no!   I don't want to see it if I can't do anything about it!

Although the signers referred to themselves innocuously as the Committee of One Hundred, the appeal marked the re-emergence of the People's group, long since buried in the on-slaught of Massive Resistance and Organization politics. The petition had all the markings of a People's production: The inspiration for it came from former Mayor Pretlow Darden in col-laboration with Frank Batten, president of the parent company that owned Norfolk's two daily newspapers and its major radio and television stations. Darden and Batten had hand-picked the group of eligible signers, and then per-sonally carried it to the chosen, going first to their old allies from the Silkstocking days. Former People's campaign chief Charles Kaufman, now chairman of the Norfolk Rede-velopment and Housing Authority, polished the wording of the final draft, just as he had done for every major campaign announcement a dozen years before. Besides Darden and Kauf-man, the list was spotted with names of those activists and appointees who had helped to lend credence to the People's crusade: John Alfriend, Charles Burroughs, Richard Cooke, C. W. Grandy, George Foote, Henry Clay Hofheimer, John Jenkins, Clarence Robertson, Dan Thorn-ton, Thomas Wilcox, and Rives Worsham (Dar-den). More than anything else, the Committee of One Hundred was the purest representation of the city's financial elite that had sur-faced in a decade--a veritable roster of the

banking and business fraternity, highlighted
by the realization that at least ten of the
signers no longer lived in Norfolk.

The statement by the Committee of One Hundred was both an opinion-maker and the most
important milestone in marking how far public
sentiment had shifted in the past week. Once
the city's major business and financial leaders had so openly crossed the power and authority of the Mayor, it was both safe and
fashionable for others who had been long silent to express their own pro-school sentiments. Typical of the community's gratitude at
the eleventh-hour conversion of its former
Silkstocking leadership was the action of one
downtown florist who sent a red rose to each
of the signers. Also symbolic was the appeal
of Harvey Lindsay, Jr., and 35 young business
and civic leaders--too young to have been a
part of the People's regime--who ran their own
advertisement so that their voice could be
counted (*Norfolk Virginian-Pilot* 1/28/59).

One example helps to underscore both how
committed the Mayor was to continued resistance, and just how opposed he was to the surrender sentiments of the Silkstocking crowd.
The same day that Pretlow Darden and others
approached him with their appeal, but well
before the existence of their effort was made
public, Mayor Duckworth had the perfect opportunity to turn the statements to his own personal and political advantage. The Committee
For Public Schools had brought suit against
the Mayor and the City Council, seeking to enjoin them in its *James v. Duckworth* litigation
from cutting off the School Board's funds and
closing more schools. Armed with the still-
secret knowledge of the Committee of One
Hundred, Duckworth could have appeared as the
initiator of the appeal by withdrawing the
city's defense in the suit, thereby conceding
the issue and effectively dropping the school
closing plan. Instead, he argued all the more

forcefully for the funds cut-off plan, specifically detailing his fears about potential
racial violence if the schools were allowed to
reopen (*Norfolk Virginian-Pilot* 1/27/59).

The Mayor had badly miscalculated if he had
hoped that the usual plodding pace of litigation before the federal courts would give him
time to reconsolidate his political power and
position. With unprecedented speed, Federal
Judge Walter Hoffman--a Norfolk native with
strong ties to the Silkstocking establishment
--ruled against the Council the very next day,
the same morning that Norfolk citizens were
reading in their papers about the Committee of
One Hundred. The very existence of the Silkstocking appeal, and the fact that it had been
sent to the Committee For Public Schools to
strengthen their legal position, was important
in negating, as far as Judge Hoffman was concerned, the Mayor's fears of racial violence
(Hoffman); in any event, the evidence that a
substantial portion of the community now
favored reopening the schools enabled Hoffman
to enjoin the City Council from engaging in
any action which might withhold funds or
otherwise interfere with the School Board's
plans to reopen the closed institutions (*Norfolk Virginian-Pilot* 1/28/59).

The speed and impact of this new ruling was
a shocking reversal for the Mayor, doubly so
because it increased the perception that the
Silkstocking crowd had fought him and won.
Even so, the Mayor was not entirely defeated:
He still had two courses of action open, either of which would preserve his status as the
hero of Massive Resistance and advance his
standing within the statewide Byrd Organization. The Defenders were urging him to declare
the closed school buildings as surplus and
quickly sell them to the T.E.F before they
could be reopened by the court (*Norfolk Virginian-Pilot* 1/28/59). The Byrd Organization
was apparently urging him to defy Judge Hoff-

man, continue to withhold the school funds, and appeal the ruling. Either course would risk a contempt of court citation and possible imprisonment, but this was a prospect that the Organization actually relished, and was even then urging upon Governor Almond as well (*Richmond Times-Dispatch* 2/10/80). The sight of a political leader behind bars to preserve the freedom of choice rights of the majority was just what the Organization wanted to promote its Massive Resistance plan as a *cause célebré*: If Duckworth or Almond would but risk personal martyrdom, they would be treated to national media attention, public prayer vigils, certain canonization in the Organization's ranks, and an endless stream of little old ladies, housewives, and mothers bearing baked goods and other wares for their jailed hero (*Norfolk Virginian-Pilot* 6/9/64). On the other hand, there was no guarantee that the Mayor could get a majority vote on the Council if he chose either route: Roy Martin's opposition a week before had been the purest political gamble--a bet that had paid off already in the flurry of following events--and there was every reason to expect additional resistance in the changed political atmosphere that was emerging after the Committee of One Hundred's statement. Finally, his options were limited by the fact that the School Board was ready to open the schools anyway, even if the City Council continued to withhold funds in defiance of the courts: The Board apparently had enough surplus funds, coal, and other supplies remaining to open for a few days even without Council's support (*Norfolk Virginian-Pilot* 1/27/59).

It was these latter considerations--Mayor Duckworth could not risk losing a bitterly split vote on the Council for a point that would be rendered useless anyway by the School Board--that probably weighed heavily in his decision to abandon the struggle. In spite of

the dire warnings of Senator Byrd that his
Organization would be "wiped out" if Virginia
gave in to integration (*Richmond Times-Dispatch* 8/4/74), Massive Resistance was over, at
least in Norfolk. The Mayor bitterly refused
to discuss the matter further, flatly telling
all comers to a historic Council session that
marked the end of his own resistance: "We [the
Council] have been taken out of the school
business [by the court]. Anyone who came here
to talk about schools can go to the School
Board (*Norfolk Virginian-Pilot* 1/30/59)."
Thus, there was no obstacle to the schools
reopening on Monday, February 2 (1959), as the
Board had promised the Court. Duckworth, in
admitting defeat, was doing his best to retain
whatever was left of his old Harmony coalition
in spite of the setback.

If Mayor Duckworth's fall from the heights
of municipal and political power was dizzying,
it was no less dramatic than Governor Almond's
sudden about-face on Massive Resistance. The
Governor, who usually possessed a calm and
rational demeanor, punctuated by both a thorough knowledge and deep appreciation of the
law, was also on occasion given to stentorian
bombast (Dabney 1970, 539). These two facets
of his personality--his keen legal sense and
his equally cutting rhetorical style--had col-
lided. Although Almond had been the studious
legal brains behind legislative efforts to
block integration, he must have known that
this house of cards would one day tumble down.
The Governor's fiery bombast following the
double court orders to reopen the schools--"We
have just begun to fight"--may have also been
partly responsible for Mayor Duckworth's overly repressive reaction. Almond explained in
later years that he was tired, distraught, and
just not thinking clearly when he made "that
damn speech" in defiance of the court orders.
He had meant to assure Virginians that he
would do everything possible to preserve seg-

regation, even though he knew a few schools would have to integrate, but the rumble of his rhetoric got the best of him, and by the time he got to the conclusion, he had falsely led many to think that he was still saving one more legal gambit to preserve Massive Resistance (Dabney 1970, 542-3). It was a much quieter and rational Almond who now stood before a special session of the Virginia General Assembly--only eight days after his rabble rousing rodomontade, and just two days after Judge Hoffman canceled Duckworth's funds-cut-off plan--to inform them that he could not prevent integration in Virginia (*Norfolk Virginian-Pilot* 1/29/59): The best he could do was to minimize the racial mixing that would occur. The Massive Resisters were thunderstruck, and a few even referred to him as "Benedict" Almond (Dabney 1970, 543), especially after he threatened to veto the last-ditch efforts of Mills Godwin and the Southside legislators (*Norfolk Virginian-Pilot* 1/30/59). Instead of legal obfuscation, Almond pressed for a more moderate program to modify tuition grants, repeal compulsory attendance laws, strengthen prohibitions against violence, and establish a commission to recommend additional proposals (Dabney 1970, 543).

With both the Mayor's and the Governor's surrender, Massive Resistance in Virginia was finally dead. There was now no legal obstacle to the schools opening on Monday, February 2 (1959), as the School Board planned. The only stumbling block lay not in the politicians, but in those other individuals who had resisted so massively, and who even now were not prepared to drop the cause. The Mayor's fears of possible racial violence were very real; even in Norfolk there still existed an element of rabble that would stop at nothing to prevent or disrupt school integration. They were, however, unable to rally much support: local newspaper, radio, and television news reporters remained faithful to a private understanding not to publish stories of or lend credence to rumors of racial violence or intimidation that would lead to "another Little Rock." Even a cross-burning across from Norview High and within sight of the black homes in Coronado went unreported (*New York Times* 2/1/59). Behind the scenes there was at least one other hopeful force moving to assure a peaceful resumption of classes: The Silkstocking crowd, relishing their recent reemergence, were not now content to sit back and rest on the laurels of their newspaper advertisement. Besides lending their collective voice quietly to those who were calling for an orderly resumption of classes, Norfolk's business and civic leaders sought a more active role by promoting a "Back to School, Keep It Cool" movement. They turned their efforts to their youthful counterparts in the hierarchy of the school's social and service clubs. The Key Clubs (Kiwanis-sponsored) of the closed high schools purchased billboards and bought newspaper advertisements that pleaded, as their Silkstocking elders had petitioned, with youth and adults alike "that the orderly reopening be completed as smoothly and as quickly as possible so that we may proceed with our immediate objective--to obtain an education (Reif 1960, 15)."

Monday morning, February 2, 1959, would prove to be a crucial test of Silkstocking diplomacy when schools reopened integrated after months of Massive Resistance hysteria. There was a widespread fear among the city's leadership that in spite of all their preliminary precautions, more was still required to signal once and for all the end of Massive Resistance. As the representatives of the nation's leading newspapers, magazines, radio, and television networks poured into Norfolk that final weekend in January, the Silkstocking business establishment began to realize just

how much would be at stake Monday morning. One
single, isolated racial incident, or worse,
one random act of violence, once it had been
flashed around the world in newspaper headlines and television broadcasts, could erase
more than a decade of concentrated effort to
restore the city's once-fallen reputation. Not
since the lusty wartime days of booze, racke-
teering, prostitution, and the sleazy honky-
tonks of East Main Street--already undergoing
demolition--would so many eyes be on the city;
not since the Staylor Raid of 1948 was it so
completely at the mercy of its hoodlum elements.

So much was riding upon peaceful resumption
of classes that the city's leadership dared to
approach Norfolk's most effective proponent of
Massive Resistance for a final symbol of defeat and racial reconciliation. Behind the
scenes that weekend there was one final effort
to arrange instead a visual image that would
ensure both domestic tranquility and Norfolk's
good name. Friends, business associates, civic
leaders, relatives, and even minor political
kingpins descended upon the Mayor, urging him
to make the most difficult decision of his
political career: He must walk, they argued,
with the handful of black students that were
to enroll in the previously all-white schools
in Norview (Darden; Mason). If there was to be
violence or racial incidents, the media were
betting that they would occur at Norview High
School, and indeed the crush of cameramen, reporters, photographers, and correspondents
that would surround Norview on Monday could
well encourage potential neighborhood trouble-
makers--identified in the local vernacular as
"suedes" because of their reputed addiction to
suede shoes (*New York Times* 2/1/59)--to show
off. There was more than just the reputation
of the local toughs, however, that had earmarked Norview as the focal point of Monday
morning's news coverage: The area had been one

of the most fruitful bastions of Massive Resistance sentiment, evidenced by the recent
cross-burning incidents there; the rhetoric of
Norview whites was still salted with vague
references to the bombings and racial strife
that had taken place four years earlier in
nearby Coronado; as a newly annexed territory,
Norview was one of the few areas that did not
owe any allegiance to the calm, deliberative
progress of the Silkstocking reign; and finally, in these largely blue-collar neighborhoods, the official pronouncements of the
business and civic elite probably counted for
less than elsewhere in the city.

The course now urged upon the Mayor by the
delegations that descended upon his private
residence was painted in the most pleasing
colors possible: One quiet, dignified walk up
the school house steps--in sharp contrast to
the tirades of Arkansas' Governor Faubus in
Little Rock--once it had been carefully immor-
talized by the electronic eye of the nation's
media, would do more to promote the city, the
Mayor, and even the Byrd Organization than any
other step he could take. Business leaders
argued that it was the one action that would
help to focus positive national attention upon
the city's cosmopolitan image, the integrity
of its leadership, its spirit of rejuvenation,
and its efforts to attract new industry. Political leaders argued that both the Mayor and
the Organization had the most to lose at the
hands of the local voters if violence marred
the resumption of classes. Further, they im-
plored, that with such a visual event, the
Mayor could upstage Governor Almond's split
with Senator Byrd, and cut short efforts to
unify opponents of Massive Resistance into a
threat to the Organization. Finally, they
urged, this was a ready-made opportunity for
both the Mayor and the city to escape the onus
of school closings--a chance for him to prove
his political resilience, re-establish his

rapport with the rapidly shifting mood of the people, and solidify his base of support in the business community. Unless he took some such action to insure the tranquility of the reopening ceremonies, the mantle of political leadership would pass from him to the School Board, Roy Martin, and other "moderates" who personally supported segregation, but who also had the courage to oppose the final stages of racial retribution associated with Massive Resistance.

No one really knows how close Mayor Duckworth came that weekend to accepting this unusual reversal: On its surface the offer was attractive enough, but, it also involved a good deal of betrayal of principle and admission of guilt. The decision, however, was his and his alone; no other political, civic, or governmental leader could substitute for him and have such impact. Mayor Duckworth, however, would have no part of such a gesture, and no one will ever know whether personal pride, prejudicial animosities, devotion to principle, or more mundane political considerations figured most prominently in his decision. An increase in uniformed police, the heightened visibility of school personnel, and the welcoming gestures of the principal would have to suffice; when school opened on Monday morning, the Mayor was nowhere near the waiting cameras at Norview High.

9

A Second School Crisis

All was calm as Norfolk's closed junior and senior high schools reopened. In spite of the presence of almost one hundred journalists and television cameras, most of them massed outside of Norview High School, there was nothing unusual to report: Stories noted that there were "a few instances of name calling," but that the "windy 26-degree weather discouraged parents from lingering." The *Virginian-Pilot* praised the "display of sanity, poise, and dignity that made a difficult day a notable one." President Eisenhower, who received hourly reports of the progress through a special telephone connection in the federal court house (Hoffman), telegraphed his congratulations to the 63 students who led the "Back to School, Keep It Cool," campaign (*Norfolk Virginian-Pilot* 2/3/59); the *New York Times* viewed the scene as a "turning point for integration (*New York Times* 2/1/59)"; and the televised footage of orderly students reporting to class stood in sharp contrast to events in Little Rock, Mobile, and other points across the South. Norfolk's calm reopening was praised across the nation, and at least a portion of its ugly wartime image had been erased. The *New York Times* ironically, credited "redevelopment and public housing" as factors in pre-

serving "comparatively good race relations."
The paper went on to report that "a number of
handsome new Negro schools have been built
[here] in the last decade," and that: "Norfolk
is distinctive among Southern cities in that
it has a powerful and articulate group of
moderates who balance off the Defenders and
their followers on the school controversy (*New
York Times* 2/1/59)."

Although the *Times* obviously had the Silkstocking Committee of One Hundred in mind, its
appraisal came as something of a shock to the
Committee for Public Schools and others who
had labored without much success during the
five months of closings to provide a counter-
point to the Defenders (Stern; White 1959b);
nevertheless the *Times* was only one of many
publications to note that Norfolk was unique
in that the critical legal action to reopen
the closed schools came from white parents,
and not Black plaintiffs. In reality, the only
really "powerful and articulate" opposition to
Massive Resistance came from Lenoir Chambers,
and the editorial staff of the *Virginian-
Pilot*, who richly deserved the Pulitzer Prize
he received for his efforts to keep the public
schools open.

Other researchers have perpetuated the myth
that "a powerful public school movement organized very quickly" in Norfolk to defeat
Massive Resistance (Crain *et al*. 1968, 231).
In point of fact, the Committee for Public
Schools, the school teachers, and others who
hoped to spark a pro-school movement were
relatively powerless until after the schools
reopened, and the Committee of One Hundred,
who had played almost no role during the controversy, only meant to signal that it was
time to surrender in Norfolk, not signal any
opposition to either Duckworth or the dominant
Byrd Organization (Darden). Duckworth, however, misread their intent, and instead helped
to promote the ragtag elements of opposition

during the school crisis into a full-blown resistance movement a few months later.

Duckworth could have easily retreated with grace and blamed the collapse of Massive Resistance on Governor Almond, as U.S. Senator Harry F. Byrd, Sr. apparently did (*Norfolk Virginian-Pilot* 6/9/64). Certainly the Mayor personally done more to keep Massive Resistance alive than even the staunchest Defender could have expected. Even though Pretlow Darden and others in the Silkstocking establishment tried repeatedly to counsel him to adopt such a course (Darden), Duckworth refused to retreat from the battle lines he had drawn. Norfolk, for all its cosmopolitan image, was still a Southern city, and its voters continued to harbor strong segregationist sentiment. Even as late as the week of January 26-31 (1959), after the court decisions but before the schools reopened, a team of researchers from the University of North Carolina found that almost 80 percent of Norfolk's white residents clung to their support for segregated schools: More than a third still denied the legality of the federal courts to order desegregation, and 40 percent thought the city should resist further. However, only one adult in five thought that continuing segregation was a viable option, and there was almost no sentiment for sacrificing public education to preserve segregated schools (Campbell *et al*. 1960, 56-61). It was precisely this last sentiment that Duckworth now misread.

In commenting on the reopening of schools in Norfolk, the *New York Times* indicated that although a major victory for public education had been won, this was a "Gettysburg," a turning point that signaled a retreat, and not an "Appomattox," or final surrender of the Massive Resistance forces (*New York Times* 2/8/59). Duckworth and the Byrd Organization seemed bent upon continuing the fight, even though the tide of war had turned against them. Almost before the national press departed the city, Mayor Duckworth fired the first salvo in what was to be a continuing attack against the School Board and its efforts to continue public education in the city. At a meeting with the Board, the Mayor warned that the City Council was going to "cut the devil out of the 1960 [school] budget," and as to prospects for any more funds for school construction, "it will take an act of Congress to get it out of us." Duckworth then disclosed a plan to build a number of three-room-school houses, each accommodating 90 pupils in grades one through three, in the eastern half of the city. In commenting on the proposal, the *Virginian-Pilot* editorialized that: "While the plan apparently would slow down desegregation of the first, second, and third grades through the creation of smaller school districts, councilmen stressed it was prompted by the need for inexpensive schools (*Norfolk Virginian-Pilot* 2/22/59)." Although the educational drawbacks were evident, the School Board found itself giving serious scrutiny to the Council's minischool proposal. Still, it refused to be stampeded into adopting this flawed approach, especially when it held such dire long-term consequences. A biracial task force appointed to study the proposal found instead that buildings with 16 to 20 classrooms were the "ideal" size for a three-grade primary school (Campbell 1959). The committee nevertheless approved of the idea of using smaller schools "strategically located to relieve crowding" in several areas of the city, and then proceeded to list nine such areas (Lindenwood, West, Clay, Goode, Carey, Titus, Jackson, Bowling Park, and Young Park) already served by small black schools (*Norfolk Virginian-Pilot* 3/13/59). In the end, however, the School Board was forced to bow to the pressures of the Council, and five "vest-

pocket" schools were built for whites during
the next year: East Ocean View, Easton, Fairlawn, Pretty Lake, and Poplar Halls (Brewbaker
5/21/59; 5/29/59) (see Figures 8 and 9). The
Board also included an "emergency ordinance"
condemning a 2.5-acre site in the Coronado
area, "a predominantly Negro section," for six
demountable classroom units. Reporter Luther
Carter noted that:

> The opening of the Coronado school will
> have the effect of reducing, if not en-
> tirely eliminating, the number of poten-
> tially qualified Negro applicants in
> Coronado for Norview Elementary . . . The
> proximity of the Coronado schools [Oak-
> wood and Coronado] would give the School
> Board a valid reason to assign Coronado
> children there even should they meet the
> academic and other standards for a nearer
> white school. . . . [The Coronado school]
> will represent a modification of the City
> Council's "little red school house"
> [plan]. [It] . . . would not have a cafe-
> teria, auditorium, playgrounds, and cer-
> tain other facilities which have been
> incorporated in larger elementary schools
> (*Norfolk Virginian-Pilot* 7/8/59).

Black leaders were understandably upset by the
proposal, and complained that the new school
would be both "educationally unsound" and an
"obvious attempt to circumvent" the courts.
The School Board attempted to reassure the
black leaders that the "same facilities will
be lacking at some new white schools now being
built." They explained that the Board did not
want to build a large, expensive school that
might be in the path of an interstate highway
then under consideration, but a cafeteria, an
auditorium, and additional classrooms would be
added to the Rosemont combination elementary
and junior high school for blacks in the same

Figure 8
New School Buildings, 1959

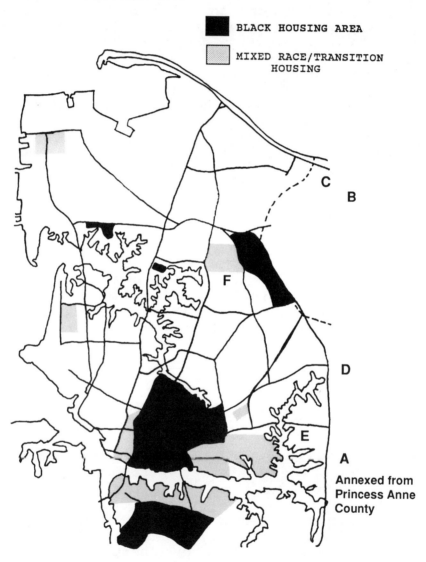

A Easton Elementary   D Fairlawn Elementary
B East Ocean View Elem.   E Poplar Halls Elementary
C Pretty Lake Elementary   F Coronado Elementary

Figure 9
School Construction Statistics, 1952-1959

Year	School	Square Feet	Acreage	Race
1952	Calcott Elementary	58,254 sq.ft.	12.0	White
1952	Lakewood Elementary	58,254 sq.ft.	12.0	White
1953	Bowling Park Elem.	58,254 sq.ft.	12.3	Black
1953	Lindenwood Elem.	40,635 sq.ft.	9.5	Black
1953	Diggs Park Elem.	44,400 sq.ft.	10.6	Black
1954	Young Park Elem.	50,540 sq.ft.	8.0	Black
1955	Suburban Park Elem.	48,919 sq.ft.	15.0	White
1956	Northside Jr. High	114,375 sq.ft.	14.5	White
1956	Oceanair Elementary	57,242 sq.ft.	17.7	White
1957	Lansdale Elementary	53,100 sq.ft.	18.7	White
1957	Sherwood Forest Elem.	53,100 sq.ft.	13.3	White
1958	Rosemont Elem./Jr.	40,000 sq.ft.*	13.0*	Black
1959	Coronado Elementary	7,500 sq.ft.	2.2	Black
1959	East Ocean View Elem.	10,790 sq.ft.*	1.2	White
1959	Pretty Lake Elem.	10,790 sq.ft.*	1.2*	White
1959	Poplar Halls Elem.	22,000 sq.ft.*	17.8	White
1959	Easton Elementary	12,000 sq.ft.*	11.7	White
1959	Fairlawn Elementary	22,000 sq.ft.*	16.4	White

* estimate of size and area at time of construction;
  does not reflect later additions and expansions.

237

area (*Norfolk Virginian-Pilot* 7/21/59). The
city's black leaders were not impressed by
this defense, and promptly filed suit in federal court seeking to enjoin what they called
"makeshift schools . . . constructed for the
purpose of pursuing the policy of racially
segregated schools (*Norfolk Ledger-Dispatch*
8/20/59)."

While it was fighting this battle over what
the papers were calling the Mayor's "little
red schoolhouse" proposal, the School Board
also had to worry that Duckworth would make
good on his promise to "cut the devil" out of
the rest of Norfolk's public school program.
Since school districts in Virginia are dependent upon their municipal government for financial support, the School Board lacked any taxing or funding power of its own. When the City
Manager announced his spending priorities for
the up-coming fiscal year, he proposed a re-
duction of more than five percent in school
funds. Even a cut of this magnitude was not
enough to satisfy the Mayor, and the Council
proceeded to remove additional funds (*Norfolk
Virginian-Pilot* 5/13/59). By the time the budget was passes, the School Board found that
local funding for public schools had dropped
by 13.4 percent from the previous year. The
Virginian-Pilot indicated that the Mayor hoped
to eliminate any possibility that the Board
would be able to give raises to the teachers
who had helped to sabotage Massive Resistance
(*Norfolk Virginian-Pilot* 10/25/59). Moreover,
the effect of this cutback fell disproportionately upon blacks, since most whites could
afford to supplement the education of their
children or send them to private schools with
the support of the state's substantial tuition
grants. Thus Duckworth was finding that he
could skillfully use his powers of the purse
to keep Massive Resistance alive by keeping
the white schools small enough to be immune
from integration or else so overcrowded and

unattractive that blacks would resist further efforts to desegregate.

Not only did the Board have to worry about loss of funding support and the pressure to build small, inadequate, but integration-proof (under the court standards of the day) school houses, it also found that the City Council was reneging on its promise to build the badly needed secondary schools that had already been promised. Lansdale Junior High, which had been approved by the Council two-and-a-half years earlier, completely designed, and accepted by the state (*Norfolk Virginian-Pilot* 6/6/58), was never built; Lakewood Junior High suffered a similar fate. Although there were problems with the suitability of the sites at both locations, both schools had been promised for the 1959-1960 school year. The *Virginian-Pilot* intimated that the delay was linked to other, more political concerns: "The State Board of Education approved the plans in the fall of 1957, but the project[s] failed to move forward. . . . Months went by, and nothing happened. It finally became apparent that the Council was waiting to see the outcome of the impending desegregation crisis (*Norfolk Virginian-Pilot* 8/8/59)." Additional annexation and the impact of the redevelopment projects closer in town was putting a tremendous burden on the schools in the eastern half of the city (*Norfolk Virginian-Pilot* 1/3/58). A disastrous annexation decision--Norfolk had sought 33 square miles in the western portion of old Princess Anne County, but instead had ended up with only 13, a large part of which were the airport and water-system lakes which it already owned--was exacerbating the problem. Norfolk was stuck with the students, but none of the schools which served them, and this urgent need was in part responsible for the School Board's acceptance of the "vest pocket" schools being erected (Martin). The fact that the School Board would be facing the school

year with reduced funds, badly overcrowded
schools (*Norfolk Virginian-Pilot* 11/11/59),
and nothing but inadequate minischools in the
works was prompting a second school crisis,
and one in which the Board and the pro-school
forces were again pitted against the Mayor and
the City Council.

Public schools, or at least the quality of
public education in Norfolk, were again under
political attack, and it seemed clear that the
Mayor had not given up the hope of making Massive Resistance work in Norfolk. The Council,
which had appealed its earlier reverses in
federal court, indicated its intention to continue the earlier fight to cut off the funds
to both black and white secondary schools
(*Norfolk Virginian-Pilot* 5/2/59). The School
Board was apparently unwilling to back the
Council on this and other anti-education measures, because the Mayor and the city's Byrd
Organization legislators, began to advance a
bill that would expand the number of positions
on the Board from six to seven members, and
shorten the terms of service from three to two
years. The bill would have allowed the Council
to replace all six of the Board members (*Norfolk Virginian-Pilot* 4/23/ 59) who had worked
so diligently to save public schools. Board
member Francis Crenshaw summed up the politics
of the situation:

> At the present time, I believe there is
> a difference of opinion between members
> of the school board and the council as to
> [the] proper handling of the integration
> problem. . . . The legislation pending in
> Richmond will . . . bring the board more
> closely under councilmanic control. I
> know of no other reason for adding a sev-
> enth member . . . nor can I otherwise
> account for a reduction in the term of
> office from three to two years (*Norfolk
> Virginian-Pilot* 4/22/59).

Fortunately this new school crisis found a
political outlet before public education was
irreparably damaged. It was in response to
public opposition to the effort to fire the
School Board that Mayor Duckworth let his
guard slip in public enough to threaten his
Massive Resistance coalition. When an officer
of the Norfolk Committee for Public Schools
(Dorothy Attaway) inquired whether it was the
intent of the Council to reappoint the incumbent members of the School Board if the bill
passed, Mayor Duckworth replied, "I don't
think it's any of your business (*Norfolk Virginian-Pilot* 4/22/59)." Although in retrospect
the infraction does not seem severe, the pro-
school forces immediately seized upon the
incident as a new *cause célèbre* of municipal
reform. A flurry of letters to the editor, as
well as the editors themselves, questioned
whether the public had a right to know, and
whether such "despotic" behavior was proper
for a "public servant." Pro-school advocates
launched a massive campaign to isolate the
Mayor, his spirited temper, and his legendary
disregard for public participation (*Norfolk
Virginian-Pilot* 4/24-7/59), by emblazoning the
slogan "none of your business" on match book
covers, key chains, and other tokens. Even so,
the pro-school forces probably could not have
made the issue stick had not the timing of the
outburst coincided perfectly with the upcoming
Democratic Primary for the state legislature.
Two seats were open because of the retirement
of incumbents; the Byrd/Prieur Organization,
the pro-school forces, and the Defenders of
State Sovereignty and Individual Liberties all
had candidates in the race. In addition, an
incumbent state senator (Edward L. Breeden)
was under attack by a coalition of Defenders
and the most conservative elements of the
Organization because he had backed away from
last-ditch efforts to save Massive Resistance
(*Norfolk Virginian-Pilot* 4/15/59). The elec-

tion hinged entirely on the Massive Resistance
issue, and all sides posed the question of
their election based upon their view of public
education (*Norfolk Virginian-Pilot* 7/15/59).
On election day, the pro-school group claimed
total victory, winning both the disputed house
and senate seats (*Norfolk Virginian-Pilot*
7/19/59); in doing so, they launched the political career of Henry Howell and a force of
progressivism that would be a major player in
city and state politics for several decades.
The force included an alliance with the city's
black voters, who up to that point had voted
solidly Republican (*Norfolk Virginian-Pilot*
10/30/59). The Defenders were crushed, and
never appeared in Norfolk again as a major
political power.

With champions in elected office for the
first time, the pro-school forces found that
their cause quickly took on a more authorita-
tive air. The antischool policies of the Mayor
and the City Council soon came under attack
from this new quarter (*Norfolk Ledger-Dispatch*
11/23/59), and it was not long before the Organization was in full retreat before a growing coalition that was emerging between the
"little people" of the pro-school movement,
the city's black leaders, and the mainstream
of its business community (*Norfolk Virginian-
Pilot* 10/25/59; 12/8/59). Shortly thereafter,
Prieur Organization stalwart George Abbott, a
seventeen-year veteran of the Council, resigned from office and was quickly replaced by
School Board Chairman Paul Schweitzer. Observers saw the move as an attempt to create a new
"Harmony Ticket" with the business establishment, or at least an effort to "cut the ground
from under" the emerging pro-school coalition
(*Norfolk Ledger-Dispatch* 2/16/60). In spite of
this move, however, the pro-school forces, now
under the leadership of Henry Howell (*Norfolk
Ledger-Dispatch* 6/15/60), endorsed Schweitzer
(*Norfolk Ledger-Dispatch* 6/10/60) and advanced

two business candidates of its own, both of whom had sought to re-open the schools during the School Crisis. Although only the candidacy of Sam Barfield was successful, the victory was seen as a direct rebuff to Duckworth, his "dictatorial rule," the Council's actions in the school crisis, and the secrecy of the process of city planning and governmental decision-making (*Norfolk Ledger-Dispatch* 6/15/60). Fred Duckworth declined to seek re-election in the next race, and the office of Mayor was turned over to Roy Martin, the one councilman who had dared to break with the Organization in order to continue public education in the city.

Norfolk had thus come full circle, and although the process of government became more contentious as decision-making came back into public view, the primacy of councilmanic support for public education was never again at issue; the biracial coalition of pro-school advocates, the Silkstocking business elite, and the city's black leadership that emerged to promote educational issues following the crisis strengthened and matured into the dominant political force for the next three decades. Not even the shift to a ward system of politics in 1992 could shake the grasp of this coalition. The election as mayor of Dr. Mason Andrews, the one member of the Norfolk Committee for Public Schools who remained anonymous so that he could better court the Silkstocking crowd, is proof that the lessons, the alliances, and the commitment to public education advanced during the Norfolk school crisis continue to provide vision, direction, and leadership for the city. Thus the intensity of Norfolk's experience with the forces of prejudice in the 1950s has been the glue that has bound its citizens together in what has been an arduous climb back to a point where they can at last look back with pride at the record of their united accomplishment.

10

Conclusion

Although the United States Supreme Court's decision in the *Brown v. Board of Education* cases sent shock waves of protest across most of the South, only the extent of the decree actually came as a surprise those who were charged with the planning and leadership of Southern cities. That some sort of decision from the Court overruling a portion of the South's elaborate system of segregated education was a foregone conclusion among many in leadership roles; clearly the "separate but equal" facilities maintained by communities, particularly those in rural areas, were so far from equivalent that only the most callous court could disregard the distinction. Moreover, desegregation had already begun in the nation's military, transportation, public accommodation, and recreational facilities, either through administrative action or legal intervention, and it was hard to imagine that a nation that had so recently fought repression overseas would allow its own schools to remain as the last bastion of racial subjugation at home. The main thesis of this work is that the individuals charged with the leadership and management of Southern cities had ample time, plenty of opportunity, and strong

motivation to plan for the demise of school
segregation in their community, that this
planning process began well before the *Brown
v. Board of Education* cases were ever decided,
and that it grew increasingly intense as the
prospect of court-ordered integration became a
reality. Moreover, this research found that
these leaders took deliberate steps to use the
powers at their disposal, including both the
more obvious control over school-plant planning, educational administration, and student
attendance, as well as the more subtle power
over land-use planning and redevelopment activities, to delay court-ordered school desegregation in their communities. The study
focuses on the link between school desegregation and urban renewal activities in one community, Norfolk, Virginia, that most nearly
fit the hypothesized variables.

Since 1938 the National Association for the
Advancement of Colored People (N.A.A.C.P.) had
advanced a withering legal attack upon the peculiar practices that provided the basis for
maintaining segregated schools. Although this
assault was aimed first at discrimination in
graduate education, their intent was to amass
an irrefutable body of precedent that would
lead the U.S. Supreme Court to a decision
striking down once and for all the logic that
separate schools could be equal in America.
For this reason, knowledgeable Southerners
knew that the Supreme Court would have to
follow these same precedents if it were faced
with similar circumstances in public schools,
that is, the absence of a facility for blacks,
separate facilities for blacks that were inadequate or inferior, or instances of separate
and degrading treatment of black students.
Four of the five cases accepted by the Court
in its 1952 session were designed to do precisely that. In the title case, *Brown v. Board
of Education*, the Court was presented with the
appeal of a black elementary student who lived

in a mixed-race area. Although Topeka had integrated its secondary schools, Linda Brown
was forced to ride a bus across town to the
black elementary school, while whites in her
area walked to school. The N.A.A.C.P. contended that in light of earlier precedents,
such separate treatment was degrading, and
thus contrary to constitutional guarantees of
equal treatment. Although most Southern leaders expected to lose the Prince Edward County,
Virginia (no equal facilities), Clarendon,
South Carolina (unequal facilities), and Delaware (unequal treatment) cases, where the
quantifiable differences between black and
white schools could be remedied short of desegregation, the defeat in *Brown* proved to be
the most troublesome, since it could only be
remediated by school integration. Even if the
South were to build literally hundreds of new
and largely unneeded schools, it still might
have to integrate some buildings in order to
comply with the *Brown* dictate that similarly
situated students not receive separate treatment merely to maintain racial separation.
Nevertheless, the *Brown* precedent, because it
focused on the long crosstown bus ride, cut to
the core of what many Southerners, both black
and white, felt was most unjust about the separate but equal system of education then in
use (Darden; Crenshaw).

The most immediate effect of the *Brown* decision was to strike down the laws requiring
segregated schools (i.e., *de jure* segregation)
in seventeen states (Texas, Oklahoma, Alabama,
Missouri, Arkansas, Louisiana, Mississippi,
South Carolina, Georgia, Florida, Tennessee,
North Carolina, Kentucky, Virginia, Maryland,
West Virginia, and Delaware) and permitting
them in four others (Kansas, Arizona, New
Mexico, and Wyoming) (*Southern School News*
9/3/54). Although the focus of the decisions
was upon state laws requiring segregation, the
impact would be felt more directly in the lo-

cal schools of thousands of communities across
the Deep South and border states of the Con-
federacy. The decision, however, left in tact
the kind of separate-race schools found in
cities of the North, West, and Midwest, where
segregation, although not absolute, was due to
choice of neighborhood, that is, *de facto* segregation. Thus, substantially equal schools
that served separate race neighborhoods were
still permitted by the Court; only the particular circumstance presented by Linda Brown, a
black living closer to a white school than a
black one, was first found unconstitutional.

For this reason, most communities could
comply with the dictates of the Supreme Court
with only a minimum of integration, and most
schools could continue as essentially single
race schools, except in the few areas of each
city where there were mixed race neighborhoods, transition areas, or where two racially
distinct areas would have to be served by the
same school. Even then, Southern cities could
copy the elaborate system of gerrymandered
districts, transfer policies, "schools of
choice,"inschool segregation by tracking,
staggered enrollment, and other quasi-legal
devices used elsewhere to avoid large-scale
integration and keep whites from attending
predominantly black schools (Williams and Ryan
1954, 45, 57, 102, 240-2, 443). This careful
distinction between continued segregation by
place of residence and court-ordered integration was one reason that the *Brown* decree was
met with only mild reaction in most areas of
the border states where there was a relatively
small black population, concentrated in a
large, central section of the downtown area,
and only occasionally found in small settlements in other parts of the city. This distinction meant that the Northern model of *de
facto* segregation could be adopted without
undue hardship, except in those few Southern
cities with large concentrations of black pop-

ulations, a history of racial strife, or vast
social class distinctions between their black
and white citizens (Williams and Ryan 1954,
40, 80-110).

One finding of this research is that local
officials responded to the threat of court-
ordered desegregation in the same manner as
their counterparts in state capitals, and used
every means at their disposal to delay, or defuse, the impact of school desegregation in
their community. Clearly they were as cognizant of the threat posed by desegregation as
their colleagues in the state legislatures--
N.A.A.C.P. legal defense team lawyers began
filing court challenges all across the nation
shortly after *Brown*--and the local electorate
was making the same kinds of demands as the
state-wide constituencies. And certainly local
officials were as adept as their brethren in
the legislatures in using the powers at their
disposal to frustrate and circumvent the dictates of the courts. Even so, however, most of
the case studies of local school desegregation
controversies in the South do not begin until
almost a decade or two later. The record of
school desegregation both before the *Brown*
decision and between the decree and its implementation is so blank that one major history
of school desegregation covers the entire
period between 1954 and 1962 in less than a
page (Metcalf 1983, 3); another accomplishes
it in six (Stephan and Feagin 1980, 3-9). What
happened in the intervening years has been
largely unknown, although Norfolk appears to
be representative of the overall process used
by Southern cities to deliberately move the
segregated status of their school systems from
de jure to *de facto*, a pattern which seems to
have continued well into the 1960s.

Before the threat of the N.A.A.C.P. challenges became apparent, all planning in the
South, and indeed much of the rest of the
nation, appears to have been racially based

(see Williams and Ryan 1954). In fact, it was
not until 1956, several years after *Brown*,
that courts began to strike down the practice
of dividing communities into separate race
housing zones (*Heywood v. P.H.A.* 1956, 347).
Before that time, Norfolk and most of the rest
of the South appear to have used an elaborate
system of computing the percentage of property
taxes paid by each race, and then using these
figures as determinants of how the public
works budgets would be spent. The result was
that, except for those few areas where blacks
had moved into middle-class housing formerly
occupied by whites, there were few, if any,
public amenities provided for black neighborhoods: no sidewalks, streetlights, gutters,
curbs, parks, playgrounds, or recreation areas
(*Norfolk Virginian-Pilot* 8/31/54). This lack
of services may actually have made the push to
expand into white housing areas both more attractive and more practical than waiting for
the extensive public improvements necessary to
bring most black neighborhoods up to similar
levels of service.

Because, for the most part, Norfolk's history during the 1950s is so very ordinary, it
may be used to typify the forces and concerns
that faced other areas in the urban South.
Certainly the scale of its development activity and the desperation of its school-closing
crisis make it well suited for a case study of
the interplay between the two. Although the
story of school desegregation and urban renewal in Norfolk may be more compelling than
in most communities, it is not thought to be
unique. There is good reason to believe that
what occurred in Norfolk on such a grand scale
could also be found in more subtle forms in
hundreds of other cities across the nation.
Norfolk's reaction to the threat of school
desegregation in the 1950s was not unique,
and, in fact, was so typical that it may well
serve as a model of what occurred elsewhere.

Neither is it unusual that the powers of urban renewal came to be employed during this era to achieve more political than purely economic ends--that, too, is a pattern that has been well documented elsewhere (Anderson 1964; Bellush and Hausknecht 1967). Only the scope, and not the direction, of Norfolk's response is larger and more dramatic than elsewhere. Indeed, the very magnitude of this reaction makes the story in Norfolk so exemplary of three distinct stages, all of which occurred well before the traditional starting date of desegregation studies, that are felt to characterize this response:

1. *An Attempt to Make Separate Facilities "Equal," 1950-1955*. Like their counter-parts across most of the nation, leaders in Norfolk were aware that the system of "separate but equal" schools for blacks and whites, at least as it existed in many parts of the rural South, could not long endure a withering legal challenge in the postwar era. Partly because of the overwhelming presence of the military, which had been integrated since 1948, they could see that the old barriers of segregation were falling. As part of a larger mandate to reform every phase of city administration, the People's Move-ment of 1946 deliberately set about the task to equalize both the facilities and the operation of its dual public school system. Writing in February, 1957, Judge Walter Hoffman commented on the success of this effort:

> The sum and substance of the School Superintendent's evidence is that the City of Norfolk has substan-tially complied with the "separate but equal" doctrine, which was ap-plicable prior to the decision in

Brown v. Board of Education. The
City of Norfolk is to be commended
for its rapid strides in bringing
about an equalization in physical
equipment, curriculum, teacher
load, and teachers' salaries. If
the "separate but equal" doctrine
were now in existence, there would
be no grounds for relief to be afforded these plaintiffs (*Beckett v.
Norfolk* 1957).

The progress in Norfolk caught the attention of other Southern leaders: writing
in *Look* magazine, U.S. Senator Sam Ervin
(D-N.C.), later of Watergate fame, commented that new schools for blacks, like
Young Park Elementary in Norfolk, gave
testimony to the South's effort to resolve the disparities of segregation "in
its own way (Ervin 1956, 32-33)." Between
1950 and 1955 Norfolk completed four new
elementary schools for blacks planned
during the People's reform era (Young
Park, Bowling Park, Lindenwood, and Diggs
Park), three of which were built with
federal redevelopment funds, and transferred a newly constructed junior high
(Jacox) to the black school system. In
addition, it completed a major building
program to modernize most of the aging
black facilities with new classroom
wings, libraries, cafeterias, audito-
riums, and other badly needed improvements. Teacher salaries had been equal-
ized in 1941 as a result of a lawsuit
(Rorer 1968, 69), and by 1951, Norfolk
was reporting that it spent more to edu-
cate its black children than its white,
due to the fact that black teachers had
more seniority and degrees than their
white counterparts.

Thus, the local record of attention to the fiscal and physical aspects of making separate-race schools more equal is in full keeping with efforts all across the South to maintain segregation in a more equitable setting. While the *Brown* cases were under consideration, most of the states where schools were segregated by law (*de jure*) began a deliberate effort to upgrade black schools, provide additional funding resources, equalize teacher salaries, and otherwise preserve segregation "on a voluntary basis (Workman 1957, 92)." During this same era, Norfolk made similar attempts to build other new facilities for blacks and to bring public services in black neighborhoods more into line with those that existed for whites. This effort, however, may have been more of an outgrowth of the People's reform movement than an indicator of a national trend. Thus when the Norfolk Redevelopment and Housing Authority acquired title to military housing projects in the postwar era, it quickly moved to turn a large percentage of these into public housing units for blacks, partly as a way to ease the crush of individuals crowding into traditional black neighborhoods. N.R.H.A. Project One, in addition to building new schools for blacks, also provided modern streets, parks, playgrounds, sidewalks, streetlights, curbs, gutters, and other public services that were almost non-existent in most black areas.

2. *A Transition Period, 1955-1956: from Calm to Hostility.* A confrontation over school desegregation was not necessarily inevitable; the initial announcement of the Supreme Court's decision outlawing separate-race schools was grreted calmly by most Southern leaders. Indeed, they had

expected some such determination. Only
the reversal of the long-standing legal
tradition under attack in the title case,
Brown v. Board of Education, really
caused much consternation. If federal
courts followed the letter of the decision in *Brown*, as it became increasingly
obvious they would, then it meant that
traditional school attendance patterns in
the South would have to be revised so
that every child would attend the school
closest to his or her home. This doctrine
of proximity represented a much greater
threat to segregated schools in the South
than in the rest of the country, for it
meant that not only would blacks be admitted in fairly large numbers to formerly white schools--a situation that was
rare enough elsewhere--in many Southern
communities, because of the high percentage of blacks, whites would have to attend nearby black schools, a circumstance
not found anywhere else in the world
(Williams and Ryan 1954). Part of the
reason for the initial calm of most
Southern leaders was the feeling that
their efforts to achieve equal school
facilities had been successful, and that
"voluntary" segregation could continue.
It was only when litigation was initiated
in their own community, and they realized
the problems posed by the doctrine of
proximity, that there was first panic,
and then wholesale opposition to the
Court.

Norfolk in 1950, like Orlando (Abbott
1981, 93), Charleston, Washington, New
Orleans, Baltimore, and a number of other
older, more established Southern cities,
had in addition to a large central slum,
a half-dozen or so other black housing
areas scattered around town; newer Southern cities, those that boomed after the

Civil War (i.e., Atlanta, Birmingham,
Memphis, and Augusta) were more like
their Northern and midwestern counterparts in that blacks were concentrated
almost exclusively in a single downtown
"ghetto." The newer cities could thus
adopt the Northern model of *de facto*
segregation without undue hardship; it
was only in the older Southern cities,
where the black population was more dispersed, that the doctrine of proximity
meant that large scale integration would
be required. Karl and Alma Taueber surmised that the "backyard" or "alley-
dwelling" type of housing arrangement
found in most older Southern cities, like
Norfolk, was due to the fact that almost
every white middle-class neighborhood had
its own black residential area nearby
which served as a source of domestic
laborers (Taueber and Taueber 1965, 23,
48). Residential integration in Norfolk
may have been even more pronounced than
elsewhere, because Navy housing, desegregated since 1948, presented additional
pockets of black population in former
white areas. Moreover, the fact that
blacks were spread across the city meant
that there were transition areas, blocks
where housing was shifting from white to
black, in a number of neighborhoods; it
was these areas that posed the greatest
threat to efforts to preserve segregated
schools on a "voluntary" basis.

The calm reaction of the School Board
in Norfolk to the *Brown v. Board of Education* decision was praised as a model
for the rest of the South. The Board was
confidant that the schools could be desegregated with a "minimum of integration"--"so little you'd hardly notice it
(Norfolk Virginian-Pilot 5/18/54)"--with-
out major disruption or problem. Catholic

schools, including Norfolk Catholic High, had been desegregated without incident at the start of the 1954-1955 school year (*Southern School News* 10/1/54), and the Board felt that the same results could be achieved in the public schools. Not until they actually faced desegregation litigation did the city's leaders realize the explosive potential of the issue. Politics and events quickly overtook this initial calmness: Virginia's Governor (Thomas Stanley) and many of the state's urban political leaders at first expressed sentiments that paralleled those of the Norfolk School Board, but the ferocity of the resistance building in the rural Southside counties that formed the core of the Byrd Organization's voting strength soon forced a retreat from moderation. Hostility to school segregation was fed by the fact that the city's bus system, state park, and other recreation facilities had desegregated under either court mandate or the threat of litigation. The change is most apparent in the sentiments of the city's legislative delegation, which at first supported the Board, but by 1956 was in full retreat as it faced opposition from the Defenders of State Sovereignty and Individual Liberty, Virginia's well-organized, and for the most part, well-heeled, staunchly segregationist, pressure group.

The School Board's calm, "wait and see" attitude soon gave way to a quiet reappraisal of its own building effort: Additions scheduled for black schools were delayed, and the Board began to evaluate the locations of proposed buildings in light of the critical issue of residential proximity. Plans to replace the aging Lafayette School were scrapped, as were at least four prospective sites for a badly needed (white) junior high. Some of these were rejected because they were too close to black neighborhoods to avoid desegregation under the *Brown* precedent, but the issue was clouded by the fact that Norfolk had also just annexed new areas where new facilities were also required. A similar situation appears to have existed in other aspects of municipal planning and development. Two major projects, the Cultural Center and Waterfront Quay, initiated during the waning days of the People's administration, were put on hold and finally discarded as the new leaders quietly assessed the impact of desegregation. It may well have been that with the prospect of political crisis facing Norfolk, its leaders were reluctant to commit precious funding for business development projects when the stability of its schools and neighborhoods was threatened.

The School Board found itself increasingly isolated in both spirit and approach from the rest of Norfolk's political leaders. Public reaction to the possibility of school desegregation was stiffening, partly because the city was finding that it would not be given much of a transition period to shift from segregated to desegregated schools. Any hope that local blacks would be content with newly improved facilities was quickly dashed: The N.A.A.C.P. filed a petition seeking desegregated schools shortly after the *Brown* decision was rendered, and once its administrative remedies were exhausted, proceeded directly to federal court. U.S. District Judge Walter Hoffman was also not inclined to grant the sort of delay customary elsewhere in the South, and was preparing to order several elementary schools desegregated in 1957,

an event that would have put Norfolk on
the same collision course as Little Rock.
The reaction in Norfolk was much like
that in other parts of the South (*Southern School News* 1/6/55), and indeed much
of the rest of the nation (Williams and
Ryan 1954, 237): When legal challenges to
segregation began to emerge in their own
community, white leaders tended to blame
this "interference" on the work of "outsiders," and failed to see it as a legitimate expression of local black hostility
to segregation. At first the N.A.A.C.P.
bore the brunt of these attacks, and all
across the South state legislatures focused their wrath through anti-N.A.A.C.P.
laws designed to intimidate its membership. The reaction of the white community
to the N.A.A.C.P. spilled over into other
community activities, and Norfolkians,
just like others in areas thought to be
racially moderate, had their own experience with hate mail, racist literature,
and racial turmoil. Events were particularly intense in Coronado, a formerly
white section of the city where the color
line had been successfully breached amid
the threat of firebombs, vandalism, and
hostile mobs. The crisis of housing in
the black community, in part exacerbated
by redevelopment activity, was forcing
racial change in a few other neighborhoods as well. Coronado was but one symp-
tom of the problem; similar hostilities
were evident in the Brambleton and Berkley sections of the city, both of which
by the mid-1950s had nearly completed
their transition to predominately black
housing areas, and in the Atlantic City,
Lamberts Point, and Broad Creek areas on
the fringe of the downtown section, which
were just beginning to tip. Just as in
Coronado, efforts by the black community

to develop new homes in the Broad Creek
Shores subdivision were met with strong
opposition from whites in the surrounding
areas. In fact, the pattern of housing in
Norfolk and older Southern cities, where
whites and blacks lived in greater proximity to one another, may have been in
part responsible for some of the growing
animosity between the races.

By 1956 race relations in the city,
which had been at their highest peak a
few years earlier, had deteriorated badly. No longer were blacks consulted on
major planning or development initiatives, and even when controversies arose,
like that faced in the Broad Creek Shores
development, black leaders had so few
contacts in city government that they had
to turn to the banking and financial
community for help. One black leader
characterized the situation: "In Norfolk,
there are no relations between the races
(*Norfolk Virginian-Pilot* 6/15/58)." The
School Board, too, found itself just as
isolated. In spite of the strong personal
commitment of its members to continue
public education in Norfolk at all cost,
they saw that state and local political
leaders were more than willing to let
public schools evolve into some sort of
state-sponsored private educational
system in order to preserve segregation.
Although its members had been willing to
do their part in carefully planning the
location of new facilities, increasingly
the School Board was being called upon to
go even farther in holding the line
against desegregation. As members of the
middle class, all of whom had benefitted
enormously from public education, the
Norfolk School Board, like hundreds of
others across the South, was not willing
to participate in the demise of public

education in the city. Partly because
they recognized this difference, political leaders in Virginia and a half-dozen
other Southern states moved to take from
the local boards a certain amount of the
administrative powers necessary to maintain public schools. Instead they created
a melange of state pupil-placement agencies designed to "interpose" the authority of the states between black litigants
and local school boards (*Southern School
News* 2/57).

Thus, by 1956, the School Board and
political leaders in Norfolk found themselves in the midst of a firestorm of
public unrest. The community seemed headed towards court-ordered desegregation of
its public schools, yet Virginia's political leaders were indicating that they
would not permit even the most minimal
form of integration. Also, public opposition to the courts had, by this time,
reached a fever pitch. Neither situation
was unique to Norfolk, although the particular circumstance of its dispersed
black population may have leant an extra
air of urgency to its deliberations.
Since the established political order
cannot long endure this level of public
unrest, the leadership in Norfolk, and
indeed much of the rest of the South,
felt obligated to take every legal step
possible to delay the eventuality of desegregated schools; in doing so, they
were following the lead of their counterparts in Congress and the state legislatures who were beginning to move beyond
rhetoric to open defiance.

3. *Overt Attempts to Move from De Jure to De
   Facto Segregation, 1956-1960.* The doctrine of "interposition" that began to
   emerge in the rhetoric of the politicians

found its outlet in a host of special
state laws designed to interpose the authority of the state between the federal
courts and local school officials. Most
of these laws dealt with pupil placement,
student transfer policies, attendance
(McCauley 1957, 132), and financial control of the schools, but it is just as
logical to assume that local officials
followed these same legislative trends in
their own enactments. Gradually the realization began to dawn on municipal officials that, because public education
was much more a community than even a
state responsibility, the powers of local
school boards and city councils to manipulate public school policies were even
greater than those of the state government. By extending the interposition logic already being advanced by numerous
state leaders, local officials discovered
that their own inherent powers to assign
pupils, rule on transfer applications,
build schools, utilize space, draw attendance zones, and otherwise administer
the day to day operations of the public
schools could be judiciously applied to
preventing, or at least delaying, the
eventuality of court-ordered desegregation. Norfolk officials quickly seized
on these powers and began to take the
drastic steps that would be necessary to
delay desegregation by closing threatened
schools, demolishing mixed-race neighborhoods, isolating pockets of black population, and otherwise replacing the elaborate system of *de jure* segregation with
the type of single-race schools zones already approved by the courts in northern
and midwestern cities. Indeed, it is both
the speed and the extent of the interposition activities in Norfolk that makes
these events so exemplary of the larger

process followed in most other cities all
across the country to prevent the possibility integrated schools and neighborhoods.

Even though data on the 1950s attendance
zones in Norfolk no longer exists, the application of the interposition philosophy at the
local level may still be tracked by studying
the fate of the school buildings most directly
threatened by court-ordered integration. Since
the first round of litigation followed almost
exactly the proximity precedent established in
Brown v. Board, by the winter of 1956-1957
Norfolk faced the certainty that at least two
white elementary schools, Patrick Henry and
Gatewood, would have to be integrated under
the proximity doctrine. (*Beckett v. Norfolk*
1957). Before the 1957-1958 school year ever
began, however, the School Board initiated its
first real experiment with applying its inherent powers of school administration to block
the court order. As Judge Hoffman had indicated, the two elementary schools most threatened
by court-ordered integration were both in
transition areas of the city. Patrick Henry
was located in the Atlantic City area, a once
proud working-class neighborhood that had
always maintained some black housing near the
cotton mill and seafood packing houses. In
recent years blacks had begun to move into
other portions of the neighborhood, and, by
1957, 50 blacks would have been eligible to
attend Patrick Henry under the doctrine of
proximity (*Norfolk Virginian-Pilot* 3/10/57).
Even though whites would have outnumbered
blacks by more than four-to-one, the school
was closed and converted to administrative
offices. Two other elementary schools, Benmoreell and Broad Creek Village, which served
integrated navy housing projects, were also
closed, even though both were little more than
a decade old, and, Pineridge Elementary, which

also served the Broad Creek area was closed
for a few years.

Gatewood Elementary School was located in
Berkley, another working-class neighborhood
that was isolated from the rest of the city by
the Elizabeth River. The black population,
which had once been confined to areas around
the shipyards, had begun in the previous
decade to expand into other parts of Berkley.
Gatewood remained the last white school in the
area, but it, too, was threatened by desegregation, although Judge Hoffman indicated that
the ratio of whites to blacks would have been
only eight-to-one. Just as it had with Patrick
Henry, the School Board closed the school to
its white clientele, and transferred it instead to the black school system. Whites in
Berkley would have to commute to some other
school across the river. In addition to Gatewood, the School Board also transferred John
Marshall Elementary on the edge of the downtown area from the white to black school systems, since it, too, was too close to nearby
black housing to withstand a legal challenge.
Since Judge Hoffman had already approved a
similar shift two years earlier when blacks
sought to enroll in Thomas Jefferson Elementary in Newport News (*Southern School News*
10/55), the Norfolk School Board had every
reason to feel he would approve the same tactic in the current instance. Indeed, Judge
Hoffman all but suggested a repeat of the
strategy to the Newport News Board in an opinion written at the same time that the fate of
Patrick Henry and Gatewood was being decided
(*Southern School News* 3/57).

In addition to the power to determine the
attendance zone and the actual use of buildings, the Norfolk School Board found that it
also had discretionary authority over the
size, location, and grade composition of new
schools as well. The most telling evidence
that these powers were used to forestall

school segregation may be found in the creation of the Rosemont and Coronado schools in the newly annexed Norview area. Rosemont, which early press accounts indicate was designed to serve as a combination elementary/junior/senior high school (the only such combination school in the city), was hastily erected to serve the black population threatening to integrate the schools in Norview. Not only did the papers speculate that the purpose of the school was to forestall school desegregation (*Norfolk Virginian-Pilot* 7/8/59), but the black community also fiercely resisted both the project and fact that the hastily erected building would lack many of the support facilities present in all the newer white structures. A school in the Coronado section was not planned until after the School Board had been given the names and addresses of the black litigants seeking to integrate Norview Elementary. After examining the documents, the Board discovered that, in spite of Rosemont, which was then under construction, the color lines in the Norview section had continued to shift, and some of the litigants still lived closer to a white school. When first conceived, Coronado was nothing more than six mobile classrooms pushed off the back of a truck onto a vacant lot (*Norfolk Virginian-Pilot* 7/21/59), which, like Rosemont, was designed almost entirely to place a black school in closer proximity to black litigants than the white school they sought to attend. Again, blacks complained bitterly that this "vest-pocket" school lacked appropriate facilities, and was only being built to counter their litigation (*Norfolk Ledger-Dispatch* 8/20/59). Although Judge Hoffman discussed the situation in his review of the suit, he nevertheless felt powerless to intervene as long as the School Board could point to a sound pedagogical reason (overcrowding) for creating the school (*Beckett v. Norfolk* 1958).

The strategy was even further refined, with the help of the more political Mayor and City Council, in the spring of 1959, just after the city's previously closed white schools had re-opened. At that time Mayor Duckworth proposed building three-room school-houses all across the city, indicating that these minischools could better serve "their neighborhoods." In spite of his subtlety, the newspapers (*Norfolk Virginian-Pilot* 2/22/59), the School Board (Crenshaw), and the City Council (Martin) all knew that the ploy was aimed at maintaining single-race schools. Even though the School Board had strong pedagogical reasons to oppose these minischools as impractical (Campbell 1959), it nevertheless bowed to the Mayor, and erected five buildings that met his specifications (Easton, Fairlawn, East Ocean View, Poplar Halls, and Pretty Lake) in the newly annexed eastern section of the city: "We had to build them . . . it was the only way we could get any schools at all . . . [although] they weren't quite as small as the ones Fred [Duckworth] wanted to build." Years later School Board member Frank Crenshaw would indicate that he thought these schools were partly responsible for the fact that the eastern portion of the city felt under served for decades, a grievance that he sensed underlay much of the recent pressure for its push for a ward system of elections (Crenshaw).

One other finding of this research is that city councils and other local officials, just like their colleagues on the school boards, state legislatures, and the Congress, used the powers at their disposal to frustrate and delay court-ordered integration. The minischool controversy in the spring of 1959 serves as a good introduction to the application of municipal powers to dictate school policies. The school system in Norfolk, like all of those in Virginia and most of the systems in other large cities, was a dependent district which

relied upon the city government for a portion
of its taxing and spending powers. Financing
new construction is but one element of that
financial power. Although normally unwilling
to risk the political outcry of involving itself in school affairs, a city council nevertheless has the power to appropriate funds,
and thus dictate many of the spending policies
of the school district. Because it feared independent action by the more educationally--
as opposed to politically--oriented school
boards, Virginia passed special legislation
that allowed municipal governments the power
to cut off school funds on a 30-day notice,
and several rural localities availed themselves of this power (*Southern School News*
8/55). The Norfolk City Council applied the
leverage of this tactic when it voted to appropriate school funds on a 30-day basis in
the midst of the school closing crisis (*Norfolk Virginian-Pilot* 11/26/58). Another aspect
of financial control may be found in the size
of the local appropriation: After the school
closing controversy, the City Council intimated that it would cut local school funding
because of the way the School Board and the
teachers had been opposed it during the crisis
(*Norfolk Virginian-Pilot* 2/21/59). Later the
Council made good on a portion of its threat
by substantially reducing the School Board's
budget, thereby effectively blocking raises
for the teachers who had defeated Massive
Resistance (*Norfolk Virginian-Pilot* 10/25/59).
Finally, the City Council sought legislation
allowing it to replace the incumbent Board
members in a thinly veiled move to enlarge the
membership and reduce their term of office
(*Norfolk Virginian-Pilot* 4/23/59).

In addition to the ability to influence the
operation of the schools directly through
their powers of appointment, financial control, and capital funding, local governments
also have considerable heretofore unrecognized

authority to dictate the size and shape of
school districts and attendance zones through
their powers of urban renewal. The Broad Creek
Shores controversy provides an interesting
example: By the time the area had been annexed
(January 1, 1955), a group of black developers
had already platted the Broad Creek Shores
subdivision and had a number of houses under
construction. Although faced with a *fait ac-
compli*, the city of Norfolk nevertheless moved
through its powers of *eminent domain* to seize
a large tract on the northern edge of the property, thereby isolating the black development
from nearby white neighborhoods. Even though
the stated purpose of the purchase was to buy
up land for a park and possible school expansion, neither was ever built on the site; the
land was eventually used for the National
Guard Armory and an industrial park. Much
later councilman (and later Mayor) Roy Martin
would indicate that the armory was placed
there "in order to block the black development
(Martin)," a theory that confirms reports in
the black press of the era (*Norfolk Journal
and Guide* 8/6/55). Even though there is no
other direct testimony to the fact, appearances at least suggest that Norfolk similarly
used the placement of Old Dominion University,
interstate highways, recreation areas, and
industrial parks to act as a natural barrier
between racially diverse neighborhoods and to
maintain separate race school districts. Although confirmation of such a theory must be
left to others, use of the powers of city
planning and *eminent domain* to block desegregation has long been hypothesized (Willie
and Greenblatt 1981, 189).

Perhaps the most damning indictment of the
use of municipal powers to achieve *de facto*
segregation comes from the former head of
Housing and Home Finance Agency (H.H.F.A.) in
the 1950s, who accused Southern cities of
using their powers of urban renewal to break

up integrated low-income neighborhoods in
order to draw the color lines more clearly:

> Where, in a few Southern cities, there
> had been a protest against this, a com-
> promise was sometimes reached involving
> proposed reuse for other than residential
> purposes. Thus a slum formerly housing
> both Negro and white families was pro-
> posed as the location for industry or a
> public institution. Urban renewal too
> often seemed to be an instrument for
> wiping out racially integrated living
> (Weaver 1967, 94).

Although he did not mention any city by name,
Mr. Weaver could well have had in mind many of
the projects undertaken in Norfolk during its
second phase of redevelopment. In spite of the
fact that N.R.H.A. Project One had been carefully conceived, thoroughly planned, and me-
ticulously implemented, Norfolk's second phase
of redevelopment, begun after 1956, was rushed, haphazard, and poorly planned. Humanitar-
ian concerns had been foremost in the minds of
the planners of N.R.H.A. Project One: Public
housing in the form of modern garden apartments in well designed neighborhoods replaced
some of the worst slums in the nation, and
development was implemented in carefully conceived stages so that residents were moved
first to public housing units away from the
site during demolition, and then moved back to
their old neighborhood, once it had been rebuilt. In spite of its size and scope, the
entire project took only five years to complete from the time the bulldozers first began
to roll. The Atlantic City, Downtown, Broad
Creek, and Old Dominion projects stand in
sharp contrast to the careful planning and
precision of N.R.H.A. Project One. Under
either a remarkable coincidence, or as part of
a much larger deliberate plan of action, at

almost exactly the same time that federal
Judge Walter Hoffman was ordering the desegregation of Patrick Henry Elementary School in
the Atlantic City portion of the city, the
Norfolk Redevelopment and Housing Authority
was announcing that it planned to demolish the
entire neighborhood. The coincidence theory is
hard to accept, especially since closing Patrick Henry Elementary, an action already taken
by the School Board, did not remove the threat
to segregated schools posed by the mixed-race
neighborhood: 13 of the 24 black plaintiffs in
the school desegregation suit lived in Atlantic City (*Norfolk Virginian-Pilot* 3/10/57).
Even though Patrick Henry Elementary was removed from the challenge, these plaintiffs, as
well as other blacks in the area, still lived
closer to the white schools in the Ghent portion of the city than to the black institutions further downtown. Although the N.R.H.A.
indicated that it had been planning the Atlantic City project since 1954, announcement of
it did not come until December 7, 1956 (*Norfolk Virginian-Pilot* 12/8/56), and the bulldozers began to roll seven months later. According to former Mayor and N.R.H.A. Commissioner Pretlow Darden, the second phase of
Norfolk's redevelopment was initiated by Mayor
Duckworth, who promoted the Atlantic City project as a way to "rid Ghent of the cancerous
growth approximate to it," although there is
little evidence that the blight would have
spread beyond the natural geographic barriers
that isolated Atlantic City from the rest of
the city.

Atlantic City was not a slum, at least in
the eyes of those who had the most professional knowledge of housing conditions in the
neighborhood. The 1950 census revealed that
more than half of the houses had central heat
and indoor plumbing--both still rarities in
many parts of town--were in adequate repair,
and commanded moderate rents twice those of

the areas demolished in Project One and the
Downtown Project (U.S. Census 1952 III, 38,
22). In spite of complaints of residents that
persistent rumors of redevelopment had driven
down real estate values and hastened its decline (*Norfolk Virginian-Pilot* 7/1/57), the
new black families moving in were apparently
willing to pay even higher rents than their
white neighbors due to the housing crisis in
the black community (*Norfolk Virginian-Pilot*
3/10/57). Because federal law required cities
to rehabilitate one housing unit for each one
torn down under redevelopment, the Health
Department's housing inspection division had
just completed a major code enforcement initiative in the area, one of the first major
attempts in the nation to salvage a neighborhood by concentrated enforcement efforts. Atlantic City was chosen precisely because it
was salvageable: It was "not so good that we
couldn't rehabilitate it, and not so bad that
we were wasting our time (Monola)." Because of
the link between the rehabilitation project
and redevelopment, there was close cooperation
between the Health Department and the Housing
Authority. When queried about future plans for
the area, N.R.H.A. executive director Larry
Cox reportedly indicated that it would be at
least "five to ten years" before the Housing
Authority would initiate a project in Atlantic
City. That was why Health Department officials
were so surprised to read the sudden announcement of the Atlantic City project; they had
been present for months at the cabinet meetings of the N.R.H.A., and there had been no
mention of such a plan. They were doubly upset
when they found that their own surveys were
used to declare the area a slum (Monola).

The code-enforcement project had been a major success, and almost every residential unit
had been brought up to the standard of the
city's minimum housing code. Although there
was a two-block wide strip of deterioration in

a mixed-use area of commercial, residential, and light industrial structures that ran along the present site of Brambleton Avenue, these buildings could have been demolished in the highway project, and the rest of the neighborhood saved, the course urged by the Health Department. According to the head of the code-enforcement project, Atlantic City, even in 1956, had a "surprisingly large number of owner-occupied dwellings" that should never have been demolished as slum housing. Although a structure could pass the city's minimum housing code and still have major structural defects under federal standards, a number of blocks in Atlantic City had only one or two such defects. These blocks could have been included for demolition only by carefully designing the project boundaries so that the overall project area could meet the federal requirement of five defects per dwelling. This accounts for the odd shape of the project, and why it zigged around some blocks and then zagged to pick up others.

In short, there was much that was worth saving in the Atlantic City area: Many of its brownstones, row houses, and turn-of-the-century dwellings were clearly salvageable, and would have commanded a premium price when urban pioneers rediscovered the charm of intown neighborhoods little more than a decade later. Although parts along the present site of Brambleton Avenue were dilapidated, some of the blocks closer to the downtown area exuded a "Greenwich Village flavor" and a "Bohemian and cosmopolitan character (*Norfolk Virginian-Pilot* 1/31/59)." The perception that Health Department officials were working with the N.R.H.A. to help it find new slums dealt a severe blow to the city's code-enforcement efforts. The Health Department was so upset at how its services and its surveys had been used, that a major rift developed between it and the Norfolk Redevelopment and Housing Au-

thority, a division that can be seen even in
the 1990s in the overlapping of housing inspection and enforcement authorities between
the city and the N.R.H.A. In spite of its
arguments and its expertise, the Department
was powerless to help Atlantic City residents,
many of whom were doubly bitter when they
learned that the N.R.H.A. would pay less for
their houses than they had spent in bringing
them up to code (Monola).

Neither was Broad Creek Village a slum.
Built during World War II, all of the units
were free-standing dwellings with central
heat, and modern plumbing and electrical,
systems. The 2,598 units each had two to three
bedrooms, hardwood floors, deep sash windows,
and sturdy interior construction; many, in
fact, were moved by their owners before they
could be torn down, and still survive in other
parts of the city. Moreover, residents were
proud of the community, and especially pointed
to its warmth, compassion, friendliness, lack
of crime, and sense of positive spirit, hardly
signs of deterioration (*Norfolk Virginian-
Pilot* 7/15/79). Nevertheless, the N.R.H.A. was
in a hurry to take possession of the property
from the federal government so that it could
be torn down. Since the Authority owned the
housing as a result of the federal government's gift, demolition of the project did not
have to meet redevelopment standards. Although
there was some discussion of maintaining the
area as residential, the City Council was adamantly opposed to having low-rent housing in
that portion of the city. Mayor Duckworth suggested using the land, which had rail service
as well as a prime location between Virginia
Beach Boulevard and Princess Anne Road, the
two major thoroughfares into the downtown, as
an industrial park, and its fate was sealed
(Martin). Once the N.R.H.A. took over (November 1954), the area was doomed. The Authority
never maintained the structures properly and

had no interest in renting the vacant units, so it was not long before neglect and vandalism took their toll on both the structures and the Broad Creek community. By the time bulldozers started to roll, the N.R.H.A. had been successful in creating a *bona fide* slum out of a once-decent and even modern, low-rent housing development (Monola).

These two new redevelopment projects share another common element: Both were rushed into the demolition phase so quickly that portions of the cleared land sat vacant for close to three decades. Atlantic City, especially, was poorly conceived as an industrial park: Although it had more than a 140 acres, it was long and narrow, and badly cut up by Brambleton Avenue, the new super-highway that crossed its spine. Why would an industry choose to be in this somewhat isolated spot on the edge of the downtown area when the city was also developing almost 500 acres in the Broad Creek Village Project closer to major thoroughfares and the population heart of the area? Not until the 1980s, when the Red Cross moved into the industrial park and the hospital complex eventually expanded to fill the western corner, did Atlantic City look like anything more than an urban desert. Even today most of the land in the project is dedicated to parking and governmental use by the U.S. Commerce Department, state highway projects, a largely unused waterfront park, city health department, medical school, and hospital authority facilities. If the project had been designed with more care, the city would have seized the last two blocks to the waterfront as well, and the area could have blossomed with highrise housing developments, a use it is just now discovering somewhat tenuously. In fact, Atlantic City has much that would recommend it to upscale apartment buildings, condos, and highrise residences: Partly because it is cut off from the rest of the city by both natural

geographic barriers and major transportation
facilities, it is much more conducive to residential than industrial uses. Even though it
is bounded on very nearly all four sides by
waterfront with spectacular vistas, the planners seemed to do everything possible to destroy its future use as a residential area.
Brambleton Avenue cuts across it in such a way
that only the two corner pieces of property on
Smith Creek (the Hague), one of the city's
premiere real estate assets, could be used for
highrise apartment houses; the small commercial area, with its quaint shops and artsy
flavor, was demolished; and the failure to
seize its rotting wharves and crumbling fac-
tory district has made it difficult for all
but the most persistent developer to realize
any of the great potential of the area.

In 1957, when the two projects were planned
and executed, the governing elites of the city
appeared to be violently opposed to residential use of either site. There was no talk of
demolition in phases, as had been done in
N.R.H.A. Project One, to minimize hardships or
plan for orderly expansion. In spite of the
fact that Norfolk was also clearing almost 200
more acres in the downtown business district
and starting another project near the present
site of Old Dominion University, it was just
more than a year between the time the projects
were announced and most of the demolition had
been completed. In just 16 months Norfolk appears to have torn down the homes of almost
twenty thousand people--roughly ten percent of
its population--but these were not the substandard dwellings of its poorest residents.
Instead these were the homes of working-class
white families and a few black residents attracted to decent housing. It was these latter
residents, because of the threat they posed to
school segregation, that the city wanted to
remove, but in the process, it embarked upon a
terribly destructive course.

The black families in Atlantic City and
Broad Creek Village posed more than just an
academic threat to school segregation. Because
they represented the upwardly mobile black
middle-class, they held high aspirations for
their children. For this reason, many had
taken the lead in initiating the lawsuit that
challenged the status of *de jure* segregation
in the city. Because the N.A.A.C.P. had wished
to follow the *Brown* precedent as closely as
possible, the original 24 plaintiffs, and
others like them, were probably sought out
precisely because they lived closer to white
elementary schools than the black institutions
to which their children were assigned. Nevertheless, they were willing to enlist and take
a very prominent and somewhat risky role in
the effort. Thirteen of the original plaintiffs lived in Atlantic City; another five
lived in Berkley section of the city and would
have gone to the Gatewood Elementary. Instead,
the School Board transferred Gatewood to the
black school system, thereby leaving the remaining whites in Berkley without a school,
and speeding the departure of white families
from the area. Although the other six plaintiffs resided closer to a black school than a
white institution, they lived in the black
section of Lamberts Point (*Norfolk Virginian-
Pilot* 3/10/57) that was just then in the process of expanding further towards the nearby
white neighborhoods. Even though Smallwood
Elementary (black) stood in the center of the
area (the Old Dominion University Library now
stands on the site), the city initiated a
small redevelopment project in the area to
provide land for expansion of the then two-
year junior college that was to become Old
Dominion University. The project had the
effect of bulldozing the transition areas,
stabilizing racial lines, and interposing a
large barrier of public land (the university)
between the black Lamberts Point section and

the white neighborhoods of Larchmont and Edge-
water, a result that is still obvious. Moreover, Lambert's Point, Atlantic City, and
Broad Creek were all integrating fairly peacefully (Monola), and experienced none of the
violence or intimidation found in Brambleton
and Coronado when the color lines were first
crossed there. Instead, all three of these
areas had supported a few black families for a
number of years. Because of the critical housing shortage in the black community, in part
created by redevelopment activity, landlords
could command higher rents from blacks, and
this helped smooth the transition of black
residents into additional parts of these
neighborhoods.

Thus, just as school boards could tear down
or close schools directly threatened by court-
ordered integration, cities had the power,
through redevelopment, to tear down mixed-race
or transition areas where the racial composition of the neighborhood schools would have
been equally mixed. Parallel to the power to
size schools in order to maintain single-race
districts, is the authority, through redevelopment, to adjust the size of the neighborhoods to meet the racial designation of the
schools. School boards could alter attendance
zones, but cities could achieve the same
effect by seizing land, demolishing housing,
or erecting barriers between neighborhoods
that would force resizing of the attendance
zones. The evidence that Norfolk took this
route and directly employed its powers of
school administration and urban renewal to
move the status of its segregated school
system from *de jure* to *de facto* is overwhelming.

In spite of the monumental effort of its
political leaders, the effort to forestall
school desegregation by applying the city's
powers of redevelopment, planning, and school
plant planning worked for only a single year.

The schools that would have been integrated in the fall of 1957 were either torn down or removed from service, and in many cases, the neighborhoods, too, were demolished. But for the quick use of its urban renewal powers, Norfolk may have joined Little Rock, Arkansas, as the first major battleground over court-ordered school integration. Judge Hoffman was obviously cognizant that the city was working to counter his authority. Writing before either the fate of the school or the full boundaries of the Atlantic City project were known, he indicated that redevelopment there could "substantially reduce" the number of children he would have to assign to Patrick Henry Elementary (*Beckett v. Norfolk* 1957, 339). Norfolk had both the motive and the opportunity to use its powers of urban renewal to forestall school desegregation. That it did so, and with a vengeance, seems obvious. Even so, any assessment of motive and municipal power would be incomplete without some discussion of possible rival hypotheses for the observed events. Although several alternate explanations are offered by other authors, the research supporting their conclusions comes from the 1960s or 1970s, and not the era under consideration.

Karl and Alma Taueber, in their study of residential segregation and neighborhood change, noted that in Southern cities, in sharp contrast to the rest of the country, residential segregation generally increased between 1950 and 1960. In their comments on this trend, they attribute this difference more to a number of market forces than to deliberate government policy. In a more detailed study of several selected cities, however, the Tauebers note that governmental action may have been a factor in maintaining segregated neighborhoods. They found that Charleston, South Carolina, for instance, deliberately used separate race public-housing projects to maintain segregated neighborhoods. Also, the pattern of backyard residences for black domestics in white neighborhoods that was evident before 1940, was almost nonexistent by 1960, but they were unsure whether this was caused by voluntary housing changes or official zoning and housing-code enforcement initiatives. They note that in Memphis, the planning commission blocked expansion of black housing into white areas, a pattern that the Taubers felt was quite common: "In some Southern cities informal political agreements permitting 'zoning' portions of the city for white or black occupancy may have played a part in making available the requisite land for building new housing for blacks." They also indicate that Southern cities were much more aggressive in their annexation efforts in order to "capture new areas of white population." Although Norfolk was not one of the cities selected for in-depth study, the Taueber's index of racial segregation indicates that it had one of the highest indexes of residential segregation in the country in both 1950 and 1960. By 1960 only Richmond, two cities in Louisiana (Monroe and Shreveport), and six cities in Florida (Daytona Beach, Fort Lauderdale, Jacksonville, St. Petersburg, West Palm Beach. and Miami), out of more than 200 studied, had a higher index (Taueber and Taueber 1965, 33-41, 49, 191, 124, 240).

In his major work on the history of urban America, Kenneth T. Jackson notes many of the same trends as the Tauebers, but he points to deliberate government action as one of the primary causes of the increasing segregation of America's cities. The government he blames, however, is not municipal, but rather federal. Professor Jackson provides a stunning indictment of how the federal Home Owners Loan Corporation (H.O.L.C.) of the 1930s invented redlining of urban, black, and racially mixed neighborhoods--a practice that was later followed by both the Federal Housing Administration (F.H.A.) and the Veterans Administration (V.A.). According to Jackson, realtors knew that with these red-lining practices in effect, the sale of homes in a white community to black buyers meant that future loans would be denied, and they worked to steer buyers into single-race neighborhoods and away from transition areas. In addition, since the loan standards of these federal agencies specified minimum lot sizes, set-backs, and other standards, they favored newer suburban housing over older, intown neighborhoods. Because of these rigid standards, inner-city housing was difficult to sell, thereby hastening the decline of the cities. Potential new property owners could not get federally-backed loans in mixed-race or declining neighborhoods, and this increased absentee ownership, property abandonment, and the development of slums. By the time the federal government finally reversed its red-lining practices (1966), the switch only helped the remaining white homeowners escape to the suburbs, thereby furthering the segregation of America.

The federal government's role in forcing housing segregation was more than just adherence to discriminatory lending practices. Jackson also documents how federal policies pushed public housing units into existing slum areas, thereby reinforcing segregated housing patterns and leading to the further decline of the surrounding neighborhoods. Although public housing had originally been intended for the "working poor" and the "deserving poor," by 1960 federal policies had forced it to become housing of last resort for welfare clients, thereby relegating it to a permanent home for the nation's underclass. Although cities are partly to blame for the design and location of public housing, nevertheless it appears that a number of national polices (e.g., subsidized highways, mortgage investment, and expansion

of military and government facilities) also
helped to isolate blacks in central cities,
while their white former-neighbors moved to
the suburbs. The only direct role attributed
to municipalities is the use of zoning powers
by Southern cities to enforce racial segregation of neighborhoods (Jackson 1987, 190-218,
227, 242).

Even though Professor Jackson's treatment
does not deal directly with this issue, his
thesis lends some support to the premise that
Norfolk's post-*Brown* redevelopment activity
was prompted as much by racial as economic
considerations. Atlantic City and Broad Creek
Village were not slums, but the fact that they
were integrated communities on the edge of the
downtown area meant that, according to Jackson's research, they were red-lined and in
great danger of tipping rapidly into slums.
Thus, even though the structures themselves
were sound, the fact that they could not be
sold with government-backed loans in a navy
town like Norfolk was a fatal flaw that doomed
them to continued decline. At the time of its
demise, the N.R.H.A. labored mightily to prove
to the skeptics that Atlantic City was in
danger of becoming a slum because of its increasing crime and public health problems
(*Norfolk Virginian-Pilot* 6/23/57). Later, it
would argue that the project was initiated to
give the medical center room to grow (Martin).
This justification is a little hard to accept,
especially since the entire medical complex
even today occupies only a corner of the
sprawling project. The idea of a medical
school was not advanced until well after the
entire 145-acre area had been swept bare
(Darden), and much of the land used for this
and other medical purposes could have been
acquired by *eminent domain* without tearing
down the rest of the community. N.R.H.A. Commissioner Pretlow Darden, who was also on the
board of Norfolk General Hospital, indicated

that Atlantic City was torn down more to protect Ghent than to help the hospital (Darden).
    The "white flight" theories advanced by
James Coleman (Coleman *et al*. 1975) and David
Armour (Armour 1980, 187-225) are equally
inadequate in explaining events in Norfolk,
where whites were pushed out of transition
areas like Atlantic City and Broad Creek
Village by municipal redevelopment activity.
Moreover, most of the research on "white
flight" was developed in the late 1960s and
early 1970s, and shows that whites left areas
when school integration efforts were at their
maximum and crosstown busing plans were being
implemented. These same concepts are not appropriate in the analysis of an era in which
schools were not yet desegregated: Norfolk's
redevelopment projects appear to have been
initiated more to prevent "white flight" by
keeping the schools segregated, than because
of it.   Similarly, the "tipping theory" advanced by Charles Willie and Susan Greenblatt
deals with events once large-scale integration
had begun under court orders. In their study
of ten school systems, only four of which were
in the South (Richmond, Dallas, Mobile, and
Corpus Christi), they found several instances
where federal courts cited direct municipal
actions to preserve desegregated schools: The
Boston School Committee, for instance, manipu-
lated school district boundaries and used
student attendance patterns to reinforce residential segregation. They also found that discriminatory actions by the state government
and the real estate community contributed to
residential segregation in Wilmington, Delaware. In their examination of school desegregation in Mobile, the authors describe how
that city appeared to place its interstate
highway so that it would serve as a dividing
line between the races, allowing it to zone
the school districts accordingly. In Richmond,
Virginia, which faced some of the same harsh

political restraints as Norfolk, they discovered that the city entered into a racially motivated merger with its surrounding counties in order to redraw attendance zones for white schools. In addition, there was some evidence of "block-busting" by the Richmond real estate community, especially in areas on the north side of town. The Richmond School Board also appears to have established two distinct feeder system of schools with different grade organizations to minimize transfers between the majority black and white schools: White schools operated on a grades 1-5, 6-8, and 9-12 organization, while black schools had grades 1-6, 7-9, and 10-12 (Willie and Greenblatt 1981, 33, 101, 189, 220-31). Another researcher found that the Richmond School Board, under the leadership of its chairman, Lewis Powell, later a U.S. Supreme Court Justice, deliberately built new schools to forestall school desegregation. This building plan appears to have been in response to the advice of James J. Kilpatrick, then editor of the *Richmond News-Leader*, that the desegregation problem, "especially in the cities, could be handled by the relocation of school buildings and the gerrymandering of enrollment lines (Eley 1976, 134, 36)"--advice that Norfolk followed as well.

Gary Orfield, perhaps the premier researcher in the field, offers an amalgam of all of these explanations in his description of the "ghettoization" of Chicago and other Northern cities in the late 1960s and early 1970s. His research documents both "white flight" and the rise of private and parochial schools as alternatives to extensive court-ordered integration. Like Jackson, he lays much of the blame for the failure of mixed-race neighborhoods on the federal government and its discriminatory lending practices. His indictment goes even farther, however, and accuses federal officials of permitting segregation in housing

constructed with federal funds. He also blames
federal urban renewal policies for allowing
cities to demolish black neighborhoods without
building adequate public housing or other low-
income replacement units. Unlike Norfolk, very
few public housing units were apparently built
in Northern cities for the residents of redeveloped areas, and Orfield believes that this
factor tended to accelerate the ghettoization
of the neighborhoods adjoining renewal areas
(Orfield 1978, 80-1).

His thesis is particularly applicable to a
city like Norfolk, where there was both extensive urban renewal activity and a large-scale
commitment to public housing, that, unfortunately, were not always coordinated. In the
city's first phase of redevelopment, 1950 to
1955, begun under the leadership of the Silkstocking reformers, urban renewal and public
housing were marvelously woven together as
integral parts of the same overall plan. The
city's business leaders worked closely with
officials in Washington to convert many of its
wartime housing projects into public housing
in the postwar period. N.R.H.A. Project One,
which was the first redevelopment project in
the nation, was so carefully planned that
residents of the renewal area were relocated
to offsite public housing units, their neighborhood demolished, and new public housing
units built in the project area, so that the
former residents could be moved back before
the next area was demolished. Since black
areas were torn down and new public housing
for blacks rebuilt on the same site, the action had little impact upon the segregation of
the city, and, in fact, expanded the number of
black housing units. Norfolk's second phase of
redevelopment, from 1956 to 1959, initiated
under the leadership of Mayor Duckworth, stood
in sharp contrast to Project One. First, the
scope of the projects was enormous: The city
proposed to bulldoze more than 800 acres, de-

stroying the homes of almost a tenth of its
population in less than a year and a half. Not
only were no new public housing units planned,
none of the areas being redeveloped would return to residential use. Except for the tiny
(44 acres) project around what would eventually become Old Dominion University and a portion of the Downtown Project, which was more
commercial and industrial than residential,
most of the housing torn down belonged to
white working-class residents who would not
have been eligible for relocation to public
housing. This phase of redevelopment confirms
part of Orfield's theory on the expansion of
slums, but with a twist. Since the private
real estate market could not absorb this enormous movement of people with any combination
of new construction or existing units, the
sudden, mass migration of residents out of the
project areas put tremendous pressure on the
rest of the city's housing. Private homes and
apartment buildings on the fringe of the downtown area were badly cut up and expanded to
accommodate some of this influx. The end result was that the enormous scope of the four
projects and the speed of demolition contributed to the deterioration of East Ghent, Park
Place, and other established in-town neighborhoods, and raised questions in the minds of
realtors, bankers, and the residents themselves about their future viability, especially when the burden of increasing school desegregation over the next few years fell disproportionately upon their schools. Because the
projects had also displaced black residents
and equally burdened the black real estate
market, it was not long before many of these
same neighborhoods, once they became overcrowded, began to decline, integrate, and then
"tip" as whites sought housing choices in the
suburbs. This type of "chain reaction effect,"
whereby destruction of one slum only creates
new slums, is more fully explained by other

critics of redevelopment (see Greer 1965, 56; Frieden and Morris 1968, 130; Rothenberg 1967, 68-9). The difference in Norfolk is that its redevelopment effort, because it tore down housing in areas that were still salvageable, only created slums where pleasant neighborhoods once stood.

Although Orfield's work deals with a later era, well after federal courts had ordered school desegregation in the cities under study, he reports that federal courts in a number of school desegregation cases found that the combination of federal and municipal housing policies increased school segregation in Charlotte, Wilmington, Cleveland, New York and other cities, although the focus of these findings was more on racially segregated public housing than other redevelopment and planning activities of the cities (Orfield 1978, 84). This finding is echoed by the research of Karl Taueber, who similarly reports that federal courts all across the South found that, once they were ordered to integrate schools, Southern school boards used their powers to delay the impact of the orders by closing school buildings directly threatened by integration, building new "vest-pocket" schools to minimize integration, redrawing attendance zones, and establishing liberal transfer policies (Taueber 1990, 18-24). Although both researchers deal with events that occurred in the 1960s, they nevertheless form an important part of the theoretical framework of this work, namely that cities took similar action in the 1950s, well before they actually faced the threat of large-scale school integration, to defer or delay court-ordered desegregation. The only difference in this work is the inference that in addition to relying upon school administrative and housing policies to achieve *de facto* segregation, cities also used their extensive powers of redevelopment and urban renewal to block the encroach-

ment of blacks into white housing areas and to
remove mixed-race neighborhoods that posed a
threat to the continuation of a segregated
school system. The effort of the School Board
in Norfolk to close schools, redesignate their
racial composition, redraw attendance zones,
and even demolish buildings in an era in which
enrollment was expanding so rapidly that many
schools were operating on double shifts (*Norfolk Virginian-Pilot* 2/10/56), seems to have
had little to do with rapid changes in the
white population explained by these approaches. Thus, even though "white flight" fails as
an alternate explanation, especially when applied to a time before schools were actually
integrated, it may be useful in understanding
the process of neighborhood change that precipitated such dramatic redevelopment activity.

Even though the advocates of redevelopment
enterprises have always claimed a purely
economic motive for their initiatives, the
critics, and there have been many who disapproved of the way urban renewal was handled
by cities in the 1950s, have indicated that
the economies of redevelopment have been false
and even counterproductive (Wilson 1966; Gans
1966, 540-5; Barron and Barron 1965). In essence, the argument of the critics is that
redevelopment has been a concerted attack upon
the poor, those least able to cope with the
hardship of relocation and loss of neighborhood ties; that many of the areas torn down
were still salvageable and served a useful
purpose by providing housing for the poor that
was never replaced; and that much of the land
actually developed was put to uses that could
have been accomplished without the wholesale
destruction of neighborhoods and such massive
clearance efforts.

Norfolk provides both a fascinating counter
and overwhelming confirmation of these critical approaches: Project One, because it tore

down vast tracks of what was generally recognized as some of the worst slum housing in the
country and replaced them with both well-de-
signed public housing developments and badly
needed industrial space, represents a triumph
of the planners' art, especially since the
entire 127-acre area was cleared and rebuilt
in about five years. On the other hand, the
Atlantic City and Broad Creek Village Projects, initiated suddenly in Norfolk's second
phase of redevelopment, provide confirmation
of the worst nightmares of the critics. Not
only did these projects clear away vast acres
of decent, even modern, homes, they left the
city's working-class poor without recourse in
the housing market, thereby creating future
slums by overburdening the surrounding neighborhoods. In their rebuilding phases, the
projects provided a subsidy to governmental
agencies, industries, and corporate developers
who required no such assistance. Most of the
uses for which the cleared land was eventually
developed--hospitals, universities, highways,
medical schools, government buildings, high-
rise apartments, and industrial expansion--
could have been achieved gradually and without
the awesome destruction of redevelopment.

Part of the tragedy of Norfolk's second
phase of redevelopment is that most of the
land, once cleared, sat vacant for so very
long: It took 20 to 30 years before portions
of Atlantic City and Broad Creek Village were
developed, and Norfolk's downtown area still
has 17 acres of prime real estate for which,
even now, well more than three decades after
it was cleared, there are no real prospects
for development. Norfolk's second phase of
redevelopment provided the acid test of the
"land bank" concept, whereby vast tracts of
urban land are cleared and "saved" in their
vacant state, ready for the day when a prospective developer is ready to make a withdrawal. Indeed, Larry Cox, Director of the

N.R.H.A. and later Under-Secretary of Housing and Urban Development, was one of the nation's greatest proponents of the land bank concept:

> Delays and land lying idle are inevitable if urban renewal is going to do what it should do in downtown areas. Projects involving great investments do not spring full-blown upon the scene in the average-size American community. Delay counseled by realistic appraisal of land potential is worthwhile delay. So my thesis is have worthwhile delay introduced into urban renewal, particularly in central city areas (Cox, as quoted in Brownfield 1960, 760).

Unfortunately, Norfolk's experience provides a stunning rebuttal to Mr. Cox's thesis: Except for a strip shopping center on the edge of the downtown area, a few high-rise bank buildings and office towers that would have been built anyway, and several small residential developments that are still underway in the Freemason Harbor area, almost all of the "full-blown" or major developments in downtown Norfolk--the Scope arena and concert complex, the municipal center, Waterside marina and urban marketplace, Town Point Park, baseball stadium, Nauticus maritime center, and the new convention hotel center--have all been public, not private, facilities that could have been built without redevelopment. Similarly, there was no need to "bank" vast tracts of land in the Atlantic City, Broad Creek Village, and Old Dominion project areas; all of the public and private investments there could have been achieved by timely destruction and phased development of the projects. Except for the unstated purpose of achieving *de facto* school segregation, the vast scope and destruction of these areas was both unnecessary and ill-advised. According to one contemporary of Cox:

Technical skills relating to land use design have today [1960] reached the point where . . . existing improvements need not be demolished before replacement can proceed. . . . Even those structures bad enough to be the subject of a clearance project contribute significantly to the local tax revenues. The demolition of these structures not only takes the value off of the tax roll, but also burdens the tax structure with payment of the city's share of the clearance cost, together with interest on money borrowed in order to accomplish this. . . . Analyzed in terms of planning future land use, the prudent course of action for the city is to plan first and undertake the execution of urban renewal projects only when it is apparent that the land can be advantageously put to use immediately upon completion of the clearance. Therefore, the only situation which would justify creation of a "land bank" would be the one in which the project area was so bad that the city would be better off without it, even if nothing arose in its place (Brownfield 1960, 761).

All four of the projects initiated in Norfolk's second phase of redevelopment have unquestionably contributed handsomely to Norfolk's tax base; upgrading land use from low- or moderate-income residences to predominantly industrial or commercial properties almost always greatly expands the real estate tax base, provides new jobs, and generates revenue from other tax sources. The economic assessment of redevelopment is not whether it has been profitable or even moderately successful in its stated aim of providing vacant land for development, it is rather whether these successes, most of which could have been achieved without the massive scale of destruction, the

disruption of human lives, and the adverse impact on the rest of the city's housing stock,
were worth the trauma and the social cost. In
spite of the fact that downtown Norfolk is
undergoing a tremendous renaissance (largely
at public expense), the economic argument for
major portions of the other redevelopment projects pales, especially when one considers
that the second, unspoken motive of preserving
segregated schools was the prime reason for
the rush to demolish housing and "bank" the
vacant land.

In spite of the pros and cons of the economic argument, however, there has been an
undercurrent that redevelopment activities
have been guided more by political than developmental considerations (Greer and Miner
1967, 152-63). Martin Anderson coined the
phrase "black removal" to characterize what he
saw as municipal efforts across the country to
get rid of unwanted elements of the community;
by "black," however, he meant not a racial designation, but rather areas of blight, crime
infestation, and unprofitable business uses
(Anderson 1964). N.R.H.A. Project One provides a prime example of black removal at its
best: A horribly blighted section of housing,
with its massive attendant problems of crime,
infestation, juvenile delinquency, disease,
and public health menace, was removed and then
replaced with modern public housing, designed
as garden apartments and arranged to provide a
continued sense of community. Demolition of
the city's notorious East Main Street "sin
district," which brought such ill repute to
Norfolk during the war years, also represents
another element of black removal, even though
the area was still commercially viable.

Cities may be able to make a strong case
for using redevelopment to clear areas of
extensive blight, but there can be little
justification for demolishing the "gray areas
(Frieden 1966, 585-623)"--neighborhoods like

Atlantic City and Broad Creek Village--which were contributing and salvageable. If Anderson's thesis of black removal can be applied to these projects, and perhaps to other Southern redevelopment initiatives undertaken at the same time, one explanation is that the unwanted elements in these projects were in neighborhoods where blacks and whites lived too close together to be served by separate schools.

This is precisely what the plaintiffs in a number of school desegregation suits have claimed, that is that urban renewal powers were used to create segregated neighborhoods, strictly enforce well-defined color barriers, isolate black populations, relocate integrated schools, and otherwise frustrate efforts to desegregate the public school system (Taueber 1990, 18-24). Although this claim has been in part supported by demographic researchers (Orfield 1985, 161-96) and other social scientists (Taueber 1989), they have chosen to blame school boards, rather than city councils, redevelopment authorities, or planning commissions, for efforts to replace *de jure* with *de facto* segregation. Even though Norfolk provides the perfect case history for all of these charges, far from being the villain, the School Board played only a bit part in the effort to divide the city into racially distinct school districts. In fact, it is only through the somewhat heroic actions of its School Board that Norfolk still had some semblance of an operational school system left after its political leaders finally gave up their fight to preserve segregated schools.

In Norfolk, at least, the fight to preserve segregated education clearly went much farther than the School Board's efforts to close effected schools, select racially "safe" sites, redraw attendance zones, and manipulate the other factors of school plant planning and student attendance, transfer, and grade organization. In several instances (Atlantic City and Broad Creek Village), the School Board's action to close a threatened school came after the city had committed to demolishing the entire school zone. In other cases (Easton, Poplar Halls, Fairlawn, Pretty Lake, and East Ocean View), the School Board went along with the City Council's desire to build tiny, "vest-pocket" schools, even though it opposed the structures; the financial control of the City Council over capital expenditures was such that, because the city was desperately short of classroom space, the Board had to take whatever new buildings it could get. In several other areas, interstate highways (Coronado Broad Creek Shores, Brambleton, Ingleside), parks (Titustown and Benmoreell), and other major public facilities (Old Dominion University and the National Guard Armory) appear to have been used, along with natural geographic barriers, to provide both a clearcut color line between school districts and a logical limitation to the size of their attendance zones. These same barriers would make it even more difficult to provide racially balanced neighborhood schools once the effort to preserve segregation was abandoned.

Although the actions in Norfolk to preserve segregated schools were dramatic, they do not appear to be unique. Norfolk, as well as many other communities in the South, had a strong motive to preserve segregation: Public reaction to the dictates of the U.S. Supreme Court were overwhelmingly negative, and large portions of the populace indicated that they may have been prepared to engage in disruptive, even illegal, activity to block court-ordered integration. Political leaders all across the South were attempting to interpose the authority of state governments between the courts and the local schools in a legal jury rig of hastily enacted legislation controlling pupil assignment, transfer, and attendance policies.

Southern senators and congressmen had banded together in the "Southern Manifesto" to urge their constituencies to use every legal means at their disposal to oppose integration. In addition to this element of motive, which may actually have been tempered in Norfolk by the leader-ship of the School Board, the editorial writers of the *Virginian-Pilot*, and the Norfolk Committee for Public Schools, an urgency of the situation also existed, because so many areas of the city appeared to run afoul of the Supreme Court's doctrine of proximity in maintaining school attendance zones. Because it had extensive areas of integrated navy housing, a few mixed-race neighborhoods in various stages of transition, and several communities where there were pockets of black population too small to be served by their own school, Norfolk faced the prospect that it would be among the first cities in the South to face widespread school integration. In Virginia that meant political death, and the fear of being cut off from state funding was very real; for two decades after it had finally integrated its schools, local residents referred to the Norfolk area as "Tollwater," an ironic allusion to the fact that the state was punishing it for killing Massive Resistance by refusing to provide funding for the bridges, tunnels, and highways so necessary for economic growth.

In addition to the strength of opposition to school desegregation and urgency of situation, as measured by areas of mixed-race housing, the third variable determining the power of the relationship between school desegregation and urban renewal activities is an opportunity to employ the powers of redevelopment and planning unchecked by normal political constraints. All three variables were present in Norfolk to their maximum extent—that is why the story in this one city is so instructive—but Norfolk, as well as other

communities across the South, had numerous
occasions to bend the powers of school administration, planning, and urban renewal to
serve both the cause of preserving segregation
and providing economic development. Southern
cities faced a period of rapid growth in population, school enrollment, industry, land
area, and economic base. This meant that they
could use the opportunity already available in
this expansion to build new schools or change
school zones so that school districts would
remain segregated, and therefore acceptable to
the public. This at least was the course urged
by James J. Kilpatrick, editor of the *Richmond
News Leader* and chief publicist for the doctrine of interposition (Eley 1976, 36). They
could go a step farther and use the opportunity to close schools, redesignate their use, or
reallocate their grade composition as another
way to defer or delay integration in a couple
of areas of the city. Or they could go the
final step proposed by this work and make sure
that the schools in threatened areas of the
city remained segregated by using their urban
renewal and municipal planning powers to carefully position parks, highways, or other public facilities so they posed a barrier to
blacks living near a white school; municipalities could control land-use policies so that
black housing could move no closer to white
schools; and cities could use their powers of
redevelopment to tear down mixed-race areas
that proved threatening under the court's doctrine of proximity. Norfolk was not alone in
taking these extra steps; there is strong evidence to suggest that Richmond, Mobile, Memphis, Charleston, Boston, Wilmington (Delaware) and others used at least some of these
techniques. Only in Norfolk is the record complete enough to project a concerted use of urban renewal to preserve segregated schools.
    This interpretation is not meant, however,
to discredit the economic argument made for

annexation, urban renewal, industrial development, and city planning. For most of these
cities, growth in both land area and tax base
was absolutely essential for survival, and
every element of municipal government was concerned with the effort to plan for and sustain
that growth. The suggestion that the effort to
preserve school segregation was also involved
in these planning, development, and redevelopment decisions is not meant to denigrate the
purely economic considerations of such activities; it is only meant to infer that the powers of urban renewal in many cities in the
1950s was meant to serve two masters, the
public-avowed one of growth, and the privately
held determination to stay the same, at least
as far as segregated schools were concerned.
The irony in Norfolk is that the powers of
redevelopment pioneered with such pride during
the People's era to create equal facilities
for blacks, were now transformed and manipu-
lated as political weapons during the school
desegregation crisis.

    Finally, some larger historical context is
necessary to fully understand the events and
actions herein described. Other contemporane-
ous researchers (Crain *et al*. 1968) found that
appointed school boards were far more adept at
handling the controversies surrounding school
desegregation than their elected counterparts.
This is definitely the case in Norfolk: All
six appointed members of the School Board responded to the crisis in admirable, even heroic, fashion, and their calm and deliberate approach, coupled with their overriding devotion
to the concept of public education, was largely responsible for the peaceful resumption of
classes, the sense of continuity and control,
and the fact that quality schools continued in
Norfolk once the legal issues were settled.
Their courage and devotion to duty brought
them into constant conflict with the elected
leaders of their day. None of its members had

sought appointment to the Board (Crenshaw),
and, for the most part, they were not the sort
of individuals who seek election to office.
All had been chosen because of their record of
involvement in volunteer, not political, community service, and it was this experience
that served them well when the clamor of the
constituency of the day demanded short-term
approaches. There was unanimity on the Board,
the kind of calm consensus that rarely is seen
in elected bodies in times of such violent
social upheaval and conflicting values. The
Norfolk School Board had the long-term interest of public education in mind throughout the
controversy; their judgement was not clouded
by political expediency or the need to seek
reelection. Their calm reaction to crisis and
their devotion to the future of public education should give pause to all those who think
that urban school systems, especially those
beset with major problems and diverse clientele, would be better served by elected, rather than appointed, boards.

Although school boards all across the South
were vilified for their efforts to delay or
defer court-ordered desegregation efforts, in
Norfolk, at least, the School Board was but
one actor in a larger cast that included the
Mayor, the City Council, the N.R.H.A., and
other municipal officials responsible for
planning and development. While this larger
relationship has been the source of some
speculation, it is the major contribution of
this work that the interplay between school
desegregation and urban renewal in one community has been more completely analyzed. The
response to court-ordered desegregation did
not begin with the first local court case, the
traditional starting date of other histories
of the process; instead, it began with a
realization in the South that predates even
the *Brown* decision that, in order to pass
court review, "separate" school facilities for

the two races must be made more nearly equal.
Later, when it became clear that the courts
would not accept separate facilities as equal
when the pupils lived in close geographic
proximity to one another, a much larger cast
of characters than just Southern school boards
followed the dictates of their state and national political leaders, as well as their
voting constituencies, to do everything in
their power to prevent school integration.
The powers of urban renewal, school-plant
planning, redevelopment, and school administration appear to have been used liberally to
create separate-race neighborhoods and school
attendance zones, thereby replacing segregation by law (*de jure*) with the type of *de
facto* separation of races already approved by
the courts in Northern and Midwestern cities.

Although a temptation exists to fix blame
or criticism for actions that turn out now, by
modern standards, to be misdirected, judging
the motives of the 1950s by the mores of the
1990s is just as unfair as requiring the citizens of that era to share the advantage of our
own more modern perspective to receive fair
treatment. Enough time has passed to gain both
the advantage of historical hindsight and a
passionless examination of the events and
issues; few cities could withstand the judgement of a serious local history if viewed from
the high ground of both hindsight and moral
certainty. Norfolk is no better or worse than
other cities; if it is proud of its accomplishments, and it has every right to boast,
then it should not be afraid to face its failures. Judgement is not intended by this critical examination of the era; indeed, one has to
marvel at both the competence and the devotion
to cause depicted here. Mayor Duckworth and
the other members of the City Council, the
School Board, the N.R.H.A., and other public
officials were responding to a public mandate
to do everything legally possible to preserve

what was considered by the city's (white) voters to be a sacrosanct way of life. Not only
did they respond with vigor and ingenuity,
they received close counsel and guidance from
others in the state and national government
who shared their sentiment. That all of these
officials enjoyed the overwhelming support of
their constituencies is evident in the voting
patterns of the era. In a democratic society
we must be prepared to accept the fact that
powerful and passionate elected leaders will
do everything possible to respond to such a
mandate without condemning their actions or
criticizing their motives.

    Partly because Norfolk encountered its de-
segregation crisis early and faced it so precipitously, the city has been able to achieve
and maintain a level of racial and political
harmony that exists in few other areas of the
country. Norfolk emerged from its school crisis with an intensity of support for public
education that has never diminished. Even when
faced with the prospect of court-ordered
crosstown busing that was more extensive than
almost anywhere else in the country, community
support remained strong. Partly because of
this support and because it continued to offer
quality inter-racial education, Norfolk did
not experience the level of white flight found
in a number of other central cities. Also, the
new leadership of the city that emerged from
the crisis determined that they, and not the
federal courts, should ultimately determine
the pattern and extent of school segregation.
Thus, each time the School Board was faced
with a new round of court-ordered integration,
it followed the lead of the 1958-1959 Board,
drew the lines itself, and endured the outcry.
By doing so, Norfolk's School Boards have
helped it escape the fate of Boston and numerous other cities where the federal courts had
to take a more direct role of intervention. In
Norfolk, school desegregation has been "volun-

tary," albeit under pressure from the courts. Partly because of this higher level of cooperation with the courts, almost two decades ago Judge Hoffman declared that Norfolk operated a truly "unitary" school system, a step that paved the way for it to be among the first major school systems in the country to leave the phase of court-ordered busing behind and return to neighborhood schools at the elementary level. Today the Norfolk Public Schools continue to win accolades as one of the nation's few effective urban school systems: Test scores are up, dropout rates are down, white enrollment seems stable, and community support remains strong.

The Norfolk story is not a deviant case; instead the history of its desegregation crisis exemplifies the level of the struggle that took place in cities all across the South in the 1950s and then moved to the North, Midwest, and border states in the 1960s when they, too, were faced with the prospect of massive court-ordered school integration initiatives. Although perhaps more compelling than events in other cities, partly because of the collapsed time frame and the fact that Norfolk was among the first cities in the South to desegregate, the actions of its public officials to preserve racially identifiable schools were not unique. Only the scale of the battle was larger than elsewhere, but that is why the story of this struggle is so instructive.

Abbreviations

F.H.A.   Federal Housing Administration
                 (U.S. Government)

H.H.F.A.   Housing & Home Finance Agency
                 (U.S. Government)

H.O.L.C.   Home Owners Loan Corporation
                 (U.S. Government)

N.A.A.C.P.   National Association for the
                 Advancement of Colored People

N.A.T.O.   North Atlantic Treaty
Organization

N.C.P.S.   Norfolk Committee for Public
                 Schools

N.E.A.   Norfolk Education Association

N.R.H.A.   Norfolk Redevelopment and Housing
                 Authority

O.D.U.   Old Dominion University (Norfolk)

P.T.A.   Parent Teacher Association

T.E.F.   Tidewater Education Association

U.S.O.   United Serviceman's Organization

W.C.I.C.   Women's Council for Interracial
                 Cooperation

V.A.   Veteran's Administration (U.S.
                 Government)

Glossary

Atlantic City--an older middle-class neighbor-
    hood and industrial area on the edge of
    downtown Norfolk that contained about 50
    black families at the time it was slated
    for a major redevelopment project

Brambleton--an older middle-class and indus-
    trial area south of downtown Norfolk that
    was shifting from white to black by the
    mid-1950s

Broad Creek Shores--a subdivision for blacks
    that was under development at the time of
    the U.S. Supreme Court's *Brown* v. *Board*
    decision. Completion of the subdivision
    was blocked when it was found to be too
    close to white schools under the doctrine
    of proximity.

Broad Creek Village--a large navy housing pro-
    ject developed at the close of World War
    II, integrated as the military desegre-
    gated following the war, and torn down to
    make room for industrial expansion

Byrd Organization--the dominant, statewide po-
    litical machine in Virginia run by U.S.
    Senator Harry F. Byrd, Sr. (D-VA); also
    referred to simply as the "Organization "

Committee of One Hundred--the name chosen by
    an informal group of business, financial,
    and community leaders in Norfolk who
    petitioned Mayor Duckworth and the City
    Council to end their opposition to court-
    ordered integration in the city

Coronado--a small middle-class community in
    the Norview section of Norfolk that was
    the scene of racial turmoil in 1954 when
    blacks first began moving into the area

de facto segregation--the type of legal hous-
    ing and school segregation found most
    commonly in northern and midwestern cites
    where blacks and whites choose to live in
    separate race neighborhoods

Defenders of State Sovereignty and Individual
    Liberties--a statewide political pressure
    group formed to prevent the integration
    of public schools in Virginia; also re-
    ferred to as the "Defenders"

de jure segregation--the type of "Jim Crow"
    segregation found in the South before
    1954 where blacks and whites were forced
    by state laws to live in separate-race
    areas and attend separate-race schools

doctrine of proximity--the essence of the pre-
    cedent set by the U.S. Supreme Court in
    its 1954 *Brown v. Board of Education* de-
    cision. The Court held that Linda Brown
    and other blacks who lived closer to a
    white school than the black school could
    not be denied the right to attend the
    school nearest their home.

Gray Plan--a "moderate" approach in the Vir-
    ginia legislature to comply with court-
    ordered school desegregation by limiting
    the impact of integration. The Gray Plan
    was defeated, and Virginia turned instead
    to Massive Resistance (the Stanley Plan).

Harmony Ticket--the name given to Mayor Duck-
    worth's city council slate in 1950 be-
    cause it represented a forced union be-
    tween the People's (or Silkstocking)
    business reformers and the Prieur Machine
    politicians

Interposition--the centuries old doctrine that
    states have an obligation to interject
    their own authority between their citi-
    zens and an unjust action of the federal
    courts. James J. Kilpatrick and the lead-
    ers of the Byrd Organization used the
    logic of interposition to justify Massive
    Resistance in Virginia.

Lambert's Point--an integrated housing area
    near Old Dominion University that was the
    site of Norfolk Redevelopment and Housing
    Authority Project Two, also referred to
    as the Old Dominion Project

Land (or Kaufman) Committee--a group of high-
    level business, community and planning
    leaders chosen in 1954 to limit housing
    integration problems and select new sites
    for redevelopment activity

Massive Resistance--the name given to the Byrd
    Organization's attempt to prevent school
    integration by closing school buildings
    under court-orders to admit black pupils.
    Under Massive Resistance, the closed
    buildings could be sold private groups,
    who would then operate them as whites-

only private schools with tuition grants
for the students and other state support.

Norfolk Committee for Public Schools--a group
of progressive white parents who first
formed a lobby to support public schools,
and then filed lawsuits crucial to the
effort to reopen the closed schools

People's Ticket or People's administration--a
businessmen's reform movement that took
control of Norfolk's municipal government
in 1946 and then led the revitalization
of the whole area. Also called the Silkstocking Ticket by its detractors.

Prieur Machine--the local affiliate of the
statewide Byrd Organization that controlled politics and planning in Norfolk
prior to 1946 and then experienced a
rejuvenation during the 1950s

Silkstocking Takeover--the process begun under
the People's administration of replacing
partisan considerations in city government with business, planning, and professional expertise

Southside (Virginia)--the rural counties and
small cities south of Richmond that formed the base of support for both the Byrd
Organization and the Defenders of State
Sovereignty and Individual Liberties

Stanley Plan--the legal structure behind Virginia's effort to resist public school
desegregation through Massive Resistance

Summers' Plan--a local effort proposed by City
Councilman Ezra Summers to preserve segregated schools by giving students a
"choice" between attending segregated or
integrated schools

Tidewater Education Foundation--a private cor-
     poration established by the Defenders of
     State Sovereignty and Individual Liber-
     ties to operate "white flight" private
     academies in Norfolk as a replacement for
     integrated public schools

White Citizen's Councils--the name adopted by
     several racist groups in the Deep South
     that opposed integration through vio-
     lence, intimidation, protest, and polit-
     ical action

Young Turks--the name given to a group of
     younger, mostly urban Virginia legisla-
     tors, who, although part of the Byrd
     political Machine, frequently opposed the
     Organization to support racial modera-
     tion, public education, governmental
     reform, and urban development issues

Bibliography

Abbott, Carl. 1981. *The New Urban America: Growth and Politics in Sunbelt Cities*. Chapel Hill: University of North Carolina Press.

Anderson, Martin. 1964. *The Federal Bulldozer: A Critical Analysis of Urban Renewal, 1949-1962*. Cambridge: M.I.T. Press.

Agle, Charles K. 1956. *A Master Plan For The Central Business And Financial District*. Norfolk: Planning Commission, 19-20. Norfolk City Planning Department files.

Architectural Forum. 1950. "Federal Slum Clearance Gets Its First Full Scale Tryout in Norfolk, Va." May:132-138.

Armour, David J. 1980. "White Flight and the Future of School Desegregation." In *School Desegregation: Past, Present, and Future*, edited by Walter G. Stephan and Joe R. Feagin, 187-225. New York: Plenum Press.

Barron, Bryton, and Ella Barron. 1965. *The Inhumanity of Urban Renewal*. Arlington, Va.: Crestwood Books.

Beall, E. T., George W. Price, and Donald R. Locke. 1950. "Face Lifting for Better Urban Living," *Norfolk* XII, 1 (February):6-10.

Beckett, Leola Pearl, et al. v. School Board of the City of Norfolk, Va., et al. 1957. In *Race Relations Law Reporter* 2: no. 2 (April):334-340.

Beckett, Leola Pearl, et al. v. School Board of the City of Norfolk, Va., et al. 1958. In *Race Relations Law Reporter* 3: no. 5 (October):953-954.

Bellush, Jewell, and Murry Hausknecht, editors. 1967. *Urban Renewal: People, Politics, and Planning.* New York: Doubleday.

Brewbaker, J. J., Norfolk School Superintendent. 11 November 1954. Letter to H. H. George, Norfolk City Manager. Norfolk Public Schools files.

___. 8 August 1955. Letter to Sherwood Reeder, Norfolk City Manager. Norfolk Public Schools files.

___. 7 May 1956. Letter to John Corbell, Clerk of the City of Norfolk. Norfolk Public Schools Files.

___. 13 February 1957. Letter to Thomas F. Maxwell, Norfolk City Manager. Norfolk Public Schools files.

___. 21 May 1959. Letter to Thomas F. Maxwell, Norfolk City Manager. Norfolk Public Schools files.

___. 29 May 1959. Letter to Thomas F. Maxwell, Norfolk City Manager. Norfolk Public Schools files.

Brown, Oliver, et al. v. Board of Education of Topeka, Shawnee County, Kansas, et al. 1956. In *Race Relations Law Reporter* 1: no. 8 (February):6-20.

Brownfield, Lyman. 1960. "The Disposition Problem in Urban Renewal," *Journal of Law and Contemporary Problems,* XXV:4 (Autumn):736-740.

Campbell, Edmund D., and Archie L. Boswell. 1959. *Brief for Appellee,* United States Court of Appeals, Fourth Circuit, No. 7848 (*James v. Almond*), Norfolk Committee for Public Schools files, Old Dominion University archives.

Campbell, Ernest Q., *et al.* 1960. *When a City Closes Its Schools.* Chapel Hill: University of North Carolina Press.

Campbell, W. E., Assistant Superintendent of Schools. 1959. "Report of the Committee Relegated By the School Board of the City of Norfolk to Study the Proposal for Construction of Small Primary Schools." Norfolk Public Schools files.

Caro, Robert A. 1975. *The Power Broker: Robert Moses and the Fall of New York*. New York: Random House.

Carter, Luther J., former reporter for the *Norfolk Virginian-Pilot*. Interview with author, 12 January 1991. Tape Recording, Washington, D.C.

Coleman, James S., Sara P. Kelly, and John A. Moore. 1975. *Trends in School Segregation, 1968-1973*. Washington, D.C.: Urban Institute.

Community Builders of Norfolk, Virginia. 1942. Norfolk: Community Builders.

Conrad, Lewis, Assistant Norfolk City Auditor. Interview with author, 13 August 1979. Norfolk.

Crain, Robert L. et al. 1968. *The Politics of School Desegregation: Comparative Case Studies of Community Structure and Policy-Making*. Chicago: Aldine Press.

Crenshaw, Francis N., former Norfolk School Board member and legal counsel for Norfolk Redevelopment and Housing Authority. Interview with author, 7 February 1991. Tape recording, Norfolk.

Curtin, Theodore A. 1969. "A Marriage of Convenience: Norfolk and the Navy, 1917-1967." Masters thesis, Old Dominion University.

Dabney, Virginius. 1971. *Virginia: The New Dominion*. Garden City, N.Y.: Doubleday.

Darden, Pretlow, former mayor and commissioner of the Norfolk Redevelopment and Housing Authority. Interview with author, 13 August 1975. Tape recording, Norfolk.

Dillon, Gordon. 1970. "An Exceptionally Talented Lad," *Article One* I:ii (May): 17-19.

Duckworth, W. Fred, Mayor of Norfolk. 6 October 1958. Letter to J. Lindsay Almond, Governor of Virginia. Box 136 papers of Governor J. Lindsay Almond, Virginia State Archives.

Eley, James W., Jr. 1976. *The Crisis of Conservative Virginia: The Byrd Organization and the Politics of Massive Resistance, Twentieth-Century America Series*. Knoxville: University of Tennessee Press.

Ervin, Sam, Jr. 1956. "The Case for Segregation," *Look*
    20, no. 7 (April 3):32-33.

Estes, John F., former Police Sargeant. Interview with
    author, 20 September 1979. Tape Recording, Norfolk.

Frieden, Bernard 1966. "Policies for Rebuilding." In
    Urban Renewal: The Record and the Controversy, edited
    by James Q. Wilson, 585-623. Cambridge: M.I.T. Press.

Frieden, Bernard J., and Robert Morris. 1968. *Urban
    Planning and Social Policy*. New York: Basic Books.

Gans, Herbert J. 1966. "The Failure of Urban Renewal."
    In *Urban Renewal: The Record and the Controversy*,
    edited by James Q. Wilson, 540-545. Cambridge: M.I.T.
    Press.

Gragila, Lino A. 1980. "From Prohibiting Segregation to
    Requiring Integration." In *School Desegregation:
    Past, Present, and Future*, edited by Walter G. Ste-
    phan, and Joe R. Feagin, 69-96. New York: Plenum
    Press.

Greer, Scott. 1965. *Urban Renewal and American Cities:
    The Dilemma of Democratic Intervention*. New York:
    Bobbs-Merritt Co.

Greer, Scott, and David W. Miner. 1967. "The Political
    Side of Urban Development and Redevelopment." In
    Urban Renewal: People, Politics, and Planning, edited
    by Jewel Bellush and Murray Hausknect, 152-163. New
    York: Doubleday.

Gregory, L. Cameron, former reporter for the *Norfolk
    Virginian-Pilot*. Interview with author, 20 July 1979.
    Tape recording, Norfolk.

Gornto, Vernon, former campaign manager of the People's
    Ticket of 1946. Interview with author, 17 August
    1975. Norfolk.

Hagan, J. Addison, former candidate for Norfolk City
    Council. Interview with James Sweeney, 25 January
    1977. Transcript, Old Dominion University Archives.

Hanna, Ira R. 1967. "The Growth of the Norfolk Naval Air
    Station and the Norfolk-Portsmouth Metropolitan Area
    Economy in the Twentieth Century." Masters thesis,
    Old Dominion University

Harrell, Charles A. 1949. *The Norfolk Story: Annual Report for 1948*, Norfolk. Sargeant Collection, Kirn Library.

____. 1950a. "The Role of the City in America," *Norfolk* XXI:1 (February):12-14. Sargeant Collection, Kirn Library.

____. 1950b. "Norfolk--A Progress Report," *Norfolk* XII:2 (November):9-14. Sargeant Collection, Kirn Library.

Harrison, Albertis S., Jr., Attorney General of Virginia, v. Sidney C. Day, Jr., Comptroller of Virginia. 1959. *Race Relations Law Reporter* 4: no. 1 (Spring): 65-78.

Hebert, George J. 1950. "Downtown Norfolk: Commercial and Municipal Progress," *Norfolk* XXI:1 (February): 10-13. Sargeant Collection, Kirn Library.

Heywood, et al. v. Public Housing Administration. 1956. In *Race Relations Law Reporter* 1, no. 2 (April):347.

The History of Lower Tidewater, Virginia. 1954. *Family and Personal History*, vol III. New York: Lewis Historical Publishing Co.

Hoffman, Walter E. Hoffman, U.S. federal district judge. Interview with author, 8 March 1991. Tape recording, Norfolk.

Housing and Home Finance Agency. 1949. *Slum Clearance Under The Housing Act of 1949: A Preliminary Statement To American Cities*. Washington, D.C.: U.S. Government.

____. 1950. *A Guide to Slum Clearance and Urban Development*. Washington, D.C.: U.S. Government.

____. 1966. "The Operation and Achievements of the Urban Renewal Program." In *Urban Renewal: The Record and the Controversy*, edited by James Q. Wilson, 189-229. Cambridge: M.I.T. Press.

Hunter, Floyd W. 1953. *Community Power Structure*. Chapel Hill: University of North Carolina Press Press.

Jackson, Kenneth T. 1987. *Crabgrass Frontier: The Suburbanization of the United States*. New York: Oxford University Press.

James, Ruth Pendleton, et. al. v. J. Lindsay Almond, Governor of Virginia, et al. 1959. In *Race Relations Law Reporter* 4: no. 1 (Spring):46-54.

James, Ruth Pendleton, et. al. v. W. Fred Duckworth, et al. 1959. In *Race Relations Law Reporter* 4: no. 1 (Spring):55-57.

Leflar, Robert A. 1957. "Law of the Land: The Courts and the Schools." In *"With All Deliberate Speed,"* edited by Don Shoemaker, 1-14. New York: Harper & Brothers.

Martin, Roy B., Jr., former Norfolk mayor. Interview with author, 18 February 1991. Tape Recording, Norfolk.

Mason, Robert H., former editor of the *Norfolk Virginian-Pilot.* Interview with author, 27 September 1979. Tape recording, Norfolk.

McCauley, Patrick E. 1957. "Be It Enacted," In *"With All Deliberate Speed,"* edited by Don Shoemaker, 130-146. New York: Harper & Brothers.

Metcalf, George R. 1983. *From Little Rock to Boston: The History of School Desegregation.* Westport, Conn.: Greenwood Press.

Monola, G. D., former Director of Environmental Health and the Department of Community Improvement for Norfolk. Interview with author, 3 April 1991. Norfolk.

Muse, Benjamin T. 1964. *Ten Years of Prelude: The Story of Integration Since the Supreme Court's 1954 Decision.* New York: Viking Press.

Muse, Benjamin T. 1961. *Virginia's Massive Resistance.* Bloomington, Ind.: Indiana University Press.

Norfolk Chamber of Commerce. 1954. "Population and Housing Survey," *Norfolk* XVI:7 (November):10-20. Sargeant Collection, Kirn Library.

Norfolk City Planning Commission 1950. *Major Highway Plan*, Part I, *Major Highways and Collector Streets.* Norfolk, Norfolk City Planning Department files.

Norfolk Public Schools. 1959. *General Fund Budget* for the 1958-1959 school year, Norfolk Public Schools files.

___. 1960. *General Fund Budget* for the 1959-1960 school
    year, Norfolk Public Schools files.

Norfolk Redevelopment and Housing Authority 1946. *This
    Is It*. Norfolk: Norfolk Redevelopment and Housing
    Authority.

___. 1957. *Report*. Norfolk: Norfolk Redevelopment and
    Housing Authority.

___. 1975. *Annual Report to the City Council* (1974).

Orfield, Gary. 1978. *Must We Bus? Segregated Schools and
    National Policy*. Washington, D.C.: Brookings Insti-
    tute.

___. 1985. "Ghettoization and Its Alternatives," In *The
    New Urban Reality*, edited by Paul E. Peterson, 161-
    96. Washington, D.C.: Brookings Institute.

Pentecost & Courtney (Architects) (1957). "Lakewood
    Junior High School (building plans)." Norfolk Public
    Schools.

Raffel, Jeffrey A. 1980. *The Politics of School Desegre-
    gation: The Metropolitan Remedy in Delaware*. Phila-
    delphia: Temple University Press.

Reif, Jane. 1960. *Crisis in Norfolk*. Richmond: Virginia
    Council on Human Relations.

Rist, Ray. 1979. *Desegregated Schools: Appraisals of the
    American Experience*. New York: Academic Press.

Rorer, Henry S. 1968. *History of Norfolk Public Schools*.
    Norfolk: by the author. Special Collections, Old Do-
    minion University.

Rothenberg, Jerome. 1967. *Economic Evaluation of Urban
    Renewal: Conceptual Foundation of Benefit-Cost Analy-
    sis*. Washington, D. C.: Brookings Institute.

Schlegel, Marvin W. 1951. *Conscripted City: Norfolk in
    World War II*. Norfolk: Norfolk War History Commis-
    sion. Special Collections, Old Dominion University.

Schmidt, John C. 1969. "Norfolk: A City Remakes Itself,"
    Baltimore, March. Reprinted by Norfolk Redevelopment
    and Housing Authority.

School Board of the City of Norfolk. 1 July 1955. Formal
    Minutes of the Board. Norfolk Public Schools files.

___. 25 March 1958. "School Construction and Site Acqui-
sition Program." Norfolk Public Schools files.

Shoemake, Don, editor. 1957. *"With All Deliberate Speed."* New York: Harper & Brothers.

Smith, Bob. 1965. *They Closed Their Schools: Prince Edward County, Virginia, 1951-1964.* Chapel Hill: University of North Carolina Press Press.

Smith, James E., comptroller for the Norfolk Redevelopment and Housing Authority. Interview with author, 13 August 1979. Norfolk.

Staylor, Claude J., Jr., former chief of Police and Norfolk City Councilman. Interview with author, 25 July 1979. Tape recording, Norfolk.

Steadfast, Philip A., Director of the Norfolk Department of City Planning. 27 January 1976. Memorandum to Paul Smith, Assistant Superintendent for Business and Finance. Norfolk Public Schools files.

Stephan, Walter G. 1980. "A Brief Historical Overview of School Desegregation." In *School Desegregation: Past, Present, and Future*, edited by Walter G. Stephan and Joe R. Feagin, 11-17. New York: Plenum Press.

Stern, Robert L., board member of the Norfolk Committee for Public Schools. Interview with author, 22 April 1978. Norfolk.

Stinchcombe, Jean L. 1968. *Reform and Reaction: City Politics in Toledo.* Belmont, Calif.: Wadsworth.

Sugg, Harold. 1967. "1945-1965: Youth Takes Command," In *Saltwater and Printer's Ink: Norfolk and Its Newspapers, 1865-1965*, edited by Lenoir Chambers and Joseph E. Shank, 376-394. Chapel Hill: University of North Carolina Press Press.

___, former reporter and editor, *Norfolk Virginian-Pilot*. Interview with author, 17 August 1979. Tape recording, Roanoke, Va.

Suggs, Henry Lewis 1988. *P. B. Young, Newspaperman.* Charlottesville, Va.: University of Virginia.

Sullivan, Frank. 1954. "Norfolk's Redevelopment Story," *Norfolk* XVI: 7 (November): 4-25. Sargeant Collection, Kirn Library.

Sullivan, W. P., Director of Building and Grounds. 15
    September 1956. "Cost Data, Outline Specifications,
    and Facilities in the New Schools in Norfolk, Vir-
    ginia, Since 1951." Norfolk Public Schools files.

Taueber, Karl E. 1989. "Residence and Race: 1619 to
    2019." *In Race: Twentieth Century Dilemmas--
    Twenty-First Century Prognoses*, edited by Winston A.
    Van Horne. Milwaukee: University of Wisconsin.

____. 1990. "Desegregation of Public School Districts:
    Resistance and Change," *Phi Delta Kappan* 21, no. 1
    (September):18-24.

Taueber, Karl E. and Alma Taueber. 1965. *Negroes   in
    Cities: Residential Segregation and Neighborhood
    Change*. Chicago: Aldine.

U.S. Bureau of the Census. 1952. *U.S. Census of Popula-
    tion*, 1950, vol. II, *Characteristics of the Popula-
    tion*, Part 46, *Virginia*, Chapter B. Washington: U.S.
    Government.

____. 1952, v. III, *Census Tract Studies*, Chapter 38.
    Washington: U.S. Government.

Weaver, Robert C. 1967. "The Urban Complex." In *Urban
    Renewal: People, Politics, and Planning*, edited by
    Jewel Bellush and Murray Hausknecht, 90-101. Garden
    City, N.Y.: Doubleday.

Wertenbaker, Thomas J. 1962. *Norfolk: Historic Southern
    Port*. Durham, N.C.: Duke University Press.

White, Forrest P., M.D. 1959. "Will Norfolk Schools Stay
    Open?" *Atlantic Monthly* 204:iii (September):30.

____. 1959b. unpublished and untitled, Article, Norfolk
    Committee for Public Schools files, Old Dominion
    University Archives.

____. 1960. "Tuition Grants: Strange Fruit of Southern
    Integration," *South Atlantic Quarterly*, Autumn.

Williams, Robin M., and Margaret W. Ryan, editors. 1954.
    *Schools in Transition: Community Experiences in De-
    segregation*. Chapel Hill: University of North Caro-
    lina Press.

Willie, Charles V., and Susan L. Greenblatt. 1981. *Com-
    munity Politics and Educational Change: Ten School
    Systems Under Court Order*. New York: Longman.

Wilson, James Q., editor. 1966. *Urban Renewal: The Record and the Controversy*. Cambridge: M.I.T. Press.

Women's Council for Inter-racial Cooperation. 1955. "Letters to the Press: A Sampling of Public Opinion on Desegregation." *Women's Council for Inter-racial Cooperation NewsSheet*, March, Norfolk Committee for Public Schools files, Old Dominion University Archives.

___. 1959. "How Norfolk's Closed Schools Were Reopened." Norfolk Committee for Public Schools files, Old Dominion University Archives.

Workman, W. D., Jr. 1957. "The Deep South." In *"With All Deliberate Speed,"* edited by Don Shoemaker, 88-109. New York: Harper & Brothers.

NEWSPAPERS (in chronological order)

"Councilmanic Consensus on Norfolk Housing," editorial, *Norfolk Virginian-Pilot*, 4 December 1938. Sargeant Collection.

"City Administration Ticket Winners In Election," *Norfolk Virginian-Pilot*, 10 June 1942, 20.

Twiford, Warner, "Old Mother Norfolk Lets Her Hair Down," *Norfolk Virginian-Pilot*, 15 August 1945, 22.

Twiford, Warner, "The Night Before Is What Norfolk Remembers (Though Some Celebrants May Be Exception)," *Norfolk Virginian-Pilot*, 16 August 1945, 18.

Borland, Armistead (City Manager), "Defects at City Hall," guest editorial, *Norfolk Ledger-Dispatch*, 21 February 1946, 6.

"Halstead Asks City Committee to Solve White-Negro Problem," *Norfolk Virginian-Pilot*, 29 May 1946, 2-3.

"Council Asked to Stop Move to White Areas," *Norfolk Journal and Guide*, 1 June 1946, 1.

"Wrong Way to Solve the Housing Shortage Problem in Norfolk," *Norfolk Journal and Guide*, 1 June 1946, 1.

"Low Cost Housing a Paying Investment," editorial, *Norfolk Journal and Guide*, 1 June 1946, 10.

"Seven Seek Racial Answer in Brambleton," *Norfolk Virginian-Pilot*, 1 June 1946, 16.

"Ruffin Says Borland Resigned as City Manager 'In a Violent Temper'; Accuses Official of Attempting to Usurp Functions of Council," *Norfolk Virginian-Pilot*, 5 June 1946.

"Vote for Ashe," editorial, *Norfolk Journal and Guide*, 8 June 1946.

"Our 'Pig-in-a-Poke' Qualification System, editorial, *Norfolk Virginian-Pilot*, 11 June 1946, 6.

Lankford, G. Wright, "Cooke, Darden and Twohy Win City Council Election," *Norfolk Virginian-Pilot*, 12 June 1946, 1.

Sugg, Harold, "Time to Act on Housing, All 5 Councilmen Agree," *Norfolk Virginian-Pilot*, 28 November 1948. Sargeant Collection.

Sullivan, Frank, "New Norfolk Out of Old: Program Outlined," *Norfolk Virginian-Pilot*, 4 October 1949, 1.

"130 Arrested in 'Numbers' Raid; Tickets, $3,051 in Cash Taken," *Norfolk Virginian-Pilot*, 3 December 1948, 40.

Gregory, Cameron, "114 'Numbers' Defendants Fined; Total of $11,700, 16 Dismissed, 2 Continued," *Norfolk Virginian-Pilot*, 4 December 1948, 20.

"The Grand Jury's Report on the Police Department," *Norfolk Virginian-Pilot*, 13 March 1949, 6.

Kelley, George, "The Boys Don't Call Him 'Charley,'" *Norfolk Virginian-Pilot*, 4 June 1950, V-1.

"The New Councilmen," an editorial, *Norfolk Virginian-Pilot*, 14 June 1950. Sargeant Collection.

"Redevelopment Project Will Start Next Month," *Norfolk Virginian-Pilot*, 15 August 1950, 1. Sargeant Collection.

"Slum Project Approved By Council," *Norfolk Virginian-Pilot*, 22 August 1951, A-17. Sargeant Collection.

Sullivan, Frank, "Rumble of First Slum House to Be Razed Echoes 15 Years of Planning," *Norfolk Virginian-Pilot*, 12 December 1951, 1.

"New School Districts Are Formed," *Norfolk Ledger-Dispatch*, 13 December 1951. Sargeant Collection.

Kelley, George, "City Culture United under Center Plans," *Norfolk Virginian-Pilot*, 23 December 1951. Sargeant Collection.

Sullivan, Frank, "$10.9 Million Loan-Grant Executed for Redevelopment Project Number 1," *Norfolk Virginian-Pilot*, 16 April 1952. Sargeant Collection.

"A Half-Century's Blueprint," editorial, *Norfolk Virginian-Pilot*, 9 July 1952. Sargeant Collection.

"Segregation's Summing Up--Living and Evolving Law," editorial, *Norfolk Virginian-Pilot*, 13 December 1952, 5.

"Housing Authority Powers Should Not Be Abused," editorial, *Norfolk Virginian-Pilot*, 20 May 1953. Sargeant Collection.

"Cost of Negro Schooling Hits $217.55 Per Pupil," *Norfolk Ledger-Dispatch*, 21 August 1953. Sargeant Collection.

"City Council Divided on Annexation As Costs Soar Beyond Expectations," *Norfolk Virginian-Pilot*, 15 March 1954, 2-1.

"The Decision on Segregation," editorial, *Norfolk Virginian-Pilot*, 18 May 1954, 6.

Marcus, Clare, "'Keep Calm' Is Plea of Brewbaker," *Norfolk Virginian-Pilot*, 18 May 1954, back page.

"Norfolk's Dual School System," map, *Norfolk Virginian-Pilot*, 18 May 1954, back page.

Sullivan, Frank, "Kiland Asks Retention of War Housing," *Norfolk Virginian-Pilot*, 11 June 1954. Sargeant Collection.

"Negro Agent Holds Firm on Coronado Home Sales," *Norfolk Virginian-Pilot*, 30 July 1954. Sargeant Collection.

"Norfolk Will Begin to Operate Broad Creek Village October 1," *Norfolk Virginian-Pilot*, 11 August 1954, 32.

Cahill, Carl, "Home Owners of Both Races Seek Solution to Problem," *Norfolk Ledger-Dispatch*, 16 August 1954. Sargeant Collection.

"Coronado Still County Matter in Eyes of City," *Norfolk Virginian-Pilot*, 19 August 1954. Sargeant Collection.

Rodeffer, Charles C., "Home of Whites Threatened Says Resident of Coronado," *Norfolk Virginian-Pilot*, 19 August 1954. Sargeant Collection.

Smith, Robert C., "Coronado: Where Mixed Housing, through Sales, Has Generated Tensions," *Norfolk Virginian-Pilot*, 22 August 1954. Sargeant Collection.

"Newly Occupied House Shaken, Panes Broken," *Norfolk Virginian-Pilot*, 25 August 1954. Sargeant Collection.

Cahill, Carl, "State and County Police Probe Blast in Coronado," *Norfolk Ledger-Dispatch*, 30 August 1954. Sargeant Collection.

Young, P. B., Sr., "Negroes in Coronado," guest editorial, *Norfolk Virginian-Pilot*, 31 August 1954. Sargeant Collection.

McKnight, C. A., "Reporting Service to Tell School Story," *Southern School News*, 3 September 1954, 1.

"Reaction to Supreme Court Decision Calm, Resigned," *Southern School News*, 3 September 1954, 1-2.

"Coronado and the Law," an editorial, *Norfolk Virginian-Pilot*, 11 September 1954. Sargeant Collection.

"Porch, Interior of Coronado Home, Sold in June, Damaged by Explosion," *Norfolk Virginian-Pilot*, 11 September 1954. Sargeant Collection.

May, Ronald, "Blast-Ravaged House in Coronado Looted; Action by Governor Asked," *Norfolk Virginian-Pilot*, 12 September 1954.

Smith, Robert C., "Bullets Fired into Coronado Home; Two Negro Residents Are Uninjured," *Norfolk Virginian-Pilot*, 20 September 1954. Sargeant Collection.

"Virginia: Parochial Schools Integrated Calmly," *Southern School News*, 1 October 1954, 14.

"The Segregation Decision Curbs School Construction," editorial, *Norfolk Ledger-Dispatch*, 13 October 1954, 6.

"Leaders Blame Racial Communications Problems on Pressures to Integrate," *Southern School News*, 1 December 1954, 7.

"School-Building Arithmetic--It's the Hardest Subject," editorial, *Norfolk Virginian-Pilot*, 16 January 1955. Sargeant Collection.

Hopkins, Mary, "Norfolk Keeps Pace with Growing Need for Schools," *Norfolk Ledger-Dispatch*, 28 January 1955. Sargeant Collection.

Smith, Robert C., "Apprehension about the Future Seizes Broad Creek Villagers," *Norfolk Virginian-Pilot*, 24 April 1955. Sargeant Collection.

Kelley, George M., "Broad Creek Rezoning for Industry Approved With Residents' Backing," *Norfolk Virginian-Pilot*, 21 May 1955. Sargeant Collection.

"Group Study of Integration Rapidly Gains Adherents," *Norfolk Virginian-Pilot*, 3 June 1955. Sargeant Collection.

"Study Group Wins Backing," *Norfolk Virginian-Pilot*, 18 June 1955. Sargeant Collection.

Kelley, George M. "Study Seeking New Basis for Referendums Ordered," *Norfolk Virginian-Pilot*, 6 July 1955. Sargeant Collection.

"Virginia: Norfolk Board Votes 'Approval in Principle' of Integration," *Southern School News*, 6 July 1955, 10.

"Schools Lauded for Racial Stand," *Norfolk Ledger-Dispatch*, 11 July 1955. Sargeant Collection.

Phillips, Joseph V., "End to School Segregation Petition Handed to Board," *Norfolk Virginian-Pilot*, 14 July 1955. Sargeant Collection.

Kelley, George M., "Parent Could Pick School under 'Integration' Plan Summers Offers to Council," *Norfolk Virginian-Pilot*, 27 July 1955. Sargeant Collection.

"City 'Compromises' on Shores Property," *Norfolk Journal and Guide*, 6 August 1955, 1.

"Group Reports on Race Home Sites," *Norfolk Journal and Guide*, 6 August 1955, 17.

"The Kaufman Committee Report," editorial, *Norfolk Journal and Guide*, 6 August 1955, 1-2.

"Virginia: More Counties Choose to Vote School Funds Month by Month," *Southern School News*, August, 1955, 10.

"Rising Pressure for School Space," editorial, *Norfolk Virginian-Pilot*, 17 September 1955. Sargeant Collection.

"A Broad Creek Shores Plan Replaces an Issue There," editorial, *Norfolk Virginian-Pilot*, 19 September 1955. Sargeant Collection.

"The City School Program and How It May Grow," editorial, *Norfolk Virginian-Pilot*, 19 September 1955. Sargeant Collection.

"Virginia: Newport News Board Turns School over to Negroes Rather Than Integrate," *Southern School News*, October 1955, 6.

Smith, Robert C., "Integration Effect Minimized; Circumvention Effort Denied," *Norfolk Virginian-Pilot*, 5 January 1956. Sargeant Collection.

Holloway, Lin, "Progress Was By-Word in Norfolk in '55," *Norfolk Journal and Guide*, 7 January 1956. Sargeant Collection.

"From Ripley to Layton on the City Council," *Norfolk Virginian-Pilot*, 9 February 1956. Sargeant Collection.

"City Schools Fast Reducing Shift Classes," *Norfolk Virginian-Pilot*, 10 February 1956. Sargeant Collection.

"Abbott-Summers-Layton--Administration Ticket," editorial, *Norfolk Virginian-Pilot*, 6 March 1956. Sargeant Collection.

Sullivan, Frank, "Bids on Final Housing Project Opened; $2,625,982 Low Figure," *Norfolk Virginian-Pilot*, 22 March 1956. Sargeant Collection.

"Tidewater Drive Building Booms," *Norfolk Virginian-Pilot*, 22 March 1956. Sargeant Collection.

"Views on Oakwood Plan Aired," *Norfolk Journal and Guide*, 31 March 1956, 2-1. Sargeant Collection.

"Segregation on Buses Officially Discontinued," *Norfolk Virginian-Pilot*, 25 April 1956. Sargeant Collection.

Carter, Luther J., "Oakwood's Redevelopment Hangs Fire Pending Appeal," *Norfolk Virginian-Pilot*, 29 April 1956, C-1.

"Segregation Supported By Summers," *Norfolk Virginian-Pilot*, 11 May 1956. Sargeant Collection.

Henderson, Jim, "Negroes Ask for Injunction Ending School Segregation in Norfolk; Claim 'Injury,'" *Norfolk Virginian-Pilot*, 11 May 1956. Sargeant Collection.

Kelley, George M., "Norfolk Request for Special Session Includes any Ideas Beyond Gray Plan," *Norfolk Virginian-Pilot*, 13 May 1956. Sargeant Collection.

"Norfolk School Board 'Unable to Act' Alone on Desegregation," *Norfolk Virginian-Pilot*, 14 May 1956. Sargeant Collection.

"Downtown Waterfront Priority," an editorial, *Norfolk Virginian-Pilot*, 28 May 1956. Sargeant Collection.

"Segregation Policy and Laws 'Valid,' School Board Answers," *Norfolk Virginian-Pilot*, 22 June 1956. Sargeant Collection.

"Racial Status in Schools of Norfolk May Continue through '56-57 Terms," *Norfolk Ledger-Dispatch*, 3 July 1956. Sargeant Collection.

Kelley, George M., "Continued School Operation Norfolk's First Aim," *Norfolk Virginian-Pilot*, 24 July 1956, 1.

Phillips, Joseph V., "Integration Study Group Is Launched," *Norfolk Virginian-Pilot*, 6 August 1956. Sargeant Collection.

"Bold, Imaginative Agle Report," editorial, *Norfolk Virginian-Pilot*, 14 August 1956. Sargeant Collection.

"Norfolk's Other 'Center'," editorial, *Norfolk Ledger-Dispatch*, 22 August 1956. Sargeant Collection.

Stein, Tony, "Negroes Granted Free Use of Portsmouth Golf Course," *Norfolk Ledger-Dispatch*, 29 August 1956. Sargeant Collection.

"Some History Making on the Council," editorial, *Norfolk Virginian-Pilot*, 3 September 1956. Sargeant Collection.

Leslie, Joseph A., III, "City's Master Plan Opposed and Praised during Hearing," *Norfolk Virginian-Pilot*, 11 September 1956. Sargeant Collection.

Sullivan, Frank, "1,000 Dwelling Units Due for Rehabilitation," *Norfolk Virginian-Pilot*, 11 October 1956. Sargeant Collection.

"Third Party Is Operating in Quarters," *Norfolk Virginian-Pilot*, 13 October 1956. Sargeant Collection.

Carter, Luther J., "$15 Million Revised School Plan Set," *Norfolk Virginian-Pilot*, 24 October 1956. Sargeant Collection.

Smith, Robert C., "Origin of 'Hate' Pamphlets Is Exposed After 'Sneak Attacks' on Chest Drives," *Norfolk Virginian-Pilot*, 25 October 1956.

Sullivan, Frank, "Atlantic City Redevelopment Hearing Scheduled January 4," *Norfolk Virginian-Pilot*, 8 December 1956. Sargeant Collection.

"Norfolk's Deferred Projects," editorial, *Norfolk Ledger-Dispatch*, 17 December 1956. Sargeant Collection.

Williams, Paul, "Cloud over Future of New School Seen," *Norfolk Ledger-Dispatch*, 19 December 1956. Sargeant Collection.

Sullivan, Frank, "Atlantic City Redevelopment Fought by Property Owners," *Norfolk Virginian-Pilot*, 5 January 1957, 24.

"New Negro Elementary School Plans Pressed," *Norfolk Virginian-Pilot*, 26 January 1957, 27.

"Background: Power to Assign Pupils Is Studied in 7 States," *Southern Schools News*, February, 1957, 1.

Henderson, Jim, "Norfolk Schools Ordered to Integrate in Fall," *Norfolk Virginian-Pilot*, 13 February 1957, 1.

"13 Schools Affected by Integration," *Norfolk Virginian-Pilot*, 13 February 1957, A-8.

Porter, Jean Bishop, "Parents Favor More City Funds to Better Schools," *Norfolk Ledger-Dispatch*, 15 February 1957. Sargeant Collection.

Dodson, Bob, "Atlantic City Development to Cost City $7,700,000," *Norfolk Ledger-Dispatch*, 17 February 1957. Sargeant Collection.

"Court's Ruling in Newport News Case," *Southern School-News*, March 1957, 14.

Carter, Luther J., "Elementary-Junior High for Oakwood-Rosemont Studied by School Officials," *Norfolk Virginian-Pilot*, 8 March 1957. Sargeant Collection.

Smith, Robert C., "Aging Atlantic City is Next on the List," *Norfolk Virginian-Pilot*, 10 March 1957. Sargeant Collection.

Kelley, George M., "Usual Operation until Crisis Rises," *Norfolk Virginian-Pilot*, 16 March 1957. Sargeant Collection.

Kelley, George M., "In Virginia 'All of Us in Same Boat,'" *Norfolk Virginian-Pilot*, 26 March 1957. Sargeant Collection.

Carter, Luther J., "Integration Opposed By P.T.A. Council," *Norfolk Virginian-Pilot*, 30 March 1957, 28.

"Hagan, Ford, and White File for Primary Race," *Norfolk Virginian-Pilot*, 10 April 1957. Sargeant Collection.

"Two Views of 'Resistance,'" editorial, *Norfolk Ledger-Dispatch*, 8 June 1957. Sargeant Collection.

Smith, Robert C., "Atlantic City Plan Would Erase Dangers to Health, Safety, Morals," *Norfolk Virginian-Pilot*, 23 June 1957.

"Norfolk's New Councilman," editorial, *Norfolk Virginian-Pilot*, 26 June 1957. Sargeant Collection.

"A Resident," "Talk of Slums--Not the Facts--Injured Atlantic City," letter to the editor, *Norfolk Virginian-Pilot*, 1 July 1957. Sargeant Collection.

Carter, Luther J., "Old School Considered for Offices," *Norfolk Virginian-Pilot*, 9 August 1957. Sargeant Collection.

Blackford, Frank, "Mandate from Court Due Soon in Nor-
    folk," *Norfolk Virginian-Pilot*, 22 October 1957. Sar-
    geant Collection.

"Old B C V School Will Be Removed," *Norfolk Ledger-Dis-
    patch*, 21 December 1957. Sargeant Collection.

"Population Shift Will Hit School," *Norfolk Virginian-
    Pilot*, 3 January 1958. Sargeant Collection.

Dodson, Bob, "Local Legislators Moved Independently on
    Mixing," *Norfolk Ledger-Dispatch*, 10 March 1958.
    Sargeant Collection.

Carter, Luther J. "5.5 Million Program for Schools
    Drafted," *Norfolk Virginian-Pilot*, 28 March 1958.
    Sargeant Collection.

"1958 City Campaign and Its Obligations," *Norfolk Vir-
    ginian-Pilot*, 14 April 1958. Sargeant Collection.

Holloway, Lin, "Building Shifts Indicate Norfolk Popula-
    tion Trends," *Norfolk Journal and Guide*, 19 April
    1958, 17.

Carter, Luther J., "Integration May Close 6 Schools,"
    Norfolk Virginian-Pilot, 21 May 1958. Sargeant Col-
    lection.

"Landsdale Junior High to be 'One of the City's Fin-
    est,'" *Norfolk Virginian-Pilot*, 6 June 1958. Sargeant
    Collection.

Kelley, George M., "Biracial Study Goal of Petition,"
    Norfolk Virginian-Pilot, 11 June 1958, p. 1.

"At Tax Windows and Behind Bars," editorial, *Norfolk
    Virginian-Pilot*, 12 June 1958. Norfolk Committee for
    Public Schools files, Old Dominion University Ar-
    chives.

Carter, Luther J., "'Frustrated' City School Board Looks
    for Collision of Authority," *Norfolk Virginian-Pilot*,
    13 June 1958. Sargeant Collection.

"Negro Pupils' Applications by Schools," *Norfolk Virgin-
    ian-Pilot*, 13 June 1958. Sargeant Collection.

"Inter-Racial Relations," *Norfolk Virginian-Pilot*, 15
    June 1958, D-3.

Bibliography

"Bi-Racial 'Bargaining' Repudiated," *Norfolk Virginian-Pilot*, 19 June 1958. Norfolk Committee for Public Schools files, Old Dominion University Archives.

"The 'Black Eye' of Closed Schools," editorial, *Norfolk Virginian-Pilot*, 20 July 1958, D-2.

"Closing School's Doors Is 'Small Sacrifice,'" *Norfolk Virginian-Pilot*, 25 July 1958, 60.

"Clergymen Rule Out Classes," *Norfolk Virginian-Pilot*, 7 August 1958. Sargeant Collection.

Carter, Luther J., "City School Board Denies Negro Applications," *Norfolk Virginian-Pilot*, 19 August 1958, 1.

Young, P. Bernard, Jr., "Key Participants in Norfolk School Integration Suit," *Norfolk Journal and Guide*, 30 August 1958.

Brooks, John I., "Six Norfolk Schools Facing Closing Threat as Board Agrees to Admit 17 Negro Students," *Norfolk Virginian-Pilot*, 30 August 1958, 1.

Carter, Luther J., "September 22 Date for Norfolk Schools," *Norfolk Virginian-Pilot*, 3 September 1958. Sargeant Collection.

Geary, James, "Don't Assign Negro Pupils, Almond Tells Norfolk Board," *Norfolk Virginian-Pilot*, 5 September 1958, 1.

Carter, Luther J., "Southside Classes Offered If 6 Norfolk Schools Close," *Norfolk Virginian-Pilot*, 12 September 1958, 1.

"Committee Is Formed to Keep Schools Open," *Norfolk Virginian-Pilot*, 19 September 1958, 1.

"What 'Progress,' Governor?" editorial, *Norfolk Virginian-Pilot*, 25 September 1958, 4.

"654 Norfolk Students Enrolled Outside City," *Norfolk Virginian-Pilot*, 26 September 1958. Sargeant Collection.

Williams, Paul, "Mayor Suggests Ministers Use Persuasion on Negroes," *Norfolk Ledger-Dispatch*, 1 October 1958. Sargeant Collection.

Carter, Luther J. "Closed City Schools' Cost Put at
    $172,000 Monthly," *Norfolk Virginian-Pilot*, 2 October
    1958, 1.

"NEA Wants Schools Open with Mixing If Necessary," *Nor-
    folk Ledger-Dispatch*, 3 October 1958. Sargeant Col-
    lection.

Ripley, Josephine, "Virginia's Massive Resistance Cracks
    Under Court Hammers," *Christian Science Monitor*, 8
    October 1958, 3.

Brooks, John I., "Tidewater Educational Foundation: What
    Next?" *Norfolk Virginian-Pilot*, 12 October 1958.
    Sargeant Collection.

"3,000 to 3,500 Studying in Norfolk Tutor Groups," *Nor-
    folk Ledger-Dispatch*, 13 October 1958. Sargeant Col-
    lection.

Carter, Luther J., "Norfolk Students in Area Schools,"
    Norfolk Virginian-Pilot, 16 October 1958, 1.

"What 'Massive Resistance' Costs City," *Norfolk Virgin-
    ian-Pilot*, 16 October 1958. Sargeant Collection.

Carter, Luther J., "Is Norfolk 'Complacent' Since
    Schools Closed?," *Norfolk Virginian-Pilot*, 19 October
    1958, D-3.

Roberts, Gene, "The Hows and Whys of a Referendum," *Nor-
    folk Virginian-Pilot*, 19 October 1958, D-1.

"Norfolk Citizens Request Almond to Return Schools,"
    Norfolk Ledger-Dispatch, 22 October 1958, 19.

Roberts, Gene, "School Referendum Set; Board Rebuffed,"
    Norfolk Virginian-Pilot, 22 October 1958. Sargeant
    Collection.

"Help Reopen Schools, Businessmen Urged," *Norfolk Vir-
    ginian-Pilot*, 23 October 1958. Sargeant Collection.

"Little Hope Is Offered by Almond," *Norfolk Virginian-
    Pilot*, 23 October 1958. Norfolk Committee for Public
    Schools files, Old Dominion University Archives.

"Education," *Norfolk Virginian-Pilot*, 26 October 1958,
    D-3.

Carter, Luther J., "Teachers Paid Little as Tutors," *Norfolk Virginian-Pilot*, 6 November 1958. Sargeant Collection.

"State Obligation toward Schools Dead--Harrison," *Norfolk Virginian-Pilot*, 8 November 1958, A-1.

"If Norfolk Won't Stand with Us, I Say Make Them Stand--Tuck," *Norfolk Virginian-Pilot*, 13 November 1958, 1.

"Tuition Charges Allowed," *Norfolk Virginian-Pilot*, 15 November 1958. Sargeant Collection.

Dodson, Bob, "Integration Foes Win Norfolk Vote," *Norfolk Ledger-Dispatch*, 19 November 1958. Sargeant Collection.

"Vote by Precincts," *Norfolk Virginian-Pilot*, 19 November 1958, 8.

Brooks, John I., "Court Delays Its Decision in Test on Closed Schools," *Norfolk Virginian-Pilot*, 20 November 1958, 1.

Kelley, George M., "City Negro Schools in Line for Closing," *Norfolk Virginian-Pilot*, 26 November 1958, 1.

Roberts, Gene, "New Private School Going Up in Norfolk," *Norfolk Virginian-Pilot*, 5 December 1958. Sargeant Collection.

"Statewide Organization Set Up to Save Schools," *Norfolk Virginian-Pilot*, 7 December 1958. Sargeant Collection.

"Layton's School Plea Falls on Deaf Ears," *Norfolk Virginian-Pilot*, 11 December 1958. Sargeant Collection.

Sullivan, Frank, "Business and Industry Are Geared for Good Year," *Norfolk Virginian-Pilot*, 1 January 1959. "The Year Virginia Closed the Schools," editorial, *Norfolk Virginian-Pilot*, 1 January 1959. Sargeant Collection.

Kelley, George M., "Forced Integration in Norfolk Schools Foreseen by Almond," *Norfolk Virginian-Pilot*, 4 January 1959, 1.

Sofflin, Mike, "Virginia Business Recovers," *Norfolk Virginian-Pilot*, 4 January 1959, C-1.

Kelley, George M., "Southside's Suspicions toward Nor-
    folk Change," *Norfolk Virginian-Pilot*, 11 January
    1959, C-1.

"Committee on Schools Critical," *Norfolk Virginian-
    Pilot*, 14 January 1959, 8.

"The Council's Lock Out," editorial, *Norfolk Virginian-
    Pilot*, 14 January 1959, 4.

"Council Step Advances Rosemont School Plans," *Norfolk
    Virginian-Pilot*, 14 January 1959. Sargeant Collec-
    tion.

Kelley, George M. and Gene Roberts, "Negro Secondary
    Schools Face Closing Along with All White Grades Over
    6th," *Norfolk Virginian-Pilot*, 14 January 1959, 1.

Martin, (Councilman) Roy B., "Martin's Statement," *Nor-
    folk Virginian-Pilot*, 14 January 1959, 8.

"Granby Scores Cut-Off," *Norfolk Virginian-Pilot*, 15
    January 1959.

"Carter, Luther J., "'Moral Right' to Limit Education Is
    Questioned By P.T.A. of Bay View," *Norfolk Virginian-
    Pilot*, 16 January 1959, 57.

"Do They Know What They Are Doing?," editorial, *Norfolk
    Virginian-Pilot*, 16 January 1959, 4.

"Bite the Hand That Feeds Us?," editorial, *Norfolk Vir-
    ginian-Pilot*, 17 January 1959, 4.

"Chamber Voice on Schools Quiet After Committee Bid,"
    Norfolk Virginian-Pilot, 17 January 1959, 15.

"Counter-Revolution among P.T.A.'s," editorial, *Norfolk
    Virginian-Pilot*, 18 January 1959, 3-B.

Henderson, Jim and John I. Brooks, "Massive Resistance
    Laws Ruled Void by Both Virginia and Federal Courts,"
    Norfolk Virginian-Pilot, 20 January 1959, 1.

"Open Schools Soon, Schweitzer Advises." *Norfolk Virgin-
    ian-Pilot*, 20 January 1959, 1.

Kelley, George M., "Stand Fast, Governor Pleads," *Nor-
    folk Virginian-Pilot*, 21 January 1959, 1.

"Women's Boos Stop Council," *Norfolk Virginian-Pilot*, 21
    January 1959, 1.

Mulfold, Ralph, "'Lost Class of '59' Called Objective by Observers," *Norfolk Ledger-Dispatch*, 22 January 1959, 21.

"Navy Has Plans for Own Schools," *Norfolk Ledger-Dispatch*, 22 January 1959, 1.

Kelley, George M., "Norfolk School Closings Permanently Banned," *Norfolk Virginian-Pilot*, 24 January 1959, 1.

Carter, Luther J., "History of a Norfolk Tiff," *Norfolk Virginian-Pilot*, 25 January 1959, C-1.

Mansfield, Richard M., "School Problem before Congress," *Norfolk Virginian-Pilot*, 25 January 1959, C-2.

Henderson, Jim, "Cut-Off Ruling Due Today at 4 P.M.," *Norfolk Virginian-Pilot*, 27 January 1959. 1.

"A New Clear Voice Speaks in Norfolk," editorial, *Norfolk Virginian-Pilot*, 27 January 1959, 4.

"A Public Petition to the Norfolk City Council," advertisement, *Norfolk Virginian-Pilot*, 27 January 1959, 11.

"Reopen Schools, Council Urged," *Norfolk Virginian-Pilot*, 27 January 1959, 1.

"Schools Could Operate Even with Funds Cut," *Norfolk Virginian-Pilot*, 27 January 1959, 5.

Henderson, Jim, "Way Cleared for Norfolk Integration,"*Norfolk Virginian-Pilot*, 28 January 1959, 9.

"New School Plea Aimed at Council," *Norfolk Virginian-Pilot*, 28 January 1959, 13.

"T.E.F. Seeks City School Buildings," *Norfolk Virginian-Pilot*, 28 January 1959, 1.

Kelley, George M., "Gloomy Legislators Laud Governor But Still Seeking to Bar Integration," *Norfolk Virginian-Pilot*, 29 January 1959, 1.

"Ohioan Would Cut Federal Spending in Norfolk Area," *Norfolk Virginian-Pilot*, 29 January 1959, 48.

Carter, Luther J., "Norfolk Opening Set," *Norfolk Virginian-Pilot*, 30 January 1959, 1.

Kelley, George M., "Resisters Make Their Bid Today,"
    Norfolk Virginian-Pilot, 30 January 1959, 1.

"Resurrection Morn on Botetort Street," editorial, *Nor-
    folk Virginian-Pilot*, 31 January 1959. Sargeant Col-
    lection.

Phillips, Cabell, "Norfolk Schools Aim to Avoid 'Little
    Rock,'" *New York Times*, 1 February 1959, 6-E.

Lewis, Anthony, "Virginia Viewed as Turning Point for
    Integration," *New York Times*, 1 February 1959, 1.

"The Opening of Schools," editorial, *Norfolk Virginian-
    Pilot*, 1 February 1959, B-2.

Carter, Luther J., "7 Schools Desegregated Peacefully,"
    Norfolk Virginian-Pilot, 3 February 1959, A-1.

Bigart, Homer, "Virginia Integration Still Has Far to
    Go," *New York Times*, 8 February 1959, E-7.

"Schools Face Budget Cuts, Mayor Warns," *Norfolk Virgin-
    ian-Pilot*, 21 February 1959, 28.

"Commission Invites Ideas on Schools," *Norfolk Virgin-
    ian-Pilot*, 22 February 1959, 1.

Carter, Luther J., "Board Names Small-School Study
    Group," *Norfolk Virginian-Pilot*, 27 February 1959,
    56.

"Small Primary Schools Approved by Committee," *Norfolk
    Virginian-Pilot*, 13 March 1959. Sargeant Collection.

Roberts, Gene, "Young Candidates Buck Resisters," *Nor-
    folk Virginian-Pilot*, 15 April 1959. Sargeant Collec-
    tion.

"School Board May Lose Two," *Norfolk Virginian-Pilot*, 22
    April 1959. Norfolk Committee for Public Schools
    files, Old Dominion University Archives.

Crenshaw, Francis N., letter to the editor, *Norfolk Vir-
    ginian-Pilot*, 22 April 1959. Norfolk Committee for
    Public Schools files, Old Dominion University Ar-
    chives.

"Breeden Supports School Board Bill," *Norfolk Virginian-
    Pilot*, 23 April 1959, 60.

"Letters to the Editor," *Norfolk Virginian-Pilot*, April 23-26, 1959. Norfolk Committee for Public Schools files, Old Dominion University Archives.

"Committee Seeks School Suit Fee," *Norfolk Ledger-Dispatch*, 2 May 1959. Norfolk Committee for Public Schools files, Old Dominion University Archives.

"Schools Cut Opposed By Parents," *Norfolk Virginian-Pilot*, 13 May 1959. Norfolk Committee for Public Schools files, Old Dominion University Archives.

Carter, Luther J., "Demountable Classrooms for Coronado," *Norfolk Virginian-Pilot*, 8 July 1959. Sargeant Collection.

Kelley, George M., "Breeden Defeats Spencer; Howell, Childress Head to House," *Norfolk Virginian-Pilot*, 15 July 1959.

Kelley, George C. "How the Roof Fell In on Grover Outland," *Norfolk Virginian-Pilot*, 19 July 1959, C-1.

"School Board Firm on Oakwood Plans," *Norfolk Virginian-Pilot*, 21 July 1959. Sargeant Collection.

"New Junior High Indicated in Eastern Part of Norfolk," *Norfolk Virginian-Pilot*, 8 August 1959. Sargeant Collection.

Mulford, Ralph, "Negroes Make Move to Push Integration," *Norfolk Ledger-Dispatch*, 20 August 1959. Sargeant Collection.

"Little Creek to Get Junior High School," *Norfolk Virginian-Pilot*, 23 October 1959. Sargeant Collection.

Carter, Luther J., "The Politics of a Budget," *Norfolk Virginian-Pilot*, 25 October 1959, 3.

Kelley, George M., "Vote Solidly Democratic, Negroes Told," *Norfolk Virginian-Pilot*, 30 October 1959. Sargeant Collection.

"Council Acquires New School Site," *Norfolk Ledger-Dispatch*, 11 November 1959. Sargeant Collection.

"Larger School Outlay Demanded," *Norfolk Virginian-Pilot*, 8 December 1959. Sargeant Collection.

Kestner, Jack, "Paul Schweitzer Talked Over New Post with Whole Family Before Signing Up," *Norfolk Ledger-Dispatch*, 16 February 1960. Sargeant Collection.

Paschang, Chet, "Schweitzer Choice Appears Move for Harmony Slate," *Norfolk Ledger-Dispatch*, 16 February 1960. Sargeant Collection.

Stein, Tony, "He'll Work Hard and Lead Others," *Norfolk Ledger-Dispatch*, 30 March 1960. Sargeant Collection.

Stein, Tony, "Lewis Layton: Often a Compromise Is the Only Way, *Norfolk Ledger-Dispatch*, 19 May 1960. Sargeant Collection.

Dodson, Bob, "Opposition Guide Ballot to List Paul Schweitzer?" *Norfolk Ledger-Dispatch*, 10 June 1960. Sargeant Collection.

Dodson, Bob, "Sam Barfield Will Attend If 'Secret' Meetings Open," *Norfolk Ledger-Dispatch*, 15 June 1960. Sargeant Collection.

"Old School Faces Ax," *Norfolk Virginian-Pilot*, 19 August 1960. Sargeant Collection.

Carter, Luther J., "Political Change Breathes in City," *Norfolk Virginian-Pilot*, 5 September 1960, 29.

Richardson, Barrett, "Challenge Children Board Member Says," *Norfolk Ledger-Dispatch*, 29 May 1961. Sargeant Collection.

Tazewell, William L., "A New Norfolk Has Arisen Out of the Blight," *Norfolk Virginian-Pilot*, 23 July 1961. Norfolk Redevelopment and Housing Authority.

Tazewell, William L., "Businessmen Provide Push in Norfolk Development," *Norfolk Virginian-Pilot*, 25 July 1961. Norfolk Redevelopment and Housing Authority.

Tazewell, William L. "Renewal Men Spark City's Growth,"*Norfolk Virginian-Pilot*, 26 July 1961. Norfolk Redevelopment and Housing Authority.

"Norfolk Man Got $6 A Week to Start," *Richmond Times-Dispatch*, 3 February 1963. Sargeant Collection.

Carter, Luther J., "'The Senator Couldn't Be Reached,'" *Norfolk Virginian-Pilot*, 9 June 1964, A-1.

Woodlief, Wayne, "Political and Social Polish Can't
    Smooth Ballard's Face," *Norfolk Ledger-Star*, 1
    September 1964. Sargeant Collection.

Owen, Gene, "Hard Times Touched First Citizen in Heart,"
    Norfolk Ledger-Star, 22 December 1972. Sargeant Col-
    lection.

Lattimer, James, "J. Lindsay Almond, Jr.: Ordeal of a
    Governor," *Richmond Times-Dispatch*, 4 August 1974.
    Sargeant Collection.

Mason, Robert, "City Government--People and Politics,"
    editorial, *Norfolk Virginian-Pilot*, 4 July 1975,
    A-18.

Coit, John, "A Return To Broad Creek: The Way We Were,"
    Norfolk Virginian-Pilot, 15 July 1979, G-1.

Lattimer, James, "Almond in '80: On Staying in Power in
    Virginia," *Richmond Times-Dispatch*, 10 February 1980.
    Sargeant Collection.

NOTE: The Sargeant Memorial Collection of local history
memorabilia is housed in the Kirn Memorial Library, Norfolk. The Archives section of the Old Dominion University Library houses the papers of the Norfolk Committee
for Public Schools collected by the author for this
work.

Index

About the Author

FORREST R. WHITE is Director of Budget for Norfolk Public Schools. He is co-editor of *A Multidisciplinary Approach to Land-Use Planning in Virginia Beach* (1972).